Springer Series: FOCUS ON WOMEN

Violet Franks, Ph.D., Series Editor

Confronting the major psychological, medical, and social issues of today and tomorrow. *Focus on Women* provides a wide range of books on the changing concerns of women.

Claire M. Brody, Ph.D. is Adjunct Associate Professor in the Departments of Psychology, Sociology and Anthropology of the College of Staten Island, City University of New York. In addition to teaching and counseling at the City University over the past 20 years, she has also taught at Fairleigh Dickinson University and is on the Adjunct Graduate Faculty of Long Island University. She has been a school psychologist and a therapist with mental health clinics in New York and New Jersey and is in private practice in Englewood, New Jersey. She is a Diplomate of the American Board of Professional Psychology and has written articles and papers in the fields of college counseling and teaching as well as psychotherapy with women. She received a Masters Degree from the Committee on Human Development of the University of Chicago and her doctoral degree in psychology from New York University. She edited a prior book in the Springer Focus on Women series, *Women Therapists Working with Women*.

Women's Therapy Groups
Paradigms of Feminist Treatment

Claire M. Brody, Ph.D.

Editor

Introduction by Hannah Lerman, Ph.D.

Springer Publishing Company
New York

Springer Publishing Company, Inc.
536 Broadway
New York, NY 10012

89 90 91 / 5 4 3 2

Library of Congress Cataloging-in-Publication Data

Women's therapy groups.

  (Springer series, focus on women; v. 10)
  Bibliography: p.
  Includes index.
  1. Feminist therapy. 2. Women—Mental health.
I. Brody, Claire M. II. Series.
RC489.F45W68 1987   616.89'152   87-4692
ISBN 0-8261-5570-7

To my daughters
Jessica, Laura, and Naomi

"Oh, I do not like to look back at myself there,
Little among the stay-at-homes, the restabeds.
No, sting my self-contents to hunger
Till up I ride my heart to the high lands
Leaving myself behind.

Teach me to love my hunger,
Send me hard winds off the sands"

DORIS LESSING
The Marriages Between Zones
Three, Four, and Five

Contents

■ **ONE**
What are Women's Groups?

■ **TWO**
Consciousness-Raising and Self-Help Groups

■ Contributors

Kathleen A. Brehony is currently in private practice and serves as Director of Women's Programs at the Counseling Center in Roanoke, Virginia. She is also Vice President of Media Works, an independent television production company where she produces programs directed toward primary prevention of health and mental health problems in women. She has conducted workshops, seminars, and lectured on the topics of women and mental health problems. She has written book chapters on the topic of women and agoraphobia, and is co-editor of the text, *Marketing Health Behaviors* (1984). She received her doctoral degree in psychology from Virginia Tech.

Dianne S. Burden is an Assistant Professor of Social Policy and Research at the Boston University School of Social Work. She is currently conducting two federally funded research projects on the effects of combined work and family stress at home and on the job. She is the author of several journal articles and, with Naomi Gottlieb, wrote *The Woman Client: Human Services Practice in a Changing World* (1987). She received her doctoral degree in public policy from Brandeis University, and has a M.S.W. degree from the University of Washington.

Annie L. Cotten-Huston is on the psychology faculty of Central Connecticut State University. She has done academic and professional programming at the local, national, and international levels; has been a producer of media presentations on women's issues and sexual violence for television and radio; has been a consultant to life insurance companies and prison rehabilitation programs about crises of violence and sexual abuse; and has been an ambassador of People to People International to China, Spring 1986. She received her doctoral degree in human development from the Graduate School of the Union for Experimenting Colleges and Universities in Cincinnati.

Abisola H. Gallagher is a counselor at the Contemporary Counseling and Psychotherapy Institute in Teaneck, New Jersey, and is a management consultant to educational institutions and private industry. She was formerly Assistant Dean of Students at Rutgers University. She is Vice President of the New Jersey Association of Black Psychologists. She holds an Ed.D. in counseling psychology from Rutgers University.

Naomi Gottlieb is a professor at the School of Social Work, University of Washington in Seattle. She has been the coordinator of the Concentration on Women graduate program at that school since 1975. She edited *Alternative Social Services for Women* and was co-editor, with Dianne Burden, of *The Woman Client: Human Services Practice in a Changing World* (1987). Her current research includes the "late bloomer" phenomenon among older women and discontinuities in women's work lives. She received her M.S.W. and her doctoral degree in social work from the University of California at Berkeley.

Barbara J. Graham is currently a research associate at the Seattle Veterans Administration Medical Center. Her research and clinical interests include the assessment and treatment of suicidal behaviors and the development of suicide/assaultive behavior reporting systems. She received her doctoral degree in clinical psychology from the University of Washington.

Judith H. Halseth is an Assistant Professor of Social Work, and Associate Director of the School of Social Work, Western Michigan University in Kalamazoo, Michigan. She has been associated with the Van Buren County Community Mental Health Center in Paw Paw, Michigan. She received her M.S.W. from Western Michigan University and is a doctoral candidate in educational leadership.

Susan Hartman is currently the Coordinator of the Family Violence Program at Family and Children's Service, Minneapolis, Minnesota. She is also in private practice with the Minneapolis Clinical Associates in Psychiatry. She wrote a chapter in *Groupwork with Women/ Groupwork with Men*. She has an M.A. degree in counseling psychology from the college of St. Thomas in Minnesota and a M.A. degree in family social sciences from the University of Minnesota.

Monika J. Haussman is a psychologist at the Battle Creek Adventist Hospital in Battle Creek, Michigan. She has been employed at the Van Buren County Community Mental Health Center in Paw Paw, Michigan and is also in private practice in that city. She received an Ed.D. degree from Western Michigan University.

Kathy Hotelling is currently Director of the Anorexia/Bulimia Program at the Temple University School of Medicine. She is a frequent program presenter at conferences on therapeutic issues of particular interest to women, as well as the author of several articles on the same subjects. She received her doctorate in counseling psychology from the University of Missouri–Columbia.

Marilyn Johnson is currently Director of the Student Counseling Center at Rush University and Assistant Professor in the Department of Psychology and Social Sciences at the Rush–Presbyterian–St. Luke's Medical Center in Chicago. Recent publications include "Counseling Women" (with Mary Sue Richardson) in the *Handbook of Counseling Psychology* and "Psychotherapy Research and Women" (with Arthur Auerbach) in *Women and Mental Health Policy*. She received her doctoral degree in counseling psychology from the University of Pennsylvania.

Barbara Kirsh is currently Assistant Director of the Office of Corporate Quality Assurance of the Educational Testing Service, Princeton, New Jersey. She previously worked in the Educational Testing Service Research Division. She was awarded a Mellon postdoctoral fellowship to be a Radcliffe Research Scholar at the Henry A. Murray Center for the Study of Lives. Her postdoctoral research was concerned with women's life span development. Other research interests and publications have included children's concepts of friendship, gender roles and stereotypes, and consciousness-raising groups as an alternative to therapy. She received her doctoral degree in sociology from Rutgers University.

Diane Kravetz is Director and Professor, School of Social Work, University of Wisconsin–Madison, and a member of the Women's Studies Program there. She has published numerous articles on women and mental health, women in social service administration, women's consciousness-raising groups, androgeny as a standard of mental health, and career orientations of female social work students, among other issues. She received her doctoral degree in social work and social psychology from the University of Michigan.

Hannah Lerman, who wrote the Introduction to this book, is in private practice as a clinical psychologist and feminist therapist in California. She is co-founder of the Feminist Therapy Institute and has also served as the President of the Division of the Psychology of Women of the American Psychological Association. She has been a member of the clinical faculties of the Menninger School of Psychiatry and of the University of Southern California School of Medicine. She has also been Academic Dean of the California School of Professional Psychology, Los Angeles. Dr. Lerman is the author of the book *A Mote in Freud's Eye: From Psychoanalysis to the Psychology of Women* published by Springer in 1986. Her doctoral degree is in clinical psychology from Michigan State University.

Marsha M. Linehan is currently an associate professor of psychology and adjunct associate professor of psychiatry and behavioral services at the University of Washington in Seattle. She is the author of *Succeeding Socially (Asserting Yourself,* in the U.S. edition) and numerous publications on interpersonal skill training and suicidal behaviors. She has been on the Board of Directors of the Association for the Advancement of Behavior Therapy. She received her doctoral degree in personality psychology from Loyola University in Chicago.

Barbara R. Rothberg is on the faculty of the Post-Masters Program in Family and Individual Treatment, and is an Adjunct Faculty member of the Hunter College School of Social Work. She is also in private prctice. She is the author of several articles about joint custody problems as well as about working with lesbian and heterosexual couples. She holds a doctoral degree in social work from the Hunter College School of Social Work, as well as an M.S.W. degree from the Adelphi School of Social Work.

Judith E. Sprei is a licensed psychologist in Maryland and Washington, D.C. She is Co-Director of the Maryland Institute for Individual and Family Therapy, LTD, in College Park, Maryland. In her private practice, she specializes in the treatment of adults molested as children. She has conducted numerous professional training workshops and has published several book chapters, a training manual, and articles on the treatment of sexual abuse and sexual assault survivors. She serves as a consultant to several sexual assault centers. She received her doctoral degree in counseling psychology from the University of Maryland.

Frances Keith Trotman is founder and Director of the Contemporary Counseling and Psychotherapy Institute in Teaneck, New Jersey. She is also in private practice. She is former President of the Bergen County Association of Licensed Psychologists and is active in the National and New Jersey Association of Black Psychologists. She has worked as a junior high school and high school guidance counselor, a teacher, consultant, and an instructor/counselor at the college level prior to becoming a psychologist. She has published articles on race and I.Q. as well as psychotherapy with Black women. She received her doctoral degree in counseling psychology from Columbia University.

Vivian Ubell is the Director of Behavioral Sciences, Department of Family Medicine at Brookdale Hospital, Brooklyn, New York. She is also in private practice. She is the co-author, with Barbara Rothberg, of an article on working with lesbian and heterosexual couples in *Women and Therapy*. She holds a M.S.W. degree from Hunter College School of Social Work.

Lilly J. Schubert Walker is an Associate Professor and Director of Counseling at Brandon University (Brandon, Manitoba, Canada). She was selected as Western Manitoba's Professional Woman of the Year in 1985, and was recently honored as Volunteer of the Year for the Canadian Mental Health Association–Westman. She has served as reviewer for the *Canadian Journal of Counseling* and has published articles on women's issues. Her scholarly research has focused on working women, pediatric psychology, and rural stress. She received her doctoral degree from the University of North Dakota.

Katherine A. Wheeler is a nurse–community psychologist. She has been in private practice in association with the Obstetrics/Gynecology Group of Manchester, Connecticut for the past nine years. Her practice has been limited to women's problems. She recently moved her practice to Wakefield, Rhode Island. She is an R.N. who also holds a Masters degree from Central Connecticut State University.

Janet L. Wolfe is Director of Clinical Services of the Institute for Rational-Emotive Therapy in New York City. She has presented lectures and workshops in the United States and Europe on sex role issues in psychotherapy, relationship counseling, and cognitive behavior therapy. She has published numerous popular and professional articles on these subjects and has taught courses at the University of California and the New School for Social Research in New York. She received her doctoral degree in clinical psychology from New York University.

Preface

Feminist therapists have many different theoretical orientations—psycho-analytic, humanistic, behavioral—but they assume that problems often result from environmental interference with natural processes of emotional growth. Whereas traditional therapists may focus more on past family dynamics as the basis for current behavior, feminist therapists are usually concerned about the current life community in which the women clients can effect personal and environmental changes.

In an earlier volume in the Springer series, *Focus on Women*, Sturdivant (1980) reminded us that feminist therapy is "a value system—the feminist value system—around which some female therapists have begun to build new conceptualizations about therapy with women" (p. 76). The feminist value system that is echoed by the authors represented in this book views women as competent adults who are capable of controlling their own lives; they can be helped to develop self-definition and autonomy as they learn to care for and about themselves. Sturdivant pointed out that it is this commitment to these values, rather than simply keeping one's prejudices out of therapy, that differentiates feminist therapy from nonsexist therapy. What most of the chapters in this volume are about, to quote Hannah Lerman's Introduction, is the "universality of women's experience and the importance of women sharing their problems with women," as they unfold through the paradigms of a variety of group therapy approaches.

Articles about women involved in therapeutic groups have been appearing since the early 1970s. The seminal volume of Franks and Burtle, *Women in Therapy*, published in 1974, included a chapter entitled "Consciousness-Raising Groups in Therapy for Women." Much more recently, Mays (1985) writes that self-help groups are a viable intervention for stress reduction for divorced black women in white collar occupations. La Pointe and Rimm (1980) did an empirical study to compare the efficacy of a variety of group approaches—cognitive, assertive, and insight-oriented— for the treatment of reactive depression in women. In the last 15 years about 90 articles have appeared that relate to women in group therapy with women therapists or self-help and consciousness-raising groups, yet none of this large body of feminist-oriented literature has been collected in a book. Recently, Dilling and Claster (1985) published an extraordinary partially annotated bibliography on female psychology, covering the history of writings about women from Freud's original thesis to current sex role issues in psychotherapy. Most of the material on women in groups that will be referred to by contributors to this volume can be found among this extensive listing.

What *are* women's groups, and how are they different from men's or mixed gender groups as therapeutic endeavors? How are feminist and traditional groups different? What are the different variables at work in cross-cultural groups? Jones and Korchin (1982) state that the cross-cultural perspective fosters a greater sensitivity to the role that values play in the study of any ethnic group (p. 17). Consonant with goals of independence and equality, single gender therapy groups encourage women to grow, to share interpersonal issues, and to explore the social determinants of problems special to women.

Most of the chapters that follow have been written especially for this volume; a few are reprints or revisions of significant articles from the fields of psychology, social work, and psychiatry. The aim has been to collect a cross-section of statements about ways that women are working with other women in groups to help them implement change in their lives. The contributors, many of whom have developed innovative treatment strategies, represent professionals from different work settings with a variety of treatment orientations. All of them share the optimistic belief that, whatever the disabling conditions of their women clients, these can be altered and women can be successful in their efforts to redirect their lives.

This volume does not attempt to cover every pertinent topic regarding women' groups. There are gaps. For example, Alcoholics Anonymous runs women's groups, and these are not detailed here, although Graham and Linehan offer innovative material about one subset of this underserved population. Whatever the technique used or the problem area confronted, all the models of feminist groups described here are concerned with fostering women's ability to design their own destinies.

The birth of consciousness-raising groups for women was coincident with a political climate that encouraged women to become aware that their problems were not the result of personal failure in relationships, but, more often, a result of being women in a sexist society. As Johnson points out in her chapter, a review of current group therapy practice reveals that in the 1980s there has been a shift from groups focused on interpersonal issues to groups organized around specific problem areas. The intent of this book is to highlight the broad range of problems met by women in groups.

Several of the chapters diverge from the overall design of the others. For example, while the rest of the chapters deal with all-feminist *groups*, the reader might have wondered about the place of Rothberg and Ubell's chapter on lesbian and heterosexual "couples." These authors explain that just as there is a need to focus on process rather than content in groups, the same principle applies to working with couples. Also, since a systems structure is being described, there is implicit an extended family, friendships, and the larger societal system; the couple is seen as a system interacting within a larger system. By integrating feminist and systems approaches, Rothberg and Ubell reinforce the common denominator of the other contributors to this volume: the clients' and the therapists' values and options as important targets of exploration and change. These authors delineate how couple therapy conforms more to feminist therapy tenets than to traditional family therapy techniques; the latter are often "manipulative and paradoxical." In many of the therapy examples, modeling is used as an important tool, and observable concrete behavioral changes are important for assessing progress.

Cotten-Huston and Wheeler's chapter on the treatment of sexual dysfunction in women is also different from the other chapters in that it presents the results of a scientific research study as the basis for a group procedure. However, in its extensive review of relevant literature and a description of a specific group process it provides a valuable model for the treatment of a common malady of women.

"What are the differences between women's groups and all other groups?" Hannah Lerman asks in her Introduction. Women therapists leading women in groups provide a unique opportunity, as Walker has so carefully outlined in her chapter, for participants to assess themselves and to validate their feelings and perceptions while they are struggling to change. She points out the unequivocal differences from mixed-sex therapy groups and offers a framework and structure for future comparative evaluations.

In considering the range of approaches and problems dealt with, it is significant to confirm the therapeutic importance for women to share, as Lerman says, "their most intimate and troubled parts with one another." Anger, lack of power, competency fears, and unassertiveness are repetitive variables in women's experiences, and the relief of these recurring stresses span the gamut of problems and populations that women present in most therapists' practices.

What is especially important to note in reviewing these chapters is the varied socioeconomic levels, political commitments, and attitudes toward the women's movement that comprise the women described in therapy groups. The common denominator is that there is something radically wrong with the lives of women in our culture as they have been socialized to live them. With more creative efforts by women therapists helping women in groups, the prospects for changing this archaic programming become more hopeful.

In the 15 years or so that I have been working with women in groups, there have been many individuals who have influenced the evolution of my own personal style and philosophy. Starting with Ruth Cohn at the Workshop Institute for Living/Learning in New York City, I adapted a theme-centered approach to both teaching and therapy groups. In those early days, I taught a fellow professor how to apply small-group process to advantage in his introductory accounting courses! It was in my private therapy practice, however, that I discovered the importance of modeling a "respectful authority with power," a woman who trusted her own competency. Knowing that I will be modeled by my clients, I have learned to use myself as a model who can make new values sound possible without exploiting women or assigning any immediate expectations for them. A woman therapist's attitude toward her sex, her sexuality, aging, authority, dependency, risk-taking, and the women's movement are, by implication, issues that will affect her work with women.

CLAIRE M. BRODY

REFERENCES

Dilling, C., & Claster, B. L. (Eds.) (1985). *Female Psychology: A partially annotated bibliography.* Project sponsored by the New York City Coalition for Mental Health, New York.

Franks, V., & Burtle, V. (Eds.) (1974). *Women in Therapy: New psychotherapies for a changing society.* New York: Brunner/Mazel.

Jones, E. E., & Korchin, S. I. (1982). Minority mental health. In E. E. Jones & S. I. Korchin (Eds.), *Minority mental health.* New York: Praeger.

La Pointe, K. A., & Rimm, R. C. (1980). Cognitive, assertive, and insight-oriented group therapy in the treatment of reactive depression in women. *Psychotherapy: Theory, Research and Practice, 17*(3), 312–321.

Mays, W. M. (1985). Black women and stress: Utilization of self-help groups for stress-reduction. *Women and Therapy, 4*(4), 67–79.

Sturdivant, S. (1980). *Therapy with Women: A feminist philosophy of treatment.* New York: Springer Publishing Co.

Acknowledgments

I would like to pay homage here to the following:

Violet Franks, Editor of the Springer Focus on Women series, who has been consistently positive and enthusiastic about this project.

My colleagues in the Women Therapists' Group who have provided me the valuable thrust for my growth as a person and a therapist: Fran Trotman, Tamara Shulman, Marilyn McGirr, Marjorie Landes, Adele Holman, Carolynn Hillman, Judy Gurtman, and Harriet Diamond.

Laurie Brody for her considerable technical assistance with the manuscript.

Jayne Mangino whose help with editing my own chapter in the book made it come to life.

My husband, Alex, who continues to give me plenty of room to grow and work, along with his love and support.

My father, Mortimore Hudesman, who at 94 has enlightened me about the roots of my own drive for autonomy.

My granddaughters, Anna and Lily, who provide the inspiration for what the next generation of women could be like.

Claire M. Brody

Introduction

HANNAH LERMAN, PH.D.

Since 1970, we have lived through phenomenal changes in how our society views women and how women view themselves. What women have learned in various kinds of women's groups has made important contributions toward those changes. Women getting together in groups has provided one of the major avenues for the spread of new ideas to other women who are eager to explore their preconceptions about themselves and to better understand their relationship to society. It is most appropriate, therefore, that we should finally have a book about psychotherapy with women that focuses around women's experience in groups.

The group phenomenon known as consciousness-raising was how it all began. Some say this special approach to rap groups arose out of the Speak Bitterness groups of the Chinese Communist revolution. In China, following liberation from the Japanese after World War II, women individually recited to their assembled neighbors what crimes had been done to them.

> Speaking Bitterness was their first opportunity for egalitarian contact with other human beings. The process of venting anger became personally liberating. Women who whimpered at their husbands' cruelty now found the courage to call their spouses before the local Women's Association. Together the women found the strength to confront the men who previously had oppressed them, forcing these men to change their ways. (Dreifus, 1973, p. 2)

The relationship of consciousness-raising to Speaking Bitterness, however, may be myth imposed upon a phenomenon in order to make it orderly and understandable—when in fact, it was neither. The parallels to the Chinese version seem to have first become known after the fact (Dreifus, 1973). Consciousness-raising groups emerged on our scene as if a spontaneous reaction finally reached crucial mass and culminated in this unique response to all the oppression that had preceded it. The era of the 1960s had given rise to a general self-help movement and a mistrust of "experts." Consciousness-raising groups among women picked up on the self-help theme that was already present in the counter-culture. Consciousness-raising, originally a nontherapeutic activity, has, however, also eventually succeeded in contributing changes to how therapy is done in a group setting. Several chapters in this book allude in different ways to the fascinating history of the interrelationship of consciousness-raising to therapy.

Originally, the idea behind consciousness-raising was that bringing women together to talk to each other in groups would help to counteract the effects of sexism. The original impetus, obviously, did not come from therapists. The organizers particularly wanted to avoid the power dynamics that they believed to be inherent to such a one-to-one relationship as the traditional therapy setting, just as they wished to oppose the mental health theories that perpetuated the individual pathology model. The groups were not organized to be therapy groups, but myriads of women can attest to their therapeutic benefits. Women in general had been isolated from one another, with each thinking that her own dissatisfaction was her own problem and was not at all related to social circumstances. Somehow, however, in a major grass-roots undertaking that has not been sufficiently documented and recorded (and, unfortunately, probably cannot ever fully be known), women gathered themselves together to learn from each other. The groups had a specific unique structure, and, at least in the beginning, they had no leaders. The design of these groups was such that everyone could have her say, with the structure substituting for the mediational work that a leader might perform. Mental health professionals were not wanted! They were identified with the enemy, the oppressive forces of the society. Male professionals were avoided completely, and women professionals were looked at with suspicion. The assumption was that women therapists must have bought into the traditional male mental health ideology and that they could not be trusted to help women rid themselves of internalized sexism.

The next step from totally leaderless groups was having women in turn take on the role of group facilitator. Then, some women were trained or trained themselves to be facilitators and served that function for other women. When the distinction began to blur between consciousness-raising and other kinds of groups of women, the Radical Psychiatry movement led the way (Agel, 1971). This movement of lay facilitators appropriated the label "psychiatry" to demonstrate that therapists always are participating in a political process. The intent here was to bring social oppression, including the ways that traditional psychiatry participated in it, into prime focus as the root cause of alienation and diagnosed psychiatric disorders (Steiner, 1971). The work of Wyckoff epitomizes this movement, one that focuses upon women's oppression in all spheres of psychological life and the methods that can be used (mainly in group settings) to alleviate the damage (Wyckoff, 1977).

Women therapists, however, were also having their own consciousnesses raised during that period. They attended women's movement consciousness-raising groups themselves and sometimes formed groups open only to women therapists. I was a member of one such group, and it changed my personal and professional life forever. We women therapists were caught up in the movement just as other women were. We wanted to use our skills to help combat the newly identified oppression—and feminist therapy was born (Sturdivant, 1980). Using consciousness-raising as a model (Brodsky, 1973), feminist therapy groups were started. Johnson in this book discusses that part of feminist therapy history, and Kirsh in her chapter discusses some of the history of consciousness-raising and how that movement has itself changed over time.

Prior to the grass-roots rise of women's groups, the thought of same-sex groups for psychotherapy was rarely considered, particularly for women. Also rare was the idea of a woman therapist as a group leader. At best, most of the time, she was a co-leader with a male therapist serving as the senior therapist/leader. Women's own issues were rarely addressed in groups because the traditional theories did not deal with them—nor did the traditional leaders. I recall, for example, when I was first being taught sensitivity training (the forerunner of encounter groups), the target population was middle and upper management business men. Each group of 12 to 15 members, however, was carefully composed to include one or preferably two women members, whether they met the general occupational requirement or not (and very few did—in those days). Thus, women who were secretaries and clerks sat in on groups with men who were presidents of companies, individual proprietors, corporative division heads, etc. The underlying rationale was that women provided the initial focus on emotionality and cohesiveness for the group (Walker's chapter in this book focuses upon some of the relevant differences in male and female participation in groups). No woman would ever have been chosen to lead an all-male group, however, nor would two women serve together as co-leaders. Brody's chapter shows us how this has changed. Now, the idea that a woman therapist can serve as an appropriate model for other women has come to be fully accepted in group therapy.

This book, in so many ways, is an illustration of how far indeed we have come. Different chapters deal with the different kinds of groups that have evolved. Also addressed are different kinds of issues that have arisen—special-focus groups versus single-race or ethnic groups, the role of male leaders, the difficulty of incorporating feminist therapy principles in family therapy, and systems theory (Rothberg and Ubell discuss this in their chapter). Hotelling raises the question of whether Yalom's curative factors (Yalom, 1975) can be applied to women's groups.

The first section of this book discusses what women's groups are and what they can provide. Walker differentiates between traditional groups and women's groups. She looks at the group therapy literature in order to identify both differences and similarities and concludes that the gender of the therapist is a crucial factor for group activity, which is only beginning to be appreciated. She advocates additional research in order to differentiate the most relevant factors operative in the various kinds of women's groups that have evolved.

Johnson takes us through the past decade, contrasting the work of the Philadelphia Feminist Therapy Collective in the 1970s and the results of a survey of present day self-identified feminist therapists. In the present, she finds greater differentiation among therapy choices for different kinds of complaints, a relatively greater choice of individual therapy than previously, and more problem-oriented as opposed to generally oriented therapy groups.

Burden and Gottlieb provide a general introduction to the process of women's socialization and describe the power possessed by feminist groups, as opposed to more traditional group formats, for undoing many of the negative aspects of typical female socialization. They identify the factors they see as significant—nurturing, especially self-nurturing, helping women identify and distinguish personal versus political sources of their difficulties, and the process of self-empowerment.

The second section, which focuses upon consciousness-raising and self-help groups, is begun by Kirsh who documents the evolution of consciousness-raising groups themselves, from an emphasis upon political and social changes toward a more personally oriented goal, the provision of support among women. She points out, however, that, even if social change is a less overt goal at present, personal change is still approached in these groups in the context of the problems of society.

Kravetz focuses particularly upon the mental health benefits that consciousness-raising groups have provided to women. She reviews the relevant literature but emphasizes that changes in individuals can only be fully evaluated in the social context.

Hartman describes a self-help group with a therapist, one oriented toward women in abusive relationships. Her model parallels that of Brehony (whose chapter follows) in that her group has a therapist-facilitator. Hartman describes the positive benefits her group provides for this special population of women.

Brehony presents her conclusions from her work in self-help groups with agoraphobic women. In these groups, the therapist functions more as a facilitator than a traditional therapist, and self-help is emphasized. The steps that her group undergo are clearly described.

The third section of this book focuses upon special techniques and special issues. Brody introduces this section by describing group therapy from the viewpoint of the female therapist/leader. She focuses especially upon the use of the therapist as a model for positive functioning both in culturally homogeneous and mixed cultural groups.

Trotman and Gallagher describe in detail the special circumstances involved in group therapy with black women. They look at how this is likely to differ from groups with white women and offer suggestions to therapists for their conduct of groups with black women.

Rothberg and Ubell explore the problems of integrating feminism with family systems theory in work with couples, particularly lesbian couples. They present examples of instances where the integration is problematic but emphasize their commitment to feminist values even during those times when the system temporarily is given priority.

Linehan provides a description of behavior therapy in groups with a population that is not usually associated with this treatment modality, women with borderline personalities and suicidal behaviors. Her chapter provides a clear description of the group process that she utilizes as an adjunct to ongoing individual therapy with these individuals.

Wolfe presents a group format that has proved useful in her setting. This approach incorporates cognitive-behavioral aspects and rational-emotive psychotherapy into the process of encouraging autonomy among women and enabling them to free their thought processes and attitudes from previously incorporated oppressive attitudes.

The fourth section of the book is about special problems and special populations. It is opened by a discussion of the special problems of the homeless and alcoholic woman who has only recently begun to receive any attention at all. Graham and Linehan report on their work with these women in a clear and clinically useful presentation of the problems and the rewards of working with this often ignored group.

A growing amount of attention, on the other hand, is being paid to adult incest survivors. Better data about the incidence of incest has been accumulating, as has evidence about its effects. Sprei, in her chapter, presents a description of her structured group approach to incest survivors.

Haussman and Halseth present a description of a semi-structured group approach for working with depressed rural women. They see the reexamination of women's role-expectations as crucial and also emphasize bonding and self-respect, and the growth in awareness of choices for these women.

Cotton-Huston and Wheeler report research into the results of group treatment for preorgasmic women: an increased experience of orgasm and experience of sexual pleasure follows completion of group experience. Their chapter is different from others in the book in that their focus is research into group effects rather than discussion of group process and issues.

In her chapter which ends the book, Hotelling uses Yalom's curative factors (Yalom, 1975) as a focus around which to organize her description of working with women with bulimia in a problem-oriented group structure. She reviews each of Yalom's factors and relates them specifically to the process of group work with this problem population of distressed women.

What are the differences between women's groups and all other groups? That question echoes again and again throughout this book. Something about the universality of women's experiences and the importance of shared problems are mentioned by most of the chapter authors. By the time you finish reading this book, you will know more about the issues that women's groups address, more about the range of structures that different therapists have found successful, and more about the therapeutic importance of women sharing their most intimate and troubled parts with one another, as well as the political significance that the initiation and continuation of such sharing has brought to us all.

REFERENCES

Agel, J. (Ed.). (1971). *The radical therapist.* New York: Ballantine Books.

Brodsky, A. (1973). The consciousness-raising group as a model for therapy with men. *Psychotherapy: Theory, Research and Practice, 10*(1), 24–29.

Dreifus, C. (1973). *Woman's fate: Raps from a feminist consciousness-raising group.* New York: Bantam Books.

Steiner, C. (1971) Radical psychiatry: Principles. In J. Agel (Ed.), *The radical therapist.* New York: Ballantine Books.

Sturdivant, S. (1980). *Therapy with women: A feminist philosophy of treatment.* New York: Springer Publishing Co.

Wyckoff, H. (1977). *Solving women's problems through awareness, action, and contact.* New York: Grove Press.

Yalom, I. (1975). *The theory and practice of group psychotherapy* (2nd ed.). New York: Basic Books.

■ one
WHAT ARE
WOMEN'S GROUPS?

■ 1
Women's Groups Are Different

LILLY J. SCHUBERT WALKER

Groups provide a unique opportunity for participants to assess themselves, validate their experiences and perceptions, attempt personal, behavioral, and attitudinal changes, express feelings, and receive feedback. A significant evolution in group therapy during the past two decades has been the increase in the number and variety of women's groups run by women for women. These women's therapy groups [i.e., consciousness-raising (CR), assertiveness training, women's self-help groups, and feminist group therapies] have developed in response to critical evaluations of traditional psychotherapy (Broverman, Broverman, Clarkson, Rosenkrantz, & Vogel, 1970). Therapy groups for women eliminate the unconscious sexism that is present in mixed groups and provide a supportive environment in which participants can discover and experience the commonalities of being a woman. Articles continue to be published outlining the benefits of all-female therapy groups (Glaser, 1976; Klein, 1976; Meador, Solomon, & Bowen, 1972; Sullivan, 1983; Wolman, 1976) and providing evidence for the therapeutic effectiveness of nontraditional forms of therapy such as CR groups (Adolph, 1983; Brodksy, 1973; Eastman, 1973; Follingstad, Robinson, & Pugh, 1977; Kravetz, 1976, 1978; Kirsh, 1974; Lieberman & Bond, 1976; Lieberman, Solow, Bond, & Reibstein, 1979; Marecek. Kravetz, & Finn, 1979; Nassi & Abramowitz, 1978; Warren, 1976).

In what ways do all-women therapy groups differ from traditional mixed sex therapy groups? This chapter reviews the group therapy literature and identifies some of the significant similarities and differences between

3

group therapy designed specifically for women and traditional mixed sex group therapy. Groups whose goals are to modify emotional states, attitudes, behavior, and interpersonal relations will be included in this discussion. The reader will learn how women's groups are distinctly different from traditional therapy groups in terms of group development, goals and structure, leadership dimensions, interpersonal relations, and communication patterns. This chapter will also summarize research findings on the similarities between the two types of groups.

GROUP DEVELOPMENT

The stages of group development of all-female groups have some commonalities and some differences from the stages of development observed in traditional mixed groups (Allen, 1970; Wolman, 1976).

Wolman (1976) described three phases of group development in female therapy groups that parallel the stages observed in mixed groups. However, there are some differences within each stage. In stage one, the common themes were dependence on and competition for the attention of the therapist as well as an inability to focus on oneself. Wolman reports this phase was briefer than the initial phase of mixed groups. During the second stage, feelings of anger and rage, disappointment, and dependency–independency dominated discussion. Group members learned to work through conflicts, express warmth and closeness, and respect one another. In comparison with mixed sex groups, the group members became much more dependent on the group. They developed an active support system and engaged in more frequent contact outside the group. Wolman (1976) notes that a greater level of intimacy develops in all-female groups than in mixed groups because the group members feel safer, and there is less need for inhibitory incest taboos. However, during the middle phase, a high percentage of group members dropped out; this attrition rate was greater than that usually observed in mixed sex therapy groups. The third stage focused on some of the issues of being female (i.e., sexism, mothering, sexuality). At this time the participants' perception of the therapists changed in that the therapist-leaders were viewed as being less omnipotent and powerful and as positive role models.

Allen (1970) has outlined four group stages that characterize the development of women's consciousness-raising groups. The first stage, "opening up," is the revelation of inner feelings and personal experiences, which usually fosters an atmosphere of intimacy and trust. The group norms of nonjudgmental acceptance and respect for feelings encourage honest self-disclosure. The second stage, "sharing," recognizes the commonalities among women and expands the discussion from the individual to the group. Members of the group reinforce one another and cooperate in helping one another solve status and role problems. The frustration and anger of this stage is hopefully channeled into personal and social change. The first two stages are similar to traditional mixed therapy groups, whereas the last two stages are distinctly different. The third stage, "analyzing," strives to combine subjective feeling and thinking with objective analysis thus directing the women to investigate the role position of women in society. During the final stage, "abstracting," the group participants examine institutions and determine how they can work together to change society.

In order to summarize the observations of researchers on the progression of development in women's groups, the framework delineated by Schutz (1967) is useful. The first stage, "inclusion," involves trust building that is generally based on sharing information about one's self (testimonials) and discovering commonalities. As members take risks and self-disclose they become more aware of their feelings and more in touch with themselves. This stage differs from mixed groups in that it may be briefer, and two of the positive outcomes are the discovery of the normalcy of their discontent and the identification with female leaders as effective role models. The second stage, "control," is marked by frustration, disappointment, and anger. Members become aware of feelings they previously ignored and withheld. The insight gained through sharing and analyzing elicits anger, which may be expressed towards oneself, towards others within or outside the group, or towards society. Several authors (Halas, 1973; Kirsh, 1974; Wolman, 1976) note that the anger revealed in women's groups differs from the anger expressed by participants in mixed groups. Women's groups appear to be more conducive to the expressing and sharing of angry feelings; participants are not uncomfortable with or threatened by tears or verbal outbursts. For many women, acknowledging feelings of anger is a new and frightening experience. some groups become overwhelmed by the angry feelings, and this produces a period of group regression and depression, which may result in an extremely high rate of attrition. Other groups channel the anger into personal and societal changes. If members successfully work through the conflicts and issues of the second stage they move into the "affection" stage. Members of female groups experience an intense feeling of closeness and intimacy, which appears to be more intense than the feelings of closeness experienced in mixed groups. Members no longer hold back but talk freely and intimately about themselves (Fried, 1974). During this stage members strive for significant changes in their lives, and some resolve to work together to change society.

GOALS AND STRUCTURE

Many of the goals of women's groups are similar to the goals of mixed groups: resolution of personal problems and concerns; improved interpersonal relationships; increased autonomy; self-respect and self-confidence; honest, direct, open communication; and changes in psychological functioning.

However, some of the goals of the two groups differ. Women's groups value the exploration of the intricacies and realities of being female. All-female groups encourage participants to discover their commonalities, to build supportive relationships with one another, to share, and to explore sex roles, stereotypes, and sexism. In contrast to mixed groups, women's groups value emotional support more than personal change or personal problem-solving (Kravetz, Marecek, & Finn, 1983; Shorr & Jason, 1982). Women's group therapy generally emphasizes the importance of societal factors as a significant determinant of personal problems, whereas mixed groups are more interpersonally oriented. Women's groups vary in their emphasis on the sociocultural components of women's personal problems with consciousness-raising groups tending to be more social action and politically oriented than the others. All-women groups break the isolation of women from each other, provide new role models for self-definition, and attempt to transcend the traditional emotional dependence on male approval.

Women's therapy groups are similar to traditional mixed sex groups in that they may be closed or open ended, and the duration of the session as well as the frequency of meetings is determined by the needs of the group members. Generally, the number of participants in both groups varies between five and 15.

The actual structure of women's therapy groups varies depending on whether the group is a growth group, a feminist therapy group, or a consciousness raising group. The structure of the growth group and the feminist therapy group parallels the structure of their mixed sex counterparts. The direction, purpose, and the goals of these groups are determined by a highly trained therapist-leader. A consciousness-raising group is generally a leaderless, highly structured discussion group that promotes peer equality. CR groups eliminate hierarchical, authoritative therapist–patient relationships and draw on the knowledge and skills of each participant.

LEADERSHIP

One of the most important issues raised by the Women's Movement has been the recommendation that only women therapists should work with women clients (Johnson, 1976). Many women have questioned whether male therapists can understand and nonjudgmentally accept a woman's innermost feelings. They believe male therapists reinforce sexual stereotyped behavior, undermine women's issues (Barrett, Berg, Eaton, & Pomeroy, 1974), and disregard the impact of social determinants on women's personal problems (Klein, 1976). Others believe that the presence of a male therapist impedes progress in accepting, expressing, and working through the feelings of generalized anxiety women experience towards men (Rice & Rice, 1973).

Several authors (Kravetz, 1976, 1978; Marecek, Kravetz & Finn, 1979; Rice & Rice, 1973; Sullivan, 1983; Wolman, 1976) have written about the advantages of a female therapist treating women. They report that female therapists are more sensitive to the issues facing women, are better able to empathize with feelings, provide a positive role identification model, and may be able to facilitate the resolution of role conflicts by utilizing their own experiences. A comparison of women in feminist therapy compared with women in traditional therapy found that clients of feminist therapists rated therapy as more helpful than did clients of traditional therapists (Marecek et al., 1979).

Carter (1971) articulates some of the differences in orientation between male and female therapists. She notes that the role expectations of women reward them for expressing and understanding feelings, and female therapists are therefore more emotionally responsive, better able to allow the patient's experiences to have an impact on them, and skilled at verbalizing how they have been affected. Male therapists, on the other hand, are less affectively oriented and more cognitively oriented.

The research findings on the impact of the sex of the therapist on the therapeutic experiences of women is limited. Elrick (1977) reports that the presence of a female group leader changes the dynamics of a group. She believes that a revolt by the participants against a female leader is more difficult. She observes that there is less competition in a female-led group, because female leaders emphasize fairness and cooperation as compared to the competitive orientation of male leaders.

There is some evidence to support the observation that the leadership styles of women differ from those of men (Denmark, 1977). Even though men and women leaders display common personality traits such as assertiveness and decisiveness, upward mobility, a strong desire to achieve, and some fear of failure, women leaders demonstrate greater concern for relationships among people than men do. Women's leadership styles tend to be more heterogeneous, varying from overcontrolling and task-oriented to permissive. Male leaders are generally more exploitative and self-seeking. The nonverbal behaviors of the two sexes vary. Men more frequently initiate touch and act more relaxed. Women have been observed to smile, listen, lower their eyes, and look at a person more frequently than men. The nonverbal behavior of men asserts status and maintains distance, that of women minimizes distance and increases affiliation (Henley, 1973).

Orlinsky and Howard (1976) found in their research that for particular groups of women the sex of the therapist is a significantly important variable. Single women and women with depressive reactions report that they feel more support and satisfaction in treatment with a woman therapist. Female patients describe significant differences in specific dimensions of the therapeutic relationship as a function of the sex of the therapist. Women with male therapists talked more about the opposite sex and about their involvement with the therapist. They were more concerned about identity-related issues, felt more erotized affection, anger, inhibition, and depression. They viewed their therapists as more demanding, more detached, and less expansive. Female patients with female therapists reported significantly higher levels of satisfaction and encouragement. They described feeling more open and less self-critical.

COMMUNICATION CONTENT AND PATTERNS

Studies comparing the content or types of issues discussed in mixed groups as compared to homogeneous female groups report some interesting differences. All female groups facilitate more self-disclosure about personal feelings and significant relationships than mixed sex groups (Nassi & Abramowitz, 1978). In all-female groups, women are encouraged to talk about themselves. Female groups focus on intrapersonal issues, whereas mixed groups focus on interpersonal issues.

All-female groups encourage participants to explore and share commonalities, to affirm one another's positive strengths, and to recognize that others have similar concerns (Kravetz, 1978). Group discussions center on intrapersonal issues such as establishing independence, allowing oneself to express one's potency, resolving conflicting role expectations, and eliminating self-hatred and repression of one's abilities (Carlock & Martin, 1977). In all-female groups, women are encouraged to focus on their unique identity quite apart from their primary relationships. They begin to see themselves as people. Topics that are taboo in mixed groups such as body image and sexuality are openly discussed (Carlock & Martin, 1977; Meador et al., 1972). Initially, compared to mixed groups, participants are less here-and-now oriented, and there is a tendency to focus on outside relationships, events, and issues. Later, communication evolves, and participants discover themselves as persons and learn to relate to, trust, and enjoy other women. One of the positive outcomes of women's groups is the rediscovery of the pleasure and fulfillment of interpersonal relations with other women.

In mixed groups, much of the focus of discussion is on current interpersonal issues (Carlock & Martin, 1977). Because one of the dominant dynamics in a mixed group is pairing, there appears to be a greater reliance on game-playing as a means of developing intimacy. Carlock and Martin (1977) and Meador et al. (1972) note that due to the dominance of the pairing theme in mixed groups, women do not develop feelings of closeness with each other and compete with one another for male approval.

The interaction patterns in a mixed group reinforce traditional role stereotypes. In mixed groups, the frequency and duration of women's verbal interaction is less than men's and women are more easily interrupted and do not defend their ideas as vigorously as men (Elrick, 1977). Generally, women are more passive, frequently talk softly, and tend to withdraw (Carlock & Martin, 1977). Women in mixed groups overtly and covertly encourage men to initiate interactions (Carlock & Martin, 1977).

In mixed groups, nonverbal communication, particularly touching, is frequently male-initiated (Denmark, 1977) and follows male–female role patterns (Harris, 1975). Carlock and Martin (1977) and Harris (1975) found that in mixed groups, nonverbal messages were frequently misinterpreted; however, the most common messages had either sexual or "big daddy/little girl" connotations. In all-female groups, Carlock and Martin (1977) report that there appear to be stricter limits on physical closeness, because touch provokes high levels of anxiety. This contrasts with reports (Walker, 1981) that touch facilitates feelings of closenss and support in women's groups. Another form of nonverbal communication, tears, is more accepted in female groups than in mixed groups (Halas, 1973).

SUMMARY AND IMPLICATIONS

This chapter reviewed some of the important process dimensions that occur in women's groups that are different from those that occur in traditional mixed sex groups. Some of the goals of the two types of groups are similar. However, female groups tend to encourage greater exploration of the social determinants of personal problems rather than emphasize solely interpersonal issues. Researchers have observed that the styles of leadership and the nonverbal behaviors of female leaders differ from those of male leaders, and the themes and interaction patterns of the two types of groups vary. In comparison to the competitive orientation of male-led groups, female leaders foster the development of cooperation and affiliation. It appears that mixed groups reinforce females for maintaining the passive sex-role stereotype. In female groups, women talk more freely, more frequently, and more intimately. Mixed groups focus on the development of male-female relationships by discussing and resolving interpersonal issues and conflicts; female groups emphasize the development of trusting, caring, close female relationships by encouraging the sharing of intrapersonal issues. The developmental pace of the two groups varies. The initial trust-building stage evolves more slowly in a mixed group and appears to be more quickly attained in a female group. A dominant theme in both groups during the second stage is anger. Women in both types of groups initially have difficulty acknowledging and identifying these feelings. However, female groups are more supportive of forceful, descriptive, dynamic, open expressions of these feelings. There is some evidence to indicate that although both groups must successfully resolve these conflict issues and feelings before progressing into the next stage of group development, this can be an especially vulnerable time for a female group.

This chapter is intended to facilitate an understanding of major differences between mixed and female groups—differences that should help alert therapists to the unique demands of group psychotherapy as a function of sex of group members. Practitioner awareness of group dynamics can be important in ascertaining the advantages and disadvantages of particular therapeutic alternatives, in assigning patients appropriately, and in developing personal leadership styles and strategies. For example, since the sex of the therapist appears to significantly influence the content of discussion and the course of the group, this information can be utilized in selecting a therapist who can best facilitate the goals of the group. Also, therapists can avoid some of the common communication problems that occur in female groups during the various stages of group growth by utilizing appropriately timed interventions that encourage self-disclosure and the safe expression of positive and negative feelings.

The findings reviewed here provide some initial understanding of the dynamics of female therapy groups. If we are to more precisely define the critical differences between female and mixed groups there are several areas in which more empirical research is needed. More data should be collected to validate the developmental progression of female groups. Although the available evidence suggests that female leaders bring a different dimension to the therapeutic encounter, the significance of gender on group process needs to be studied more systematically. In order to differentiate the relative advantages and disadvantages of female groups and to control for such variables as ideology, goals, and structure, studies comparing the various types of women's groups (i.e., self-help, consciousness-raising, and traditional psychotherapy) with their mixed sex and male counterparts need to include more experimental rigor (i.e., random assignment to treatment and control groups). Research in these areas will add significantly to our understanding of group psychotherapy and to a more efficient utilization of various treatment options.

REFERENCES

Adolph, M. (1983). The all-women's consciousness-raising group as a component of treatment for mental illness. *Social Work with Groups, 6(3-4),* 117-131.

Allen, P. (1970). *Free space: A perspective on the small group in women's liberaton.* Washington, NJ: Times Change Press.

Barrett, C. J., Berg, P. I., Eaton, E. M., & Pomeroy, E. L. (1974). Implications of women's liberation and the future of psychotherapy. *Psychotherapy: Theory, Research and Practice, 11(1),* 11-15.

Brodsky, A. M. (1973). The consiousness-raising group as a model for therapy with women. *Psychotherapy: Theory, Research and Practice, 10(1),* 24-29.

Broverman, I., Broverman, D., Clarkson, F., Rosenkrantz, P., & Vogel, S. (1970). Sex role stereotypes and clinical judgments of mental health. *Journal of Consulting Psychology, 34(1),* 1-7.

Carlock, C. J., & Martin, P. Y. (1977). Sex composition and the intensive group experience. *Social Work, 22(1),* 27-32.

Carter, C. A. (1971). Advantages of being a woman therapist. *Psychotherapy: Theory, Research and Practice, 8(4),* 297-300.

Denmark, F. L. (1977). Styles of leadership. *Psychology of Women Quarterly, 2,* 99-113.

Eastman, P. C. (1973). Consciousness-raising as a resocialization process for women. *Smith College Studies in Social Work, 43(3),* 153-183.

Elrick, M. (1977). The leader, she: Dynamics of a female led self-analytic group. *Human Relations, 30(10),* 869-878.

Follingstad, D. R., Robinson, E. A., & Pugh, M. (1977). Effects of consciousness-raising groups on measures of feminism, self-esteem and social desirability. *Journal of Counseling Psychology, 24(3),* 223-230.

Fried, E. (1974). Does women's new self-concept call for new approaches in group psychotherapy? *International Journal of Group Therapy, 24(3),* 265-272.

Glaser, K. (1976). Women's self-help groups as an alternative to therapy. *Psychotherapy: Theory, Research and Practice, 13(1),* 77-81.

Halas, C. (1973). All-women's groups: A view from the inside. *Personnel and Guidance Journal, 52(1),* 91-95.

Harris, A. (1975). The Tori model of change and the changing woman. *Training and Development Journal, 29(8),* 22-29.

Henley, N. M. (1973). The politics of touch. In P. Brown (Ed.), *Radical psychology.* New York: Harper & Row.

Johnson, M. (1976). An approach to feminist therapy. *Psychotherapy: Theory, Research and Practice, 13(1),* 72-76.

Kirsh, B. (1974). Consciousness-raising groups as therapy for women. In V. Franks & V. Burtle (Eds.), *Women in therapy: New psychotherapies for a changing society.* New York: Brunner/Mazel.

Klein, M. H. (1976). Feminist concepts of therapy outcome. *Psychotherapy: Theory, Research and Practice, 13(1),* 89–91.

Kravetz, D. (1976). Consciousness-raising groups and group psychotherapy: Alternative mental health resources for women. *Psychotherapy: Theory, Research and Practice, 13(1),* 66–71.

Kravetz, D. (1978). Consciousness-raising groups in the 1970's. *Psychology of Women Quarterly, 3(2),* 168–186.

Kravetz, D., Marecek, J., & Finn, S. E. (1983). Factors influencing women's participation in consciousness-raising groups. *Psychology of Women Quarterly, 7(3),* 257–271.

Lieberman, M. A., & Bond, G. R. (1976). The problem of being a woman: A survey of 1700 women in consciousness-raising groups. *Journal of Applied Behavioral Science, 12(3),* 363–379.

Lieberman, M. A., Solow, N., Bond, G. A., & Reibstein, J. (1979). The psychotherapeutic impact of women's consciousness-raising groups. *Archives of General Psychiatry, 36(2),* 161–168.

Marecek, J., Kravetz, D., & Finn, S. (1979). Comparison of women who enter feminist therapy and women who enter traditional therapy. *Journal of Consulting and Clinical Psychology, 47(4),* 734–742.

Meador, B., Solomon, E., & Bowen, M. (1972). Encounter groups for women only. In L. Solomon & B. Berzan (Eds.), *Perspectives on encounter groups.* San Francisco: Jossey-Bass.

Nassi, A. J., & Abramowitz, S. I. (1978). Raising consciousness about women's groups: Process and outcome research. *Psychology of Women Quarterly, 3(2),* 139–157.

Orlinsky, D. E., & Howard, K. I. (1976). The effects of sex of therapist on the therapeutic experiences of women. *Psychotherapy: Theory, Research and Practice, 13(1),* 82–88.

Rice, J. K., & Rice, D. G. (1973). Implications of the women's liberation movement for psychotherapy. *American Journal of Psychiatry, 130(2),* 191–195.

Schutz, W. C. (1967). *Joy.* New York: Grove Press, Inc.

Shorr, S. I., & Jason, L. A. (1982). A comparison of men's and women's consciousness-raising groups. *Group, 6(4),* 51–55.

Sullivan, M. (1983). Introduction to women emerging: Group approaches. *Journal for Specialists in Group Work, 8(1),* 3–8.

Walker, L. J. S. (1981). Are women's groups different? *Psychotherapy: Theory, Research and Practice, 18(2),* 240–245.

Warren, L. W. (1976). The therapeutic status of consciousness-raising groups. *Professional Psychology, 7(2),* 133–139.

Wolman, C. S. (1976). Therapy groups for women. *American Journal of Psychiatry, 133(3),* 274–277.

■ 2
Feminist Therapy in Groups: A Decade of Change

MARILYN JOHNSON

Celia was having marital problems; Linda had felt depressed since her mother's psychiatric hospitalization eight years ago; Janie wanted a life as an independent craftswoman, but her fears about her competence prevented her from leaving a deadly job; Irene's relationship with friends and family were in constant turmoil, because she was so often critical and angry; Carol was becoming an academic superstar, but she couldn't sustain an intimate relationship with a lover; Lily couldn't organize her life to work sufficiently at her painting to win a necessary scholarship; and Ruth felt unable to set up her own home, because attempts to do so upset her parents too greatly.

Clinicians reading these descriptions in 1987 might recommend a variety of therapies (or nontherapies) to these women. Clinicians at the Philadelphia Feminist Therapy Collective in the early and mid 1970s nearly always recommended group therapy, and, in fact, the women described above were typical of the collective's clients. It is this contrast in therapists' preferred modes of treatment and clients' presenting problems that I would like to address in this chapter. The perspectives of some early consumers of feminist therapy services and the views of current feminist therapists will demonstrate some of the changes of the past 10 to 15 years.

GROUPS IN THE 1970s

In 1976 I published a paper describing the group therapy conducted at the Philadelphia Feminist Therapy Collective between 1972 and 1975, and my comments about the collective in the present chapter refer primarily to this period. To reread the earlier paper is to recall the *zeitgeist* of that time (Johnson, 1976). The collective therapists were, of course, exclusively female; nearly all of the therapy provided in the first years of the collective's life was group therapy, because of our belief in the power of women in groups (Brodsky, 1973). Nearly all (80%) of the first clients were feminists; two-thirds of our clients had previously had individual therapy with male therapists and were determined to work with feminist therapists the second time around. Therapists and clients came together empowered by the energy of the revitalized Women's Movement.

Two factors that characterized practice during the early life of the collective are relevant here. First, women with a variety of presenting problems were assigned to groups on the basis of convenience. No attempt was made to build groups around similar concerns. The influence of consciousness-raising (CR) groups on group therapy was greater then than it is now, and this influence stressed that, in women's groups, individual differences were minimized and that a sense of common concern was maximized (Bernardez, 1983). The collective groups focused attention on common sources of oppression, on interpersonal issues among group members, and on the strength of sisterly support. The therapists were guided by principles later delineated by Butler (1985).

The second factor was that the presenting problems or target complaints of the collective clients were typical of those of other women at that time. In the 1976 study, 24 collective clients were compared with a sample of 26 women of similar age and education who had completed a course of individual therapy at the University of Pennsylvania. These two groups defined quite similar problems, and several of these could be subsumed under a label of mild depression (e.g., low self-esteem, inertia and directionlessness, uncertainty about the future, and discomfort with oneself). No one named physical abuse or work stresses, and only 17% of the collective clients and none of the Pennsylvania clients named compulsive overeating. These problems surely existed at the time, but widespread attention had not yet been focused on psychological services for treating them.

The emphasis on group therapy at the collective was effective, according to the posttherapy evaluations of the early clients who were compared with the women from the Pennsylvania study. Although the mean length of therapy for the collective clients was only four months compared to 10 months for the other sample, the two groups were virtually identical in the severity of their pretherapy target complaints and posttherapy target complaints and in the degree of their satisfaction with therapy. Certainly two of the nonspecific factors that contributed to therapeutic success among collective clients were the shared political philosophy of clients and therapists and the enthusiasm therapists felt in finally being able to conduct therapy as they wanted to. Some other curative factors will be discussed later.

GROUPS IN THE 1980s

The decade since the publication of the collective study has been marked by greatly expanded psychological services for women. The current group therapy literature indicates a shift from groups focusing primarily on interpersonal issues to groups organized around specific problem areas. This may be a reflection of growing sophistication on the part of group therapists who saw that the single issue emphasis of self-help groups could accelerate change. Also, there has been an expansion of the concerns focused on by these groups. The feminist influence on psychotherapy has legitimized the fact that psychological trauma suffered by victims of rape, physical abuse, and other causes is worthy of therapeutic attention.

Survey of Feminist Therapists

In order to ascertain the depth of these changes, I recently surveyed feminist therapists to answer the following questions. How many of them conduct groups? Do these groups resemble the interpersonal process groups of the early collective days, or do they emphasize single issues? Has interest in women's therapy groups increased or decreased? Why? Do today's therapists view group therapy's curative powers similarly to or differently from early collective clients? For what client problems would therapists regard group therapy as the treatment of choice? And finally, do therapists differ on these questions as a function of their professional discipline or of the region in which they practice?

Sample

A seven-item survey was sent to 135 members of the Feminist Therapy Institute, Inc.; 81 (60%) responded. As Table 2.1 indicates, the majority of the

TABLE 2.1 Characteristics of Feminist Therapist Sample

Age	N	%	Discipline	N	%	Region	N	%
20–29	1	1	Social work	19	24	Northeast	20	25
30–39	24	30	Education	4	5	Southeast	8	10
40–49	39	48	Psychology	51	63	Midwest	17	21
50–59	11	14	Nursing	1	1	Southwest	8	10
60–69	6	7	Psychiatry	1	1	West	21	26
70 and older	0	0	Pastoral care	0	6	Northwest	7	8
			Other	5				

respondents were between 30 and 49 years of age, were social workers and psychologists, and practiced in the northeastern, midwestern, and western sections of the country.

RESULTS AND DISCUSSION

Group Therapy Involvement

Several of the survey questions will be examined as they were answered by the total group of feminist therapists, by the disciplines of social work and psychology, and by the region in which the therapists practice. Although 11 therapists indicated disciplines other than social work or psychology, there were too few to make comparisons.

First, therapists were asked if they conducted women's therapy groups, and the majority (65%) stated that they did. When regional differences were examined, there was a wide range from 43% (northwestern therapists) to 88% (southeastern therapists). The other groups were as follows: southwest 50%, northeast 65%, west 66%, and midwest 71%. The groups at the high and low extremes were two of the three small samples; it may be that the addition of data from more therapists would bring the northwestern and southeastern therapists' activity more in line with that of the other groups. There was only a minor difference between the percentage of social workers (74%) and psychologists (63%) who conducted groups.

Therapists were then asked to indicate the type(s) of group they conducted. Three options were provided: (1) the participants were women—no further specification; (2) the participants were women working on interpersonal issues; and (3) the participants were women working on specific single issues such as compulsive eating, assertiveness, etc. The rationale for this question was to assess to what degree therapists were conducting groups like those described in the 1976 paper, that is, groups of women working on interpersonal issues. Of 53 therapists who stated that they conducted groups, 52 indicated the type(s) of groups. A total of 73% conduct at least one of the three types of groups, 25% conduct two types, and one person checked all three types of groups.

A total of 51% of the therapists indicated that they conducted specific issues groups; the remaining half was evenly divided between the other two choices. Therefore, only one-quarter of the therapists were conducting groups like those at the collective in the early 1970s. All of the northwestern therapists who conduct groups offer specific issue groups, as do 80% of the southwestern therapists. All regional groups offer a higher percentage of specific issue groups than of the other two types, although one-third of the northeastern, southeastern, and western feminists offer groups on interpersonal issues as well. Both social workers (63%) and psychologists (48%) conduct more specific issue groups than any other type of group; 31% of the psychologists conduct interpersonal relations focused groups, whereas only 19% of the social workers do so.

Perceptions of Group Therapy

As I noted above, the group therapy literature of the 1980s indicates a sharp decrease in articles concerning the women's therapy groups recommended by Brodsky (1973) and conducted at the collective and in other sites during the 1970s. To what can we attribute this decline? Do groups focused on specific issues now serve the purpose of the earlier groups? Have women clients moved back toward a desire for individual therapy? Are women's groups generally perceived as less valuable than they were? Broadly speaking, is the change a reflection of changes in the larger society (renewed emphasis on individualism, some backlash towards feminism), or is it a sign of the refinement of psychological services for women?

These questions were asked of the feminist therapists in this sample. Because the growth of specific issue groups has been so great, I asked the therapists to contrast them with the interpersonal issue types of groups defined above. That is, did the therapists believe that the demand for women's therapy groups focused on interpersonal issues had increased, decreased, or remained the same, and if they had seen a decrease, to what did they attribute this decrease?

The majority of the sample (58%) stated that there had been a change in the demand for women's groups/women's interpersonal relations groups; 22% saw no change, and 20% did not respond. Only the southwestern group differed on this point, with only 38% indicating change. Therapists from the northeast and midwest were tied at 65%, with those from the west and northwest tied at 57%. More of the social workers (68%) than psychologists (53%) indicated that a change had occurred. There was agreement that change had occurred, but the group split on the direction of the change, with 32% saying that demand for these groups had increased and 28% reporting a decrease. Unfortunately, 40% of the therapists did not respond to this question, so this finding is not a solid one.

Four reasons were given to explain why interpersonal issue groups might have decreased; therapists were asked to check as many as they wished. All four of the options were selected by approximately one-fourth of the therapists. The most frequently selected options stated that women's groups in general are less popular than in the past (28%) and that women find specific issue groups more helpful than other types (28%); 25% felt that more women want individual therapy than groups, and 23% agreed that therapists emphasize the value of specific issue groups more than other types of groups. There were few regional differences. Nearly half of the northeastern therapists agreed that women's groups are less popular now than in the past, and one-third of the western therapists indicated both that specific issue groups and individual therapy may be more helpful and popular now. The social workers and psychologists were very similar in giving almost equal weight to all of the options.

Curative Factors

In Yalom's (1975) classic book on group psychotherapy, he conceptualized group therapy's impact in the form of a number of curative factors. These factors spelled out the numerous means by which group therapy leads to positive change. Some of the factors could apply to group psychotherapy alone (e.g., group cohesiveness, a sense of universality, etc.), whereas others could occur in other kinds of psychotherapy as well (catharsis, insight, etc.). For the collective study, I developed a checklist of 20 curative factors, 11 of which were taken from Yalom's list, and nine were feminist therapy items that I wrote. Some of the feminist therapy items referred to the curative effect of closeness to other women, some to the value of having women as therapists, and others to clients' perceptions of themselves as women. Collective clients rated this checklist at the termination of therapy.

In the current survey, feminist therapists were presented with the 10 curative factors most frequently cited by the collective clients and were asked to rank them in terms of their curative value. Table 2.2 compares the rankings of the collective clients and the feminist therapists.

TABLE 2.2 Group Therapy Curative Factors Ranked by Feminist Therapies and Collective Clients

	Feminist therapists (N = 81)	Feminist Therapy Collective clients (N = 27)
Universality: Learning that one is not very different from other people	1	7
Group cohesiveness: Belonging to and being understood and accepted by a group	2	1
Insight: Learning why one thinks and feels the way one does	3	4
Interpersonal learning (input): Learning about the way one relates to other people	4	2
Interpersonal learning (output): Learning how one comes across to others	5	6
Catharsis: Getting things off one's chest	6	5
Importance of other women: Discovering that other women are central in one's life	7	9
Competent therapists: Seeing female therapists as competent women	8	3
Shared client–therapist experience: Knowing that female therapists share much of one's experience	9	8
Identification: Admiring and behaving like the therapists or another member of the group	10	10

For both groups, nearly all of the most curative factors are a function of the group process rather than of elements of feminist therapy. Only one feminist therapy item (seeing female therapists as competent women) was ranked in the top half of the items by clients. The climate of the times of the collective study and those clients' previous poor experience with male therapists may have led the collective clients to emphasize this factor. With regard to the Yalom curative factors, collective clients are similar to those studied by Marcovitz and Smith (1983), Yalom (1975), and Maxmen (1973) in naming group cohesiveness, insight, and interpersonal learning output and input as dominant curative factors.

Referral Patterns

Therapists were asked to name the type(s) of referrals they would make for women with the following complaints: panic attacks, physical abuse, work stress, compulsive eating and starving, relationship problems, and mild reactive depression. The types of referrals from which they were asked to choose were individual psychotherapy, a consciousness-raising group, a self-help group, a professionally-led psychotherapy group (subsequently called group therapy), or some other form of assistance. Their choices were examined for the group as a whole, for each regional group, and for the two most heavily represented disciplines, social work and psychology.[1] Many therapists made more than one choice for the various complaints. When therapists listed more than one type of therapy, these choices were assigned to a single category entitled "combined treatment."

Panic attacks. Of the entire sample, 65% would refer such clients for individual therapy. The majority of therapists from all regions selected individual therapy as the treatment of choice, and the social workers and psychologists were nearly identical in choosing individual therapy first, followed by group therapy and combined therapies.

Physical abuse. For the group as a whole, the only two choices made with any frequency were combined treatments (42%) and group therapy (36%). The most frequently recommended set of combined treatments was that of individual therapy and group therapy. The only regional differences were that therapists from the northeast recommended self-help groups more frequently than did therapists from the other regions. The psychologists and social workers differed somewhat, with 50% of the social workers pre-

---

[1] A copy of tables containing raw numbers and percentages for each subgroup can be obtained from the author.

ferring combined treatments (individual therapy plus group therapy) and with 43% of the psychologists choosing group therapy and 39% choosing the same combined treatment as that of the social workers.

Work Stress. For the total sample, self-help (28%) and combined treatments (26%) were recommended most frequently. No one combined treatment predominated for this problem. There were regional differences with therapists from the west, southwest, and northwest recommending self-help groups, and those from the other areas preferring combined treatments or consciousness-raising. The two disciplines were quite similar, with about one-third of each group opting for different choices. Both social workers and psychologists agreed that self-help groups were good choices for this problem. Of the psychologists, 15% also recommended CR, whereas only 6% of the social workers did so.

Compulsive eating and starving. Overall, group therapy was the first choice (42%), with combined treatments a close second (39%). The combination of individual therapy and group therapy was the choice of 63% of those therapists who chose combined treatments. Therapists from the southeast and southwest preferred group therapy, northeasterners chose combined treatments, and the others chose both options equally. Social workers and psychologists agreed about equally on the two treatments.

Relationship problems. The two most preferred treatments were group therapy (29%) and combined treatments (36%), primarily individual therapy with group therapy. There were some regional differences. The majority of therapists from the northeast, midwest, and west preferred combined therapies, whereas the others divided their choices across all options. The social workers and psychologists made relatively similar recommendations.

Mild reactive depression. The most frequently recommended treatment was individual psychotherapy (34%), with combined therapies (25%) and group therapy (21%) next. Several combinations of therapies were recommended for this problem, with none being clearly more popular than any other. The majority of therapists from every region except the northwest made this choice; 50% of northwestern therapists chose consciousness-raising and none of them recommended individual therapy. Nearly half (42%) of the psychologists preferred individual therapy, whereas the primary choice for the social workers was evenly divided between individual therapy and combined therapies.

Preference for Group Therapy

A final question concerns the preference of group therapists for this mode of treatment for a variety of problems. Do group therapists select professionally-led therapy groups as the preferred treatment for more presenting complaints than do therapists who do not conduct groups? Of the therapists, 65% conduct groups at the present time. Those who do and do not conduct groups would refer women to groups in relatively similar numbers.

None of the therapists selected group therapy as the treatment of choice for all six complaints. Approximately 20% of each group would recommend professionally-led group therapy for two or three of the six problems, and approximately 33% would do so for at least one complaint. The recommendation for professionally-led group therapy in combination with another form of therapy was made for at least one complaint by 20% of each group. However, more of the group therapists (62%) recommended this combination over the six complaints than did the nongroup therapists (43%). These findings suggest that group therapy is the treatment of choice for certain complaints, and that group therapists believe it is also a good addition to other therapies for a number of complaints.

In summary, then, individual therapy was the clear choice for women suffering panic attacks and, to a lesser extent, for women experiencing a mild reactive depression. In all other cases, some use of group therapy was recommended, alone or in conjunction with individual therapy. For work stress, a self-help group was the treatment of choice, but for women seeking help from physical abuse, eating difficulties, and relationship problems, a professionally-led group was recommended.

The six complaints considered here could be divided into two categories. One is comprised of problems for which women (and men) have long sought therapy: panic attacks, depression, and relationship difficulties. The other category consists of concerns for which women in large numbers have sought therapy only relatively recently: physical abuse, compulsive eating and starving, and work stress. The therapists in this survey recommended individual therapy for two of the three "traditional" problems and group therapy for all of the "new" problems. Perhaps the social oppression embodied in the "new" problems emerges more readily within a group setting than in a one-to-one encounter.

The regional and professional differences reported here may be of interest to individual therapists for comparative purposes, but they do not suggest any significant division among feminist therapists. It seems clear that most of them, regardless of training and location, believe that groups are generally more therapeutic for women than is individual therapy.

There is, of course, a caveat: the respondents may have reacted to my survey's focus on group therapy by choosing a group option more frequently than they would otherwise have done. Nevertheless, it is encouraging to find that the curative powers and feminist values of women's groups are still esteemed by feminist therapists.

In the future, we may see a renewed appreciation for the groups that focus on interpersonal relations. Not all women seek therapy for single problems, and not all women begin therapy with a clear understanding of the problems they seek to solve. Such women may respond well to the interpersonal relations group. Therapists should be encouraged to compare the effects of single issue and interpersonal relations groups for women suffering with similar concerns. This would be a worthy effort over the next decade.

REFERENCES

Bernardez, T. (1983). Women's groups. In M. Rosenbaum (Ed.), *Handbook of short-term therapy groups*. New York: McGraw Hill.

Brodsky, A. (1973). The consciousness-raising group as a model for therapy with women. *Psychotherapy: Theory, Research and Practice, 10(1)*, 24–29.

Butler, M. (1985). Guidelines for feminist therapy. In L. Rosewater & L. Walker (Eds.), *Handbook of feminist therapy: Women's issues in Psychotherapy*. New York: Springer.

Johnson, M. (1976). An approach to feminist therapy. *Psychotherapy: Theory, Research and Practice, 13(1)*, 72–76.

Marcovitz, R. J., & Smith, J. E. (1983). Patients' perceptions of curative factors in short-term group psychotherapy. *International Journal of Group Psychotherapy, 33(1)*, 21–39.

Maxmen, J. (1973). Group therapy as viewed by hospitalized patients. *Archives of General Psychiatry, 28(3)*, 404–408.

Yalom, I. (1975). *The theory and practice of group psychotherapy* (2nd ed.). New York: Basic Books.

■ 3
Women's Socialization and Feminist Groups

DIANNE S. BURDEN and NAOMI GOTTLIEB

The gender-based socialization that women experience sets two major tasks for group work with them. First, group work needs to counteract the dysfunctional consequences in women's general behavior and attitudes that result from life-long reinforcement of sex-specific and subordinate roles. Second, feminist group work with women needs to attend to the particular ways in which women usually respond in group situations, especially mixed sex groups. Strategies used in feminist groups can then be based on what is known about traits women generally exhibit in society at large and in groups in particular, as a result of their socialization. The purpose of this chapter is to ground feminist group activities in what is known about the effects on women of sex-role socialization and gender-based discrimination.

This chapter makes selective use of the considerable literature on women's socialization to set an agenda for feminist group work. From that literature, the case is made about the overall problematic effects of how women are raised and the related ramifications for how women usually respond in groups. Strategies in group work are then recommended that build directly on this analysis.

DYSFUNCTIONAL CONSEQUENCES OF
WOMEN'S SOCIALIZATION

The focal point of women's socialization is the primary role as wife and mother. Women are expected to be family- and home-oriented. Much of women's world view and behaviors stems from that basic conception. Several themes will illustrate the connection between sex-role socialization and women's subsequent cognitions and behaviors. These themes will demonstrate the nature of the dysfunctions that feminist groups might counteract. The emphasis on affiliation with and caretaking of others, the power differentials and dependence inherent in the marital role, particular attributions of control, the devaluation of other women, and limitations on achievement are essential characteristics of women's external and internal world and derive from their pervasive socialization into traditional roles. These outcomes of socialization impose constraints on a full range of options for individual behavior and result in problems for many women.

Several cautions need to precede the discussion of these themes as problems for women clients. First, social changes, e.g., the Women's Movement and the accelerated labor force participation by women, may be leading to a dilution of the primary emphasis on women's family role. Ongoing empirical inquiry into the lives of the younger generation of women may lead to shifts in grounded knowledge about women's development and social status. Second, scholars continue to raise constructive questions about earlier conclusions concerning girls and women (Maccoby & Jacklin, 1974, 1976; Weitzman, 1984) and about how knowledge is developed by feminist social scientists (Acker, Barry, & Esseveld, 1983; Gottlieb, 1987). The relatively new knowledge base derived from feminist scholarship may require continual revisions, and the analysis in the present discussion, though grounded, must be considered tentative. Third, some of the consequences for women included here as problematic may not be inherently so. For example, women's affiliative behavior and concern for the well-being of others have been discounted in some discussions of sex-role socialization. They need to be redefined as valuable traits to be balanced in women with other valued traits and to be shared by men as well. Gilligan's (1982) analysis suggests a different, not an inferior, moral development in girls and women. As we argue for a fuller appreciation for women's distinctive issues, long hidden by male-oriented scholarship, we also advocate a healthy skepticism about the current state of knowledge and an acknowledgment of a continually changing world. Finally, the empirical studies on which many of these observations are based have, by and large, relied on the experiences of comparatively young, white, middle-class heterosexual women. The knowledge base will be enhanced as we add the differences and similarities for the women who are not represented in those categories.

Emphasis on Affiliation

From the earliest months of life young girls are taught to derive their greatest satisfaction from positive emotional response and approval of others and not from an internal sense of achievement from their own accomplishment (Rubin, Provenzano, & Luria, 1974). Young girls are encouraged to be more passive, dependent on their parents for approval, and family-oriented than are boys. Girls are groomed from an early age to be both physical and emotional caretakers and to gain their sense of identity from the opinions of others. The reality for most women's lives is that their economic future depends on achieving and maintaining approval in marriage. Women must remain attractive and desirable. To maintain her husband's acceptance, a woman may need to downplay her own achievements if they interfere with the demand to please him (Marciano, 1981).

Caretaking Role

An adjunct to the affiliate imperative is the expectation that women will be family caretakers, attending to both physical and emotional well-being. They are socialized at an early age to be responsible for household chores and emotional support activities, which are generally held in low esteem compared with other societal roles. Combined family and work roles mean that caretaking responsibilities added to workplace demands are major components of most women's lives. This is true for the more than half of married women who work and for the large majority of women who are single parents. These multiple demands are being made even more complex for many women by the changing demographics of an aging population. Women are increasingly responsible for caring for their aging parents as well as their own children and frequently their grandchildren. Most men do not share equally in these tasks (Burden 1983, 1985; Condran & Bode, 1982). Aside from the practical demands of these roles and their lifelong character, the important issue for this discussion is that women appear to accept the inequitable requirements of their roles. Caretaking and maintaining the emotional well-being of others are high on their list of priorities (Gurman & Klein, 1980). Maintaining the family equilibrium usually requires that women place their own needs for nurturing and self-enhancement at a low priority.

Power Differentials

The realm to which women are consigned is clearly not the seat of political power in this society. From elementary school textbooks that display a wider variety of economic and political options for men (Russo, 1984; Weitzman, Eifler, Hokada, & Ross, 1972) to wage differentials in sex-segregated occupations (Lloyd & Niemi, 1979), the message to women is clear. Men have the power, not only in economic and political circles, but in individual households as well (Steil, 1984). As Weitzman (1984) comments, "children understand the relative worth of the two sexes at quite young ages. The little girl is therefore aware that she is being pushed, albeit gently, into behaviors that are neither considered desirable nor rewarded by society at large" (p. 171). Women know that their husbands hold jobs with higher pay and social status and that to depend on their own salary would mean a decline in standard of living for themselves and their children. The young girl being socialized to her societal role is well aware of these circumstances. Rossi's (1964) description of children reared in an egalitarian home makes this point well by contrast. In Rossi's conception, children would see both mother and father employed in well-paid work outside the home and sharing home responsibilities equally. Girls could then visualize a future in which their potential for paid work could be realized and in which caregiving responsibilities were neither demeaned nor relegated exclusively to women.

Young girls are effectively taught that attributes associated with power—aggressiveness, a sense of strength, flaunting of worldly knowledge—are considered inappropriate for women. The importance of men, and particularly their connection with affairs that matter beyond the family, are pervasive in the experience of girls and women and are reinforced throughout their lives. Women feel uncomfortable in exercising power in large part because of the lack of permission or experience in doing so. Lipman-Blumen (1984) maintains that women accept their weaker position as "inevitable," as a "result of their own inadequacy," and as "the best available situation under the circumstances" (p. 9). The harmful effects on women of the power imbalance in traditional marriages have become evident as scholars have introduced sociopolitical factors into analyses of family relationships (Marecek & Kravetz, 1977).

Dependence

A close corollary of the emphasis on affiliation in women's lives and the power imbalance they experience is the essentially dependent role that women assume in society and in their central personal relationships

(Greenwood-Audant, 1984). Women, in general, are more passive than men and learn to defer to them. They are socialized to avoid risktaking behavior and to stay close to home. Powerlessness and dependence have important consequences for personality and self-image. Gurman and Klein (1980) employ major psychological theories to demonstrate that, across theoretical frameworks, women's socially inferior position is seen as leading to personality dysfunction. To cite some of their examples, within object relations theory, the woman's dependency in both family of origin and marriage does not allow her to differentiate herself as an autonomous individual; within behavioral theory, women are viewed as failing to learn effective problem-solving skills; within a cognitive framework, dependency and powerlessness are described as external- and helplessness-oriented attributes.

The reality of women's poor economic prospects reinforces the personal difficulties to be encountered in standing on their own. A bargain appears to be struck between men and women in the traditional family formation pattern. Women will provide physical and emotional caretaking functions in return for financial and personal security. Women will enhance men's self-esteem by deferring to men's higher status and perceived greater value. Men, on the other hand, will increase women's self-esteem by providing her a measure of success (i.e., acquisition of a male partner) in the view of the family and society.

This bargain, however, has the potential for serious negative outcomes for women. In the reality of the modern world, women can no longer rely on men for financial and emotional security. However, women still exhibit sex-typed behaviors of lack of assertiveness, dependency on others for identity, and deferral to men for leadership roles. The bargain has been particularly dysfunctional in its tendency to foster an inequitable political and economic situation of women at home, in the labor force, and in the larger society. As has been documented elsewhere, women and their children are at high risk for poverty and the social isolation of living alone (Pearce, 1979). Traditional sex-role socialization has provided little support in equipping women to deal with the exigencies of their lives. Socialization to expect to be cared for by others, combined with real life requirements for a growing proportion of women that they care for themselves, is a powerful combination for depression (Guttentag, Salasin, & Belle, 1980). Many of the problems that women come into counseling to address are those exacerbated by this poor fit between expectations and reality. Single parents, battered women, and displaced homemakers are all examples of women clients who may perceive that they have fulfilled their part of the bargain but feel betrayed and immobilized, because their expectations have not been met by others. The negative effects of sex-role socialization for these women leave them ill-equipped to deal with the stresses of their lives.

Locus of Explanation and Control

The expectation ingrained in women that they are responsible for the well-being of others appears closely related to their tendency to blame themselves when things go awry (Brewin & Shapiro, 1984; Dweck & Repucci, 1973). Conversely, because women do not have a well-developed and reality-reinforced sense of control over their circumstances, they tend to attribute successful outcomes to factors outside their control. If they are successful, it is due to good luck. Both tendencies—to self-blame and to refuse self-credit—further exacerbate a sense of powerlessness to affect successfully the world around them.

Devaluation of Other Women

As girls are socialized to a role that does not carry appreciable weight in society, the process of devaluing women is set in motion. They see themselves and other women as less important and less powerful, and therefore, they do not esteem same-sex friendships. As they enter adulthood, many heterosexual women transfer their approval-seeking behavior from their parents to men. Personal success and economic security depend on the acquisition of a husband. Other women become rivals in the crucial marital game. This competitive position vis-a-vis other women for marital partners occurs not only in early adult life but, in view of the current divorce rate, continues throughout the life cycle.

Conflicts in Achievement

Previous sections have asserted that women are not powerful and autonomous actors in this society. The specific impact of this circumstance on their abilities to achieve needs special emphasis. The socialization messages and the reinforcing reality are clear: a sense of personal value is to be obtained mainly through the family role and the accomplishments of others; achievements outside the home are constrained by a limited number of sex-segregated occupational choices, all paid comparatively poorly; the wife must not exceed her husband's accomplishments or salary. Conflicts result when a woman's sense of her potential is not congruent with how she must act in order to insure social and economic security via marriage (Horner, 1972). For these reasons, women tend to depress their expectations for their own competencies and to derive satisfaction mainly from the achievement of others—husbands and children. However, the possibilities for change in these perceptions is evident in the higher achievement motivations found in daughters of career-oriented mothers (Huston-Stein & Higgins-Trenk, 1978). These findings also suggest the potential for constructive modeling to counteract socialization forces toward limited expectations of self.

CONSEQUENCES OF SOCIALIZATION FOR WOMEN IN GROUPS

These general characteristics of women derived from their socialization suggest a set of behaviors and attitudes that women are likely to exhibit in groups. They will likely try to please other people, particularly men, and may find it difficult, because of lack of practice, to identify their own needs. The need for the approval of others, as a central motivation in interpersonal relations, will carry over into group interaction and will be intensified in mixed-sex groups. Women group members may attempt to act out their caretaking in the group. As in other circumstances, they may need to give higher priority to pleasing others than to expressing their own needs. They may tend not to value the experience and opinions of other women nor to put much store in their own competencies.

Group work with women clients can be a powerful antidote to the immobilizing consequences of sex-role socialization. Before describing a feminist approach to group work with women, the impact of sex-role socialization for women in traditional groups must be addressed. A traditional group may be a long-term, open-ended therapy group for both men and women. The group may be led by a male therapist—possibly with a female co-therapist. For many women clients this type of group will simply reinforce their dysfunctional sex-role socialization patterns and may provide a further obstacle to women achieving their full personal power. In stressful situations, both men and women tend to revert to familiar sex-role behaviors. Group settings for women, whether they be therapy groups, staff meetings, or classroom situations, tend to be particularly stressful. As a result, men tend to dominate, and women tend to defer to them (Baird, 1976). Both revert to familiar patterns, where men are expected to take charge, and women are expected to defer to men's higher status and to provide support through listening. Women run the risk of appearing domineering if they talk too much. Women's deferring behavior may be exacerbated by group leaders' tendency to reinforce male participation and to extinguish female participation. Women in mixed groups, therefore, are less likely to talk freely, less likely to express their anger toward men, and less likely to assume leadership roles.

Dependence on a group leader, frequently male, simply reinforces women's sense of external locus of control and identity through approval of parental or male others. As a result, women are encouraged to adjust to their situation, not to challenge it. They may be encouraged to focus on an intrapsychic or interpersonal interpretation of their problems rather than a social, political, or economic interpretation. Because women clients are continually on the lower end of the male/female or therapist/client power differential, they may not find it possible to move beyond sex-role socialized cognitions and behaviors in a traditional group setting (Lerman, 1976).

Counteracting Negative Sex-Role Socialization Patterns

A feminist approach to group work with women clients counteracts the negative consequences for women of sex-role socialization by making explicit the impact of socialization and social policy factors throughout the group process. The explicit nature of the approach serves to diminish the magical quality of the therapy intervention and to reduce the power imbalance between women clients and the group leader. (See Brody's discussion of therapist as group model in Chapter 8.) Women are resocialized during the course of the group (1) to value the support they can gain from other women; (2) to distinguish the personal from the political by focusing on the impact of social and political factors on their lives; (3) to gain a sense of internal locus of control through developing competencies at problem-solving and skill-building; and (4) to gain power through the development of leadership skills. All of these strategies serve to counteract traditional sex-role socialization, which encourages women to be isolated from other women in the competition for approval from men and to deny their own needs for personal growth in favor of family demands. The following sections discuss in greater detail the major components of a feminist approach to group work with women and their counteracting influence on sex-role socialization.

Support to Decrease Isolation

Women who enter groups for women frequently mention that it is their first experience in real interactions with other women in their situation. A single mother, for example, for some time after separation from her spouse may remain in a community that is primarily married couples and may be ostracized by married friends. If she is in a work setting where she is isolated in an office doing clerical work, as is true for many women, she may have no contact with other single parents. Social isolation is a major problem for single mothers as they try to balance the many demands of their lives with little support from former friendship networks (Burden, 1980). Similarly, battered women are frequently characterized by the intense isolation that is imposed upon them by their spouses. A husband may jealously guard his wife in the home, prevent her from driving, or forbid her to visit with friends in an escalating attempt to control her. The isolation experienced in both of these situations may lead a woman to feel she is alone with her problem and, therefore, is deviant, bad, and to blame. The isolation both stems from and reinforces sex-role socialization, which encourages women to be husband- and child-centered and discourages them from developing cooperative group- or team-building activities with women or men outside of the family. From a political power perspective, women's isolation serves to diffuse the potential power they would derive from organized support both within the family and in the larger society.

Feminist group work reduces the impact of sex-role socialization by making the isolation of women explicit. Group members learn from the commonalities that they all experience that they are not alone in their situation. They learn the world is full of other single mothers, other abused women, and other displaced homemakers facing the same struggles, fears, and anger. For many, the group provides the first experience at interacting with other women in a noncompetitive way. They learn to value and trust other women and by extension to value their gender and themselves (Gottlieb, Burden, McCormick, & Nicarthy, 1983).

Women who come to groups have frequently been emotionally starved by inadequate nurturing. They have been socialized to be the caretakers of their husbands, their children, their churches, the PTA, their bosses, and their own aging parents. They receive little nurturing in return. The result may be depression, dependent behaviors toward children or ex-spouses, inappropriate anger, overeating, or reliance on alcohol, drugs, or prescription medication. A major function feminist groups fulfill is to provide women with the opportunity to be nurtured themselves. Women learn that they can gain tremendous support, understanding, and caring from other women in their situation. Such a discovery provides a major impetus to a woman gaining her own sense of internal locus of control.

Personal Versus Political Sources of Problems

A key component of feminist women's groups of all types has been their consciousness-raising (CR) focus. Women have traditionally been socialized to internalize the blame for their problems and to assume that their difficulties stem from personal inadequacies. Their isolation leads them to believe that everyone else is functioning well and that they are alone in their inability to cope. Feminist group work offers an alternative explanation for much of the difficulty that women experience. The impact of the social, political, and economic origins of women's difficulties is made explicit. This approach refuses to accept society's analysis that women have problems because they are defective, i.e., because they do not budget their welfare check well, because they had too many children, because they are too lazy to work, because they were not good wives and mothers. A feminist approach suggests that women have difficulty finding affordable child care and housing for example, not because women are inadequate, but because the political system provides inadequate subsidized child care and housing, while the economic system makes it highly unlikely that a woman will be able to earn a high enough wage to exist on the free market. The result of such a bind for women is predictable stress due to the inequities of the job, home, and childrearing demands on them combined with inadequate time for themselves.

A CR component gives permission and provides a supportive environment for women to express their long-standing feelings of unfairness and anger at men and at the political and economic system. The acknowledgment and ventilation of women's anger at the unfairness of their condition is an important step in reduction of self-blame and in the mobilization of energy toward developing strategies to solve specific problems.

Educational and Skill-Building Component

Closely related to the consciousness-raising focus of feminist group work is an emphasis on education and skill-building to reduce the negative effects of sex-role socialization. Group members learn from each other as well as from the group leader. They provide modeling and reinforcement among themselves to learn both about the dynamics of their situation and about strategies to solve their problems. Single parents, for example, who are experiencing the high anxiety period of recent separation can look to women in the group who have been divorced longer to discover that they too will feel better in time. Longer-term single mothers, on the other hand, who feel stressed by the boring grind of their lives can gain a measure of how far they have progressed from the anxiety inherent in immediate post-separation. Similarly, battered women who are new to the group can learn from longer-term members that the dynamics of battering are similar from case to case, and the problem is one that is likely to get worse with time, not go away. Women who have been away from the battering situation longer may reaffirm their resolve to stay away by viewing the distress of newer women to the group (Gottlieb et al., 1983).

The group also offers the opportunity for members to request information on a range of issues about which they were given little knowledge during their socialization process. The group leader can provide an important resource for the group by bringing in requested material on such issues as parenting skills, sex-role development in children, financial skills, assertion-building skills, time management, career and life planning, and female sexuality. In a safe environment with other trusted women, group members may for the first time be able to express concerns about the development of male children's sexual identity in a female-headed family, or about fears of handling their own finances, paying bills, and completing tax forms. Much of the utility of a feminist approach to working with women clients lies in the focus on providing practical skills and tools that will empower a woman to solve problems, take new risks, and gain a sense of her own competency to function as an independent adult.

Problem-Solving Approach

If the goal of group work with women is to empower them to take charge of their own lives through support from other women, then the power of each member must be reinforced by focusing on the partnership that exists among group members and leader. As long as a power differential is maintained between leader and members, women members will be encouraged to stay in their traditional sex-typed dependent roles. A problem-solving approach to group work provides an effective means of reducing the power imbalance and of focusing on the joint effort of solving specific problems. Women clients frequently feel so overwhelmed by the multiplicity of their problems that they have difficulty identifying one or two specific problems. Life may seem hopeless and unmanageable. Such is the result of socialization patterns that channel women into accepting an external locus of control. That is, if someone else (a husband) is expected to provide financial support and happiness, a woman's only recourse may be to try to exert control over him. If he is no longer there, she may be left helpless, confused, and in a rage. Or, as in the case of a battered woman, if he is physically abusing her, she may feel helpless to change that pattern since he, not she, has been the one in control.

A problem-solving approach attempts to demystify problems by pinpointing and separating them and then by prioritizing them. Once problems are identified and prioritized, group members select one specific problem to be their project for the remainder of the group. This approach moves women from simply talking about their situation to taking active steps toward changing that situation. Women may select projects such as moving to a better apartment, finding a new job, asking for a raise, getting children to share with household responsibilities, taking legal steps to deal with a violent ex-spouse, making a career plan, or returning to school. Part of each group session may then involve planning and monitoring implementation strategies. Group members experience not only their own successes but each other's as well. In an assertion training group, for example, members may plan and carry out specific strategies for handling situations that have been intimidating in the past. These may include dealing with a demanding boss or negotiating more equitable relationships with family members. The group provides a supportive place to vent anger, devise strategies, practice new behaviors, and report on results. Since women frequently have been socialized to feel that assertive behavior is unfeminine and even dangerous, they are often fearful of the results. The group provides the nurturing and support necessary to change long-held socialization patterns.

The key outcome that a problem-solving approach engenders is an increase in internal locus of control for women in the group. This factor alone serves to counteract socialized beliefs about incompetency and the need to rely on men to survive. The approach also counters the belief that problems are indicative of personal defects within the woman. Problems come to be seen as external obstacles that require planning, strategizing, action, and mutual support to overcome.

LEADERSHIP AND GROUP FACILITATION SKILLS

As has been mentioned, a major focus of feminist group work is on reducing the power differential between leader and group members. The minimization of the power differential counteracts socialization patterns that encourage women to be dependent on parental figures and to seek approval from outside of themselves. Group leadership then consists of structured group sessions in the early phases of group development to foster a safe atmosphere where members can participate freely. In a feminist approach, there are no covert agendas. The leader makes the process explicit from the beginning, discusses objectives and motivations of the group, and lets group members know what they can expect from participation. Since the leader as a woman shares the same sex-role socialization process as the members, self-disclosure and role modeling become important strategies of participant empowerment. The group is encouraged early on to determine the structure and content of the sessions. The leader becomes a resource person and professional consultant to the group in assisting members to achieve their objectives. Other group members, however, are as important as the professional facilitator in giving members permission to be angry, to be assertive, to be nurtured, take risks, and be leaders. This element of permission, along with the elements of skill-building, the reinforcement of newly acquired cognitions and behaviors, and the encouragement to take control of their lives are vital factors of feminist groups that counteract dysfunctional sex-role socialization of women. Whereas sex-role socialization essentially prepares women to be compliant to the wishes and needs of others, feminist group work resocializes them to take risks, be leaders, and trust in their own judgment about the world.

FORMAT ISSUES OF FEMINIST GROUP WORK

A few words are in order about format issues in a feminist approach to group work. The format in itself may tend to counteract the impact of sex-role socialization. In order to counteract dependency on the group and group leader, for example, feminist groups are frequently quite structured and time-limited. Identification of explicit objectives, rather than free association type therapy sessions, reinforces the view that much of women's difficulties are due to external factors that can be changed or resolved. In other words, women can do more than simply cope with their situation or analyze the intrapsychic or familial and interpersonal patterns that some theorists identify as the cause of women's problems. In a structured problem-solving format, group members can distinguish between the personal and political aspects of their situation and begin to develop explicit strategies to deal with both.

A feminist approach to group work strives to lessen environmental barriers to women receiving assistance by providing childcare and transportation options to enable women to attend groups. Rather than accepting the societal assumption that women should be responsible on their own for their children, feminist groups encourage women to feel they have a right to ask for and receive assistance with their childrearing responsibilities. They have a right to expect the community to take some communal share or responsibility for childrearing.

Key questions frequently asked about groupwork with women are whether women need to be in groups that exclude men and whether women's groups require women leaders. A feminist approach to group work does advocate the need for all-women groups at least in the initial stages of group development. The entire sex-role socialization process is aimed at making women desirable, compliant caretakers of men and children. Most heterosexual women are so focused on pleasing men, attracting men, and providing emotional sustenance to men that the presence of men in a group greatly lessens women's ability to express themselves, particularly their anger, freely. The presence of a male leader establishes the same conflicting pattern and reinforcement of traditional sex-role behavior. Successful counteraction of dysfunctional sex-role socialization outcomes requires a hiatus from traditional male/female power differentials and a factoring out of the inhibiting effects of males on a group of women. As women learn to trust their own perceptions and gain assertiveness through support and mutual reinforcement, they become more able to interact with men from a position of equal strength.

CONCLUSION

This chapter has identified major elements of sex-role socialization of women and has discussed their negative impacts on women's lives. It has also discussed how socialized sex-role cognitions and behaviors are reinforced by traditional group experiences for women. The chapter has focused on key characteristics of feminist group work with women clients that counteract negative outcomes of sex-role socialization. A feminist approach to group work provides a resocializtion process that gives women the right to be nurtured as well as to nurture, that helps women distinguish between the personal and political sources of their difficulties, and that empowers women through skill building, problem-solving, and leadership-training techniques.

REFERENCES

Acker, J., Barry, K., & Esseveld, J. (1983). Objectivity and truth: Problems in doing feminist research. *Women's Studies International Forum, 6*(4), 423–435.

Baird, J.E. (1976). Sex differences in group communication: A review of relevant research. *Quarterly Journal of Speech, 62*(2), 179–192.

Brewin, C., & Shapiro, D. (1984). Beyond locus of control: Attrributions of responsibility for positive and negative outcomes. *British Journal of Psychology, 75*(1), 43–49.

Burden, D. (1980). Women as single parents: Alternative services for a neglected population. In N. Gottlieb (Ed.), *Alternative social services for women.* New York: Columbia University Press.

Burden, D. (1983). The interaction of job and homelife responsibilities: A comparison of married and single parent employees. (Unpublished doctoral dissertation, Brandeis University, Waltham, MA.). *Dissertation Abstracts International, 45,* 961A.

Burden, D. (1985). *Preliminary report on the managing of job and homelife demands in corporations study* (Progress report No. 3). USDHHS Office of Human Development Services, Washington, D.C.

Condran, J., & Bode, J. (1982). Rashomon, working wives and Middletown. *Journal of Marriage and the Family, 44(2),* 421–426.

Dweck, C., & Repucci, N. (1973). Learned helplessness and reinforcement responsibility in children. *Journal of Personality and Social Psychology, 25(1),* 109–116.

Gilligan, C. (1982). *In a different voice.* Cambridge, MA: Harvard University Press.

Gottlieb, N. (1987). Dilemmas and strategies in research on women. In D. Burden & N. Gottlieb (Eds.), *The woman client: Recent developments in knowledge and research.* NY: Methuen, Inc.

Gottlieb, N., Burden, D., McCormick, R., & Nicarthy, G. (1983). The distinctive attributes of feminist groups. *Social Work with Groups, 6(3/4),* 81–93.

Greenwood-Audant, L. (1984). The internalization of powerlessness: A case study of the displaced homemaker. In J. Freeman (Ed.), *Women: A feminist perspective.* Palo Alto, CA: Mayfield Publishing Company.

Gurman, A., & Klein, M. (1980). Marital and family conflict. In A. Brodsky and R. Hare-Mustin (Eds.), *Women and psychotherapy: An assessment of research and practice.* New York: The Guilford Press.

Guttentag, M., Salasin, S., & Belle, D. (1980). *The mental health of women.* New York: Academic Press.

Horner, M. (1972). Toward an understanding of achievement-related conflicts in women. *Journal of Social Issues, 28(2),* 157–176.

Huston-Stein, A., & Higgins-Trenk, A. (1978). Development of females from childhood through adulthood: Careers and feminine role orientations. In P. Bates (Ed.), *Life-span: Development and behavior.* New York: Academic Press.

Lerman, H. (1976). What happens in feminist therapy? In S. Cox (Ed.), *Female Psychology: The emerging self.* Chicago: SRA.

Lipman-Blumen, J. (1984). *Gender roles and power.* Englewood Cliffs, NJ: Prentice-Hall.

Lloyd, C., & Niemi, B. (1979). *The economics of sex differentials.* New York: Columbia University Press.

Maccoby, E., & Jacklin, C. (1974). *The psychology of sex differences.* Stanford, CA: Stanford University Press.

Maccoby, E., & Jacklin, C. (1976). The psychology of sex differences—summary and commentary. In Cox, S. (Ed.), *Female psychology: The emerging self.* Chicago: SRA.

Marciano, T. (1981, Fall). Socialization and women at work. *National Forum,* pp. 24–25.

Marecek, J., & Kravetz, D. (1977). Women and mental health: A review of feminist change efforts. *Psychiatry, 40(4),* 323–329.

Pearce, D. (1979). Women, work and welfare: The feminization of poverty. In K.

Feinstein (Ed.), *Working women and families.* Beverly Hills, CA: Sage Publishing.

Rossi, A. (1964). The quality of women: An immodest proposal. *Daedalus, 93,* 607-652.

Rubin, J., Provenzano, F., & Luria, Z. (1974). The eye of the beholder: Parents views on sex of newborns. *American Journal of Orthopsychiatry, 44*(4), 512-519.

Russo, N. (1984). Sex-role stereotyping, socialization and sexism. In A. Sargent (Ed.), *Beyond sex roles.* St. Paul, MN: West Publishing Company.

Steil, J. (1984). Marital relationships and mental health: The psychic costs of inequality. In J. Freeman (Ed.), *Women: A Feminist Perspective.* Palo Alto, CA: Mayfield Publishing Company.

Weitzman, L. (1984). Sex-role socialization: A focus on women. In J. Freeman (Ed.), *Women: A feminist perspective.* Palo Alto, CA: Mayfield Publishing Company.

Weitzman, L., Eifler, D., Hokada, E., & Ross, C. (1972). Sex role socialization in picture books for pre-school children. *American Journal of Sociology, 77,* 1125-1150.

■ two
CONSCIOUSNESS-RAISING AND SELF-HELP GROUPS

■ 4
Evolution of Consciousness-Raising Groups

BARBARA KIRSH

This chapter will discuss the evolution of women's consciousness-raising groups, their historical origins, and their resulting function, ideology, and structure. While the main features of the groups' structure and the core of ideology have remained quite constant since they first appeared, the function is the most notable feature to have evolved.

We can find the explanation for the changes as well as the relative constancy in the history of the women's movement and its social context over the past two decades. In addition, we can look for explanations in the enormous amount of social science research performed during this same time period that has added to our knowledge about sex roles and women's status—key concepts for understanding the women's movement and consciousness-raising groups. Indeed, the main ideology of consciousness-raising groups is that the conflict and discomfort felt by the individual woman are caused by culturally prescribed sex roles and social statuses.

CHANGING SEX ROLES

Gender is one of the first roles superimposed on individuals from birth. Gender or sex role is pervasive, with strong expectations of role conformity in the majority of life spheres (family, education, occupation, and religion).

Yet sex roles have been changing rapidly over the past 20 years, creating conflict for both sexes and also between the sexes. Some conflict is therefore inevitable. It is partially because change seeps through a society differentially that people experience so much conflict concerning sex roles.

Learning about social roles continues throughout life and, for modern adults, gets increasingly complicated and confusing. We choose our roles and derive images of ourselves through reflections of how others see us compared to how we want to be seen. We pick and choose from possible behaviors and put our roles together in ways we hope will be reinforcing or get us what we want. We run into difficulty when we are faced with sudden change, feel conflict in our roles, and need to clarify expectations made of us. At such times, individuals often search for support mechanisms like CR groups or therapy. In the process of offering support, consciousness-raising groups have also challenged assumptions about sex roles. The research has meanwhile helped prove the assumptions wrong.

During the 1970s, a great deal of social science research was devoted to theories concerning sex roles. As Kelly (1983) states, theorists in the 1970s challenged three key assumptions about sex roles. These three assumptions are that (1) individuals should "normally" develop in a manner stereotypical for one's gender; (2) that masculine and feminine traits and behaviors form a bipolar continuum, so that "well-adjusted" men and women possess opposite characteristics; and (3) that sextyping is psychologically adaptive for the individual (Kelly, 1983).

A large body of social science research now shows that very few, if any, traits considered masculine or feminine are innate (see, for example, Maccoby & Jacklin, 1974). Most all the behaviors we consider gender-linked are taught during early socialization. For example, children in the United States receive strong messages about conformity to sex roles directly from parents, school, peers, and the media. (For an insightful discussion of pressures to be feminine, see Brownmiller, 1984.) After much criticism of bipolar masculine-feminine scales (such as Constantinople, 1973), social scientists devised new measures in which separate, nonoverlapping scales tap traits associated with males and females. Individuals can be high in both masculine and feminine traits and considered to be androgynous (Bem, 1974; Spence, Helmreich, & Stapp, 1975).

Social scientists are not the only people to believe that the continuum of opposite male and female behaviors is a social myth. A popular illustration of the concept of androgyny (a positive combination of traits functional to both genders) is the 1980s phenomenon of the yuppie: young, urban professional. The concept of the yuppie is truly androgynous, and although it is at times used in a derogatory way, it pinpoints an important social fact. This fact is the presence of hard-working young men and women who want career, relationship, material comfort, and family. The image of a yuppie is similar for both men and women: the gray or navy suit with tie, jogging before work, walking briskly to the office clad in running shoes, climbing the job ladder in determined fashion, preparing the latest haute cuisine in the Cuisinart, and picking up gourmet take-out dishes for dinner while holding the baby in front in a Snugli.

Adversity in combining motherhood and career and finding large pockets of sexism in the corporation will surely induce the sort of conflict in young women that has generally led to feminist enlightenment. Meanwhile, the yuppie phenomenon benefits other women in illustrating that androgyny is possible. Consciousness-raising groups support their members in integrating and developing traits that are positively valued, both so-called masculine and feminine traits.

Social scientists have also worked on disproving the myth that sex roles are adaptive for mental health. Some of the problems women have are caused by conformity to elements of the feminine role, problems that include agoraphobia, depression, sexual dysfunction, bulimia and anorexia, passivity, and low self-esteem (Franks & Rothblum, 1983). However, elements of sex roles may well be satisfying at certain times in life and in some situations; yet, at other stages in life, they may contribute to emotional distress. A growing literature has developed during the past decade on life transitions (see, for example, Baruch & Brooks-Gunn, 1984; Block, Davidson, & Grambs, 1981; Giele, 1982). The most written-about transitions are adolescence (the change from childhood to adulthood) and mid-life (the transition between young and older adulthood). There still exists a blurring of concepts related to these transitional stages, but one certainty is that sex-role behaviors and attitudes are intrinsically involved in the changes experienced by individuals at these transitions.

Adolescent girls frequently exhibit strongly stereotyped feminine characteristics to carefully define themselves as young women. One reason contributing to the skyrocketing rate of adolescent pregnancy is that motherhood is the clearest female role possible. In mid-life, many women shift out of an emphasis on motherhood as a central role and need to find other identities. Stress and confusion frequently accompany these transitions, and conscious searching for support mechanisms is typical.

Consciousness-raising groups appeared during a time when large numbers of women were experiencing role-related stress and confusion and when the female role had become more problematic than satisfying.

BRIEF HISTORY OF CONSCIOUSNESS-RAISING GROUPS

The first women's consciousness-raising groups appeared in scattered locations across the United States in 1967 and 1968 as women involved with left-wing political movements began to focus attention on their own devalued status as females in male-defined movements. Student power, anti-war, and civil rights movements were the predominant sources of activity from which feminist consciousness arose. Much has been written about the second-class status women were allotted by their male colleagues in 1960s political organizations (e.g., Freeman, 1984; Hole & Levine, 1971; Piercy, 1970).

While the National Organization for Women (NOW) was formed slightly earlier in 1966, it addressed women's issues in a reformist, formal manner. Compared to the members of the early consciousness-raising groups, NOW's founders were somewhat older and more committed to a traditional structure with elected office holders. They worked for change through existing channels—political and legal processes, education, and the media. In contrast, the consciousness-raising groups developed in a grass-roots fashion, with the earliest members generally in their 20s or college students.

Because of their leftist or countercultural affiliations, consciousness-raising group members attempted to create new nonhierarchical institutions where each person was equally responsible for what happened during the group meetings. There was a belief that consensus ought to create decisions and that structure should be minimal. Moving the group along spontaneously in intuitive fashion was preferred over planned activities.

There was no real organization linking the individual consciousness-raising groups during the late 1960s and early 1970s except newsletters and whatever ties the groups had to national organizations, such as NOW. Although the two segments of the women's movement had begun as independent units, women desiring to locate a consciousness-raising group could most easily link up by contacting the local chapter of NOW. NOW quite rapidly became a national organization with a proliferation of local chapters with advertised meetings and easily found phone numbers. In a survey administered in 1974, Kravetz (1978) found that most groups were formed by word of mouth among acquaintances, by information in women's publications, or by women's organizations.

In an article about the formative years of the Women's Movement in the 1960s and early 1970s, Freeman (1984) remarks that, "From a sociological perspective, the rap group is probably the most valuable contribution by the women's liberation movement to the tools for social change" (p. 545).

Freeman contends that the groups allowed change simply by bringing women together in a manner in which they experienced themselves to have a common identity rather than being divided from each other. The second feature of the groups that worked for social change is the process of consciousness-raising itself. As the women share personal experiences and feelings with each other, they realize "that what each thought was individual is in fact common, that what each considered a personal problem has a social cause and probably a political solution" (p. 546).

As is illustrated by the above quote from Freeman, few people writing in the mid-1980s about the groups or who are now members refer to them as "consciousness-raising groups." They are more commonly called rap groups, discussion groups, support groups, or women's groups. This is an important clue to the change in function that has occurred over the past two decades. As knowledge about the Women's Movement and women's issues has permeated much of our society, individuals join the groups less to have their consciousness raised about feminist matters than to find support in their efforts to change. It is ironic that the groups that started as efforts to change society took on the later role of coping or support mechanisms to deal with some of the dilemmas brought about by those social changes.

EVOLVING FUNCTIONS OF CR GROUPS

Changes in society along with the remaining problems women face are reasons why the functions of consciousness-raising groups have evolved over time. Kravetz (1978) states the case well: "As with other social movements, the first stage of the women's movement stressed raising consciousness and developing new groups with common goals and principles. Consciousness-raising was a necessary first step, and women in the early CR groups effectively promoted social awareness of the wide-ranging effects of sexism" (p. 169). (See also Chapter 5).

The media picked up the ideas of the women's movement, and by the mid-1970s, the small groups were called upon less often to function as political education or individual enlightenment. The alternative function was support. Women say they join the small groups to gain and give emotional support in a nonthreatening atmosphere. Lieberman and Bond (1976) found that political motivations for joining a group decreased in their study sample; after 1973, more personal reasons for joining a group were mentioned.

A study of group members in the mid-1970s found 70% joined a group to "examine women's roles and experiences" (Kravetz, Marecek, & Finn, 1983, p. 261). A decade later, when group members were asked why they were in a group, they voiced the need for support from peers while trying to get control of the various aspects of their lives and also to better understand women's experiences. Many women in current women's groups were members of previous groups also. They seem to seek out a group at times of stress and change when support in a caring environment is more desired than formal psychotherapy.

The functions of groups certainly vary according to the woman; for example, young women just exploring feminist issues and older women in new stages of life (divorced, postmotherhood, suddenly poor) will experience the groups more as consciousness-raising than will women who have more previous exposure to feminism. A number of women who were interviewed for this chapter claimed not to be members of consciousness-raising groups but rather women who happen to gather together with others at systematic intervals for mutual support; they called their groups "support groups" or simply, "my group." While most women in current groups would espouse general feminist beliefs, there seems to be less overt political discussion than there is conscious personal support from being women. However, women who are not feminists upon entering a group evolve into feminists as the group continues, even with a modicum of political discussion.

Groups members generally become close friends and serve as support for each other after the group ends. Single women, particularly, say they feel like family and often spend holidays together. They sometimes help each other find jobs and housing.

Some of the groups in recent years also function in ways other than giving emotional and personal support. Activist projects that the groups work on can include setting up a local women's center or women's coffee house, establishing a directory of local women's resources, writing a women's newspaper, and setting up a table with educational material on feminist issues at local events.

"Networking" became widespread in the 1970s and served some of the functions of the consciousness-raising groups. To counter the "old boy's network," women started multitudes of organizations, some formal and national and others informal and local for mutual support. These networking organizations set out to help women in instrumental ways, usually within a profession or special interest. The academic professional organizations within sociology, psychology, history, and anthropology, for example, developed feminist subunits to organize and gain power for women within each profession and to engender support for women members. Medicine, law, education, and business networking organizations developed and served some of the functions of consciousness-raising groups, in that specialized circumstances in each field needed communication among the women to analyze the sources of sexism and strategies to overcome them.

STRUCTURE AND IDEOLOGY

It is truer than ever that "many 'personal' problems women experience arise from the cultural attitude of prejudice (a stereotyped negative set of attitudes) and structural discrimination (a stereotypical negative set of behaviors)" (Kirsh, 1974, p. 328). Women still constitute a social minority group because of low access to power compared with men. Thus, the ideology of the women's groups has not changed much over the years from "the personal is political."

Not only are many women's problems rooted in society, according to this ideology, but these problems would be alleviated if societal values and structures changed. This key belief postulates that consciousness-raising groups first make their members aware of the external causes of their discomfort, and then the members will feel empowered to change the worlds in which they live. Consciousness-raising groups tend those characteristics that women would like to bestow on the larger society: nonhierarchical, democratic, noncompetitive, supportive, emotional rather than intellectual. The ideology dictates and is intrinsically related to the groups' structure.

By the mid-1980s, we can see that the usefulness of the structure of consciousness-raising groups has engendered the widespread adaptation of the model to other groups. It is common for social service agencies to set up specialized peer support groups similar to consciousness-raising groups for many kinds of constituents: pregnant teenagers, drug abusers, bulimics and anorexics, widows, single parents, prisoners, alcoholics, women with high-risk pregnancies, and rape victims.

The key features of the structure of CR groups have remained quite constant since the late 1960s. The groups are deliberately small, generally with four to 12 members so that each person gets adequate amounts of time to speak at each meeting. The group members usually sit in a circle, allowing face-to-face communication. Meetings are held at regular intervals, generally once a week or once every other week to engender a close feeling of continuity among members. Attendance is valued highly, and frequent absence is interpreted as a lack of caring about the group. Meetings are usually held in members' homes, either at a fixed location or rotated among the members. Some groups meet at a public location, such as a town library, women's center, YWCA, or university building.

Most groups are leaderless, partly because of the distrust of authority figures that was such a prominent ideology among the early consciousness-raising members and, indeed, of many young people in the late 1960s. Another reason for the groups to be leaderless is so that each individual member can serve as the expert on her own life and can be equally responsible for group processes. NOW published a pamphlet in 1976 for a more structured group in which a trained leader is in charge of guiding the women through specific discussion topics, but this seems to be a less popular format than the leaderless groups.

Some women in current groups have mentioned that they are more comfortable requesting some rules for the group than they would have been in previous groups. These rules generally concern group processes, such as beginning the evening with a short, uninterrupted speech by each person, requesting that no one get too much talking time, picking topics to discuss in advance, not giving advice or being judgmental, and dealing with issues the group feels competent to handle—and suggesting therapy for more serious problems. The very early groups seemed to avoid much in the way of rules or imposed structure, valuing spontaneity.

The meetings begin in a number of different ways, although the commonality is that each member gets a chance to talk, and personal feelings rather than intellectual ideas are the focus. One means of starting a meeting is for each woman to speak for a given amount of time about whatever concerns her; a variation of this opening is for each person to say an adjective that best describes her that moment. Some groups focus on chosen topics that are relevant to the whole group, and still others encourage the woman with the most need that evening to begin the meeting.

Many groups, at least periodically, prepare and eat dinner together before the official start of the meeting. This bonding among group members sometimes carries over to special occasions when spouses and lovers are included in discussions or meals.

It is interesting to note that the structure has remained close to that of the early groups given that the demographics of the members seem to have changed somewhat. The earliest group members were single and in their 20s, whereas the most reliable samples from the mid-1970s on suggest the group members are older, are married or divorced, better educated, and with professional or semiprofessional occupations. We might suspect that a similar cohort of women belonged to the earliest groups, some of the same individuals are group members once again in the 1980s, or, at least, some are women in the same generation as the first women's groups' members.

Women in current groups may phrase their ideology more in terms of support than politics but with clear awareness that the need for support comes from the difficulties of being a woman in the current society.

EFFECTS OF CR GROUPS

Accolades for consciousness-raising group experiences attest to the groups' successes: women go back to school, get first jobs and better jobs, leave bad jobs and marriages, write a first article, have a child, learn to drive, stop cooking; the anecdotes concerning the role and status changes encouraged by the groups are accompanied by praise for profound emotional changes. As Kravetz notes in chapter 5, no research has appeared on CR groups since the late 1970s. The listings under "consciousness-raising" that appear during the 1980s in *Psychological Abstracts* involve clinical, often hospitalized, populations. However, the research findings that do exist point to increased self-esteem, ambitions, and confidence (Acker & Howard, 1972; White, 1971); greater feelings of affinity and liking for other women (Cherniss, 1972); decreased passivity and greater self-knowledge (Eastman, 1973); and increased understanding of structural and psychological pressures on women (Micossi, 1970).

A potent effect of CR groups is changing behavior in ways that convey a changed sense of self. Small, supportive groups act as laboratories that reinforce new behaviors as group members bring in their tales of attempts to demonstrate new sides of themselves. Difficulties and negative reactions from outside the group (from spouses, lovers, employers) elicit encouragement from the other group members to try again. Some of these specific behaviors are forms of assertion and self-confidence, such as speaking in declarative sentences rather than in questions, talking in mixed-sex meetings at work and school, speaking louder, and arguing with "authorities." These very specific manifestations of change in self-esteem are easier to attempt in the safe confines of a support group. The women sometimes role-play threatening situations they find too challenging to create outside the group.

Consciousness-raising groups can also function to bring to awareness how we act and speak, so we can understand the messages we give and attempt to change them. The ways we present ourselves are important in eliciting reactions from other people. As a reason for joining a women's group, some women have mentioned learning how to speak in groups and exploring whether they speak differently with women than with men.

CONCLUSION

We have seen that consciousness-raising groups evolved as the Women's Movement attained some primary goals and continues to work for further sex-role and status changes. Now, the groups function more for support than for political revelations, although the structure remains essentially the same; this successful structural model springs up in endless peer support groups. The early ideology may be less frequently verbalized as "the personal is political," yet the essence of this slogan remains the foundation of the groups, as women see each other through personal change in the context of problems generated by society.

Breaking the semiconscious verbal taboos for each sex can result in embarrassing discomfort. However, when a woman conforms to the norms for female speech, a negative self-image may be reinforced and her speech may give the impression of incompetence, insecurity, passivity and emotionality, thereby thwarting attainment of desired goals(Kirsh, 1983).

REFERENCES

Acker, J., & Howard, M. (1972). *On becoming a feminist.* Paper presented at the American Sociological Association Annual Meeting, New Orleans.

Baruch, G., & Brooks-Gunn, J. (Eds.). (1984). *Women in Midlife.* New York: Plenum.

Bem, S.L. (1974). The measurement of psychological androgyny. *Journal of Consulting and Clinical Psychology, 42*(2), 155–162.

Block, M., Davidson, J., & Grambs, J. (1981). *Women over forty: Visions and realities.* New York: Springer.

Brownmiller, S. (1984). *Femininity.* New York: Linden Press.

Cherniss, C. (1972). Personality and ideology: A personological study of women's liberation. *Psychiatry, 35*(2), 109–125.

Constantinople, A. (1973). Masculinity-femininity: An exception to the famous dictum. *Psychological Bulletin, 80*(5), 389–407.

Eastman, P.C. (1973). Consciousness-raising as a resocialization process for women. *Smith College Studies in Social Work, 43*(3), 153–183.

Franks, V., & Rothblum, E. (Eds.). (1983). *The Stereotyping of Women: Its effects on mental health.* New York: Springer.

Freeman, J. (Ed.). (1984). *Women: a feminist perspective.* Palo Alto, CA: Mayfield Publishing Company.

Giele, J. (Ed.). (1982). *Women in the middle years.* New York: Wiley.

Hole, J., & Levine, E. (1971). *Rebirth of feminism.* New York: Quadrangle Books.

Kelly, J. (1983). Sex role stereotypes and mental health. In V. Franks & E. Rothblum

(Eds.), *The Stereotyping of Women: Its effects on mental health.* New York: Springer.

Kirsh, B. (1974). Consciousness-raising groups as therapy for women. In V. Franks & V. Burtle, (Eds.), *Women in therapy: New psychotherapies for a changing society.* New York: Brunner/Mazel.

Kravetz, D. (1978). Consciousness-raising groups in the 1970's. *Psychology of Women Quarterly, 3*(2), 168–186.

Kravetz, D., Marecek. J., & Finn, S. (1983). Factors influencing women's participation in consciousness-raising groups. *Psychology of Women Quarterly, 7*(3), 257–271.

Lieberman, M., & Bond, G. (1976). The problem of being a woman: A survey of 1,700 women in consciousness-raising groups. *Journal of Applied Behavioral Science, 12*(3), 363–380.

Maccoby, E., & Jacklin, C. (1974). *The psychology of sex differences.* Palo Alto, CA: Stanford University Press.

Micossi, A. (1970). Conversion to women's lib. *Trans action, 8,* 82–90.

Piercy, M. (1970). The grand coolie damn. In R. Morgan (Ed.), *Sisterhood is powerful.* New York: Random House.

Spence, J., Helmreich, R., & Stapp, J. (1975). Ratings of self and peers on sex role attributes and their relation to self-esteem and conceptions of masculinity and femininity. *Journal of Personality and Social Psychology, 32*(1), 29–39.

White, H. (1971). *Becoming a feminist.* Unpublished honors thesis, Douglass College, New Brunswick, NJ.

SELECTED READINGS

Broverman, I.K., Vogel, S.R., Broverman, D.M., Clarkson, F.E., & Rosenkrantz, P. (1972). Sex-role stereotypes: A current appraisal. *Journal of Social Issues, 28*(2), 59–78.

Eakins, B., & Eakins, R. (1978). *Sex differences in human communication.* Boston: Houghton Mifflin.

Kirsh, B. (1983). Sex roles and language use. In V. Franks & E. Rothblum (Eds.), *The Stereotyping of Women: Its effects on mental health.* New York: Springer Publishing Co.

Golan, N. (1981). *Passing through transitions.* New York: The Free Press.

Hacker, H.M. (1951). Women as a minority group. *Social Forces, 30,* 60–69.

Hanison, C. (1971). The personal is political. In J. Agel (Ed.), *The Radical Therapist.* New York: Ballantine.

Hareven, T., & Adams, K. (Ed). (1982). *Aging and life course transitions.* New York: The Guilford Press.

Holter, H. (1970). *Sex roles and social structure.* Oslo, Norway: Universitetsforlapet.

Laing, R.D. (1967). *The politics of experience.* New York: Ballantine.

Lakoff, R. (1975). *Language and woman's place.* New York: Harper and Row.

Nassi, A., & Abramowitz, S. (1978). Raising consciousness about women's groups: Process and outcome research. *Psychology of Women Quarterly, 3,* 139–156.

Rohrbaugh, J. (1979). *Women: Psychology's puzzle.* New York: Basic Books.

Spender, D. (1980). *Man-made language.* London and Boston: Routledge and Kegan Paul.

Weitzman, L. (1985). *The divorce revolution: The unexpected social and economic consequences for women and children in America.* New York: The Free Press.

Woman's body, woman's mind: A guide to consciousness-raising (1972, July). *Ms.,* pp. 18, 22–23.

Zimmerman, D., & West, C. (1975). Sex roles, interruptions, and silences in conversation. In B. Thorne and N. Henley (Eds.), *Language and sex: Difference and dominance.* Rowley, MA: Newbury House.

■ 5
Benefits of Consciousness-Raising Groups for Women

DIANE KRAVETZ

Over the past two decades, consciousness-raising (CR) groups have evolved as a way for women to understand the intricate relationships between public, systemic conditions and the individual aspects of their experiences. Through CR, "the personal becomes political." In addition to their significant social and political impact, CR groups have served as an important mental health resource for women. This chapter will focus on the ways in which CR groups have contributed to personal change for women.

CONSCIOUSNESS-RAISING GROUPS AND PSYCHOTHERAPY

Although CR groups have important therapeutic benefits for women, they are not a form of psychotherapy. The primary differences between CR groups and psychotherapy concern ideology, goals, structure, and process (Brodsky, 1973, 1977; Kirsh, 1974; Kravetz, 1976; Warren, 1976).

The goals of traditional psychotherapy include changing individual attitudes, behaviors, and emotional states that are assumed to be deviant, sick, or maladaptive. Whether treatment is focused on recovery from illness, modifying problematic behaviors and emotional states, gaining insight, or discovering the underlying causes of symptoms, traditional psychotheraphy is adjustment-oriented and focuses on the individual. Diagnosis and intervention are based on clinical theories and research as well as on the clinical experience of the therapist.

In contrast, in CR groups, institutional structures and social norms, as well as individual attitudes and behaviors, provide the framework for analysis. Through sharing, CR groups help women understand and deal with personal problems as they are related to their gender-role conditioning and to their experiences with sex bias and discrimination. Through this process, personal attitudes, behaviors, roles, and relationships as well as social policies and practices become targets for change. Although literature may be used to provide additional information, the personal experiences of group members are the central ingredients for understanding problems and for devising solutions, both private and public.

The structure of the therapist–client (or therapist–patient) relationship is hierarchical and relies on the expertise of a trained professional, who is generally male. Typically, it is assumed that the therapist does not share the problems of the client and will not reveal personal material. The therapist professes to be morally neutral and nonjudgmental. Authority and control are maintained by the therapist, who establishes therapy goals and treatments. Conversely, CR groups are based on equal sharing of resources, power, and responsibility. They are generally leaderless and stress principles of sisterhood and the authority of personal experience. The structure of these groups inherently assumes and promotes women's abilities to be autonomous, self-directing, and competent. There is an assumption of shared experience and shared difficulties. CR groups emphasize being supportive and nonjudgmental toward group members' behaviors and attitudes but critically examine social values and political beliefs.

Some of the processes that occur in CR groups also occur in group psychotherapy, including provision of role models, sharing the personal experience, imparting of information, peer support, identifying commonalities, instillation of hope, and cohesiveness (Warren, 1976). However, group therapy is designed to be a corrective experience, based on exploration of individual factors and emphasizing the interpersonal relationships within the group as a major factor in the change process. CR groups are not viewed as a corrective experience but rather as a process of personal growth. CR groups also minimize the importance of interpersonal learning in the group; change occurs through women's increasing understanding of themselves as part of a larger social group and through viewing personal problems within the context of common social roles and social conditions.

These significant distinctions between CR groups and psychotherapy are unnecessarily blurred when CR groups are referred to as a form of therapy or of treatment. However, based on personal accounts and research investigations of CR groups, it is apparent that CR groups serve as effective mechanisms for resocialization and personal change for women.

CR GROUPS: STUDIES OF GOALS AND OUTCOMES

CR groups generally consist of seven to 15 women, with a range of ages, educational levels, occupations, marital and parental statuses, and sexual orientations. Most groups emerge from informal friendship networks in community and work settings. Others are formed within and through political organizations, such as the National Organization for Women (NOW), and through women's centers.

Studies of CR groups primarily include women who are white, middle-class adults with at least some college education, who live in urban/suburban areas, a majority of whom are or have been married. Given the characteristics of women in the feminist movement during the late 1960s to the mid-1970s, when studies of CR groups were conducted, it is likely that these studies represent the majority of women in CR groups during that time. However, it is also true that Third World women and working class women of all races are generally not represented in traditional research; "black women's groups and white working class women's groups have been nearly invisible to all but their members" (Jenkins and Kramer, 1978, p. 69).

Many studies of CR groups have been based on participant observation and personal interviews. In her field study of 1971 to 1973, Cassell (1977) found that through CR women began to question the "automatic female assumption of domestic responsibility" and to explore ways to change their roles. Also, women developed a sense of closeness to each other and to other women, and they began to perceive themselves as members of a larger group composed of women. Some women became increasingly dissatisfied or angry, and often their new consciousness and new demands placed a range of pressures on existing female–male relationships. Although the women shared a commitment to personal change, not all women actually made major changes in their lives. For some, the group seemed to function as a safety valve and helped them to maintain the status quo. For these women, generally married women with young children, the alternatives to their current situation were often perceived as worse, and/or they were waiting until their children were in school before making major changes in their lives.

Carden's (1974) study of the Women's Movement from 1969 to 1971 included interviews with movement members in seven cities in the United States as well as participant observation of movement activities and analysis of movement publications. Like Cassell, Carden also observed a conscious change in group members' persectives on their roles and on what it is to be a woman. She found that many women changed jobs, returned to school, or went back to paid employment; some (5–15%) became (or remained) involved in feminist social action projects. Carden concludes that "the degree of reconceptualization reached does not depend upon the group's life span but upon its members' openness to radical ideas and their prior commitment to a traditional or nontraditional lifestyle" (Carden, 1974, pp. 71–72).

Based on interviews with 17 women in CR groups, Newton and Walton (1971) found five types of CR group outcomes: (1) an altered world view: understanding the political and social aspects of women's experience and seeing women as a definitive group and society as divided into females and males; (2) changes in identity, including changes in body image and feelings about sexuality; (3) an enhanced sense of self-acceptance and a lessening of guilt and self-doubt; (4) change in reference groups and interpersonal relationships: seeing women as their primary reference group, having more women friends, and having more egalitarian relationships with men; and (5) changes in job/career orientation: an ambivalence toward careerism and a tendency to change their main area of interest to be directly related to activities of the Women's Movement.

Eastman (1973) observed one CR group for nine months and interviewed members of the group. She found that members of the CR group achieved increased autonomy, self-confidence, and self-knowledge. Group members stated that they were able to overcome passivity and had a growing sense of identity with other women as a result of their group experience. Some women became starters for other CR groups and worked on the creation of a women's center as an outgrowth of their CR group experience.

There have also been quantitative studies of CR groups. In a national survey of 1,669 women in CR groups, Kravetz (1978) found that women's most important goals for the CR group experience were (1) to share thoughts and feelings about being a woman, (2) to increase self-awareness, (3) to learn about other women and their experiences, (4) to receive and give emotional support, and (5) to examine problems women have with their traditional roles. In this study, 71% of the women indicated that they had met their goals, 89% felt that they had had a constructive experience, and 89% enjoyed the experience. The majority of women in this survey actively encouraged other women to participate in a CR group and thought that many (or all) of the women they knew would benefit from being in a CR group.

Although women join CR groups to examine women's experiences and roles, Kravetz, Marecek, and Finn (1983) found that this common theme has different meanings for different women. More detailed analyses of data from the national survey revealed two central and separate motives for joining CR groups: (1) to solve personal problems and (2) to develop a more feminist perspective. The women entering CR groups for personal problem-solving tended to be housewives with children who were experiencing high levels of distress. Women who enter CR groups to develop or strengthen their feminism tended to be identified with the Women's Movement prior to joining a CR group, to be employed or students, to be "symptom-free," and not to have children. The results of this study suggested that for women who identified with the Women's Movement prior to joining a CR group, participation in CR groups reflected a desire to explore the linkages between feminist ideology and their own lives. For women who were not otherwise involved in the Women's Movement, CR groups were primarily a means for personal growth through shared understanding of problems common to women.

Follingstad, Robinson, and Pugh (1977) compared 22 women in two CR groups with a control group, using group facilitators and structured group experiences. They found significantly more self-reported profeminist attitudes and behaviors among the women in CR groups than among the controls. However, there were no significant differences on the personality measures.

Barrett (1978) compared the effectiveness for widows of three types of leader-led discussion groups focusing on "specific problems of widowhood" (self-help group), "the development of friendships" (confidant group), and "the roles of women in society" (CR groups). She found that in all three types of discussion groups, women showed more positive change in their health predictions and became less other-oriented than the controls. On items concerning the extent of help from the group and extent of learning in the group, the highest ratings occurred in the CR groups, the lowest in the self-help groups. The most frequently reported positive changes in this study were reduced feelings of unique experience, increased self-confidence, a more positive future outlook, the incorporation of help from the group, increased social contacts, and return to school. The most positive life changes occurred in the CR groups, the least in the self-help groups.

In a study of 32 women in CR groups, Lieberman, Solow, Bond, and Reibstein (1979) found that women in these groups joined with concerns about their self-esteem, self-reliance, identity, and interpersonal relationships. They did not join to deal with their psychological distress. After six months, women had significantly increased their self-respect, self-esteem, feelings of autonomy and assertiveness, and identification with the Women's Movement. In this study, levels of depression or anxiety did not change.

In contrast, Weitz (1982) found that CR group participation was related to decreased feelings of depression, helplessness, and self-reproach as well as increased self-esteem and increased positive attitudes toward women and feminism. Weitz concluded that CR group pariticipation reduces women's depression and increases their self-esteem by externalizing blame, encouraging feminism, and providing strong female role models.

To summarize, in the studies cited here and in other studies as well (Kirkpatrick, 1975; Micossi, 1970; Whiteley, 1973), the CR group outcomes most frequently reported include (1) increased self-awareness, self-respect, and self-esteem; (2) increased awareness of the effects of traditional sex roles and sexism; (3) increased awareness of a commonality with other women; (4) improved relationships and a sense of solidarity with other women; (5) development of a sociopolitical analysis of female experience and the nature of female oppression and the development of a feminist identity; (6) change in interpersonal relationships and roles; and (7) participation in a range of activities designed to change women's circumstances in the workplace and in the community.

The most prevalent findings across all studies concern changed perceptions and attitudes toward self, others, and society; there is a reorganization of attitudes and beliefs in a profeminist direction. The behavioral components or ramifications of these cognitive/emotional changes are less specifically documented but are frequently cited. Personality change is frequently noted, primarily based on self-report and observation.

These results confirm the highly positive regard held toward these groups by the women in them. Given the ever-present questions concerning sampling problems, social desirability factors, and the possible lack of "objectivity" among investigators, one must still be impressed with the consistency of findings, particularly those concerning changes in women's awareness. The reported outcomes are very consistent with the stated purpose of these groups, that is, CR.

There is some additional work that should be considered in evaluating the benefits and potential of CR groups. Some of the reported outcomes of CR groups may be related to the positive effects of all-women groups (Aries, 1976; Carlock and Martin, 1977; Jakubowski, 1977). Also, effective socioemotional behaviors continue to characterize women's performance in groups (Eskilson & Wiley, 1976; Piliavin & Martin, 1978), an example of one of the more positive aspects of traditional female conditioning. The empathy and support emphasized in CR groups, combined with an explicit group purpose that focuses on cognitive restructuring through sharing of common experiences and feelings, may contribute to the overall positive evaluation and effectiveness of these groups.

Outcomes of a CR group experience are also affected by the fact that these groups are part of a growing and influential social movement—the Women's Movement. Participation in a CR group is often accompanied by reading feminist literature and by involvement in other feminist activities. In Kravetz' (1978) study, for example, before joining a CR group, 25% of the women had been in a women's political group and 65% considered themselves to be members of the Women's Movement; 55% joined a CR group that was started by a women's organization. Therefore, for many women, feminists outside of the group serve as a reference group and provide additional role models and support.

IMPLICATIONS OF RESEARCH ON CR GROUPS

In reviewing the literature on women's CR groups, it is evident that we need to further specify the nature of these groups and extent of change related to participation in these groups. In general, women join CR groups with the overall purpose of exploring women's experiences, roles, and social conditions. However, "being a member of a CR group" does not adequately define the sample of women in these groups. Women in CR groups have different needs, personal circumstances and lifestyles, roles, political perspectives, and sociopolitical involvements. CR groups differ in terms of their purposes, the types of issues discussed, and the range of alternatives considered.

It is important to recognize that the available literature on CR groups is limited to studies conducted from the late 1960s to the mid-1970s. There are no studies of CR groups during the late 1970s and 1980s, a time during which the feminist movement has become increasingly diversified and complex.

In the 1970s and 1980s, women have multiple sources for CR, including the large, national women's rights organizations; women's caucuses within academia, business, labor, and the professions; women's studies courses; feminist service agencies; lesbian political groups; feminist music, theater, art, literature, and scholarship; and CR groups. Therefore, in the 1970s and 1980s, many CR groups have been the result of, rather than the source of, women's feminist identity.

These CR groups (often termed "support groups") have provided feminists with support, validation, and assistance as they worked to incorporate feminism into their everyday lives. In these groups, women continue to explore the social structural nature of their problems and share strategies for dealing with them; they develop feminist alternatives to apply in their work and in their personal relationships.

Also, during this time, CR groups have been among the many services offered by feminist service agencies, including women's counseling centers, rape crisis centers, and shelters for battered women. Feminist counselors, therapists, and social service workers in traditional agencies have designed programs and services to help female offenders, women who abuse alcohol and drugs, women with eating disorders, incest victims, etc. and include CR groups as one important part of their overall efforts. Research on CR groups must take into account that CR groups emerge under these different conditions and have different foci.

Finally, the feminist movement recognizes and works to change the multiple and interrelated sources of female oppression, including racism, ageism, classism, and heterosexism. Correspondingly, feminists represent many different groups of women, but the literature on CR groups does not reflect this diversity. The absence of information on Third World women's groups, working class women's groups, and lesbian groups especially limits our understanding of the nature and impact of CR groups. It is important that we document the extent to which CR groups are used by different populations of women and investigate the commonalities and differences among these groups.

Comparative Utility of CR Groups

The therapeutic value of CR groups has been well documented. Researchers have only begun, however, to assess the relative utility of various help-giving systems for women. If we are to identify the problems that require the service of professional therapists and also acknowledge the problems well served in CR groups, we must identify and assess the relative value of different systems. One approach is to compare CR groups with traditional therapy groups. Since CR is a critical component of feminist approaches to therapy (Brody, 1984; Greenspan, 1983; Rawlings & Carter, 1977; Rosewater & Walker, 1985; Sturdivant, 1980), the relative therapeutic value of CR groups should also be assessed in studies that compare the effects of CR groups with feminist approaches to therapy for women.

Meaningful comparisons of CR groups with psychotherapy may be difficult, however, since women may enter psychotherapy and CR groups with different needs and goals. Also, as discussed earlier, traditional therapies and CR groups differ significantly in ideology, structure, process, and goals; therefore, many outcome measures are not equally appropriate or relevant to both systems (Klein, 1976; Kravetz, 1976). Conformity to patriarchal models of the family is defined as healthy by many clinicians and as repression by feminists. Anger and dissatisfaction are viewed as symptoms in conventional psychotherapy but as desirable outcomes in CR groups.

It is also important to recognize that, unlike adjustment-oriented systems, change from CR groups may not produce more rewarding or more successful behavior. Presenting a self-image and behaviors that deviate from the accepted norms of society may incur increasing difficulties for women. Some relationships may become more satisfying, but others are likely to become stressful (or more stressful). Parents, spouse, children, friends, relatives, and co-workers may be ambivalent, even hostile, toward a woman's desire to make nontraditional changes in her life. Further, due to sexism in education and in the workplace, as well as in other social institutions, women may not be able to achieve the changes they desire.

Assessment of CR Groups

Assessment, then, must focus on whether or not women are behaving in a self-directing, autonomous manner and whether or not their behavior is the result of a conscious understanding of available options and a deliberate weighing of costs and benefits. As noted by Klein (1976), assessment of successful therapeutic outcomes for women must take into account changing roles and norms, as well as distinguish between soluble and insoluble issues. For assessing mental health, feminist models "are more likely to look at the processes that the individual uses to internalize and personalize values and roles, rather than at the specific content" (Klein, 1976, p. 94).

It is particularly important that studies of CR groups include assessment of the full range of relevant outcomes. In general, there has been an overemphasis on the psychotherapeutic outcomes of CR groups. Especially in the quantitative studies, there has been little evaluation of the ways in which women incorporate their new insights and awareness into ongoing roles and relationships or how these groups contribute to decisions regarding family roles, work, education, and social and political activities.

A full understanding of the nature and outcomes of CR groups is only possible when CR groups are evaluated in terms of their connections to the feminist movement. Although involvement in political action may not be a direct result of CR groups, the political nature of these groups should not be minimized. Change from CR groups is grounded in sociopolitical insights and includes shifts in sociopolitical attitudes and values. As discussed above, the mental health benefits of CR groups derive from women understanding the relationships between personal feelings and circumstances and social roles, norms, and structures. CR group outcomes consistently include development of a feminist identity and perspective and a sense of solidarity with other women.

Women's development of profeminist attitudes and values has important political significance as well. Women's oppression is supported by women's internalizing cultural views that devalue women and legitimate women's powerlessness and victimization. By altering these internalized views, CR groups challenge one of the most basic ways that oppression is maintained.

Similarly, many of the changes that occur in women's behavior are in opposition to the dominant cultural ideology. When the nature of personal change conflicts with the dominant values of society, personal change becomes political and holds broad social and political implications.

Feminist theorists and activists ground their work in analyses of the multifaceted ways in which women's personal concerns and experiences are inextricably linked to their subordinate social, economic, legal, and political status. Research investigations of women's CR groups must be done within this same analytical perspective in order for their results to hold meaningful implications for women's services. The results of such investigations would provide the basis for appropriate linkages and referrals between professionals and nonprofessionals serving women. Such research will contribute to the further development and refinement of feminist change efforts and enhance women's resources for personal and social change.

REFERENCES

Aries, E. (1976). Interaction patterns and themes of male, female, and mixed groups. *Small Group Behavior, 7*(1), 7–18.

Barrett, C. J. (1978). Effectiveness of widows' groups in facilitating change. *Journal of Consulting and Clinical Psychology, 46*(1), 20–31.

Brodsky, A. (1973). The consciousness-raising group as a model for therapy with women. *Psychotherapy: Theory, Research and Practice, 10*(1), 24–29.

Brodsky, A. (1977). Therapeutic aspect of consciousness-raising groups. In E. I. Rawlings & D. K. Carter (Eds.), *Psychotherapy for women: Treatment toward equality*. Springfield, IL: Charles C Thomas.

Brody, C. (Ed.) (1984). *Women therapists working with women: New theory and process of feminist therapy*. New York: Springer.

Carden, M. L. (1974). *The new feminist movement.* New York: Russell Sage Foundation.

Carlock, C.J., & Martin, P.Y. (1977). Sex composition and the intensive group experience. *Social Work, 22*(1), 27–33.

Cassell, J. (1977). *A group called women: Sisterhood and symbolism in the feminist movement.* New York: David McKay.

Eastman, P.C. (1973). Consciousness-raising as a resocialization process for women. *Smith College Studies in Social Work, 43*(3), 153–183.

Eskilson, A., & Wiley, M. G. (1976). Sex composition and leadership in small groups. *Sociometry, 39*(3), 183–193.

Follingstad, D. R., Robinson, E. A., & Pugh, M. (1977). Effects of consciousness-raising groups on measures of feminism, self-esteem, and social desirability. *Journal of Counseling Psychology, 24*(3), 223–230.

Greenspan, M. (1983). *A new approach to women and therapy.* New York: McGraw Hill.

Jakubowski, P. (1977). Self-assertion training procedures for women. In E. I. Rawlings & D. K. Carter (Eds.), *Psychotherapy for women: Treatment toward equality.* Springfield, IL: Charles C Thomas.

Jenkins, L., & Kramer, C. (1978). Small group process: Learning from women. *Women's Studies International Quarterly, 1*(1), 67–84.

Kirkpatrick, M. J. (1975). A report on a consciousness raising group for women psychiatrists. *Journal of American Medical Women's Association, 30*(5), 206–212.

Kirsh, B. (1974). Consciousness-raising groups as therapy for women. In V. Franks & V. Burtle (Eds.), *Women in therapy: New psychotherapies for a changing society.* New York: Brunner/Mazel.

Klein, M. H. (1976). Feminist concepts of therapy outcome. *Psychotherapy: Theory, Research, and Practice, 13*(1), 89–95.

Kravetz, D. (1976). Consciousness-raising groups and group psychotherapy: Alternative mental health resources for women. *Psychotherapy: Theory, Research and Practice, 13*(1), 66–71.

Kravetz, D. (1978). Consciousness-raising groups in the 1970s. *Psychology of Women Quarterly, 3*(2), 168–186.

Kravetz, D., Marecek, J., & Finn, S. (1983). Factors influencing women's participation in consciousness-raising groups. *Psychology of Women Quarterly, 7*(3), 257–271.

Lieberman, M., Solow, N., Bond, G., & Reibstein, J. (1979). The psychotherapeutic impact of women's consciousness-raising groups. *Archives of General Psychiatry, 36*(2), 161–168.

Micossi, A. (1970). Conversion to women's lib. *Trans action, 8,* 82–90.

Newton, E., & Walton, S. (1971). *The personal is political: Consciousness-raising and personal change in the women's liberation movement.* Paper presented at the Annual Meeting of the American Anthropological Association, New Orleans.

Piliavin, J. A., & Martin, R. R. (1978). The effects of the sex composition of groups on style of social interaction. *Sex Roles, 4*(2), 281–296.

Rawlings, E. I., & Carter, D. K. (Eds.) (1977). *Psychotherapy for women: Treatment toward equality.* Springfield, IL: Charles C Thomas.

Rosewater, L., & Walker, L. (Eds.) (1985). *Handbook of feminist therapy: Women's issues in psychotherapy.* New York: Springer.

Sturdivant, S. (1980). *Therapy with women: A feminist philosophy of treatment.* New York: Springer.

Warren, L. W. (1976). The therapeutic status of consciousness-raising groups. *Professional Psychology, 7*(2), 132–140.

Weitz, R. (1982). Feminist consciousness-raising, self-concept, and depression. *Sex Roles, 8*(3), 231–241.

Whiteley, R. M. (1973). Women in groups. *The Counseling Psychologist, 4*(1), 27–43.

■ 6
Therapeutic Self-Help Group: A Process of Empowerment for Women in Abusive Relationships

SUSAN HARTMAN

In recent years, a proliferation of self-help groups has developed that have focused on persons aiding others who are in similar situations. While most of these groups have been leaderless, a distinct form of the self-help model, the therapeutic self-help group departs from the traditional form by its use of leaders, both a professional and an indigenous chairperson.

Also during the past few years, social services have probed for the most effective ways to respond to the needs of women in violent relationships. Individual counseling, educational groups, shelters, and various forms of group-work approaches have been tried.

This author has found the therapeutic self-help model effective in working with women in abusive relationships. Since 1981 about 50 women have been served each year through this group at Family and Children's Service in Minneapolis, Minnesota. The leader of the group has been committed to the beliefs that no woman is responsible for her partner's violence and that every woman must take responsibility for protecting herself. A broad definition of violence allows women to join groups who have experienced verbal abuse, psychological abuse, and destruction of property as well as physical violence to participate in the weekly meetings.

The author thanks Jane Hynes and Carole Mae Olson for their support and suggestions.

The details of how to develop and lead a therapeutic self-help group for women in abusive relationships have been reported elsewhere (Hartman, 1983). Following will be a description of the characteristics of this model, the characteristics of women in violent relationships, and a discussion of how the model itself addresses the issues of the women and acts as an empowering mechanism.

CHARACTERISTICS OF A THERAPEUTIC SELF-HELP GROUP

A unique combination of ingredients characterize the therapeutic self-help model. Minimal entry requirements, member ownership, mutuality through peer support, and dual facilitation comprise the critical aspects of this model.

Minimal Entry Requirements

Although the Group for Women in Abusive Relationships is housed in and funded by a traditional family service agency, the typical intake interviews and forms are dispensed with in this self-help model. Any woman who is or has been in an abusive relationship may attend the meetings. "Abusive relationship" is defined as any intimate relationship with a male or female peer where there is/has been physical, sexual, or psychological abuse. Lesbians and heterosexuals, women who define themselves as abusive as well as abused, and women who are in initial crisis or at the end of a treatment plan may partake of this group.

After making phone contact with the professional facilitator ("sponsor") of the group for a description of the group, the women attend without paying fees, filling out registration forms, contracting for number of sessions, or having to provide their last name. Members may attend as many sessions as they wish and may leave and return at any time they choose. The women are encouraged to attend a minimum of four sessions and to call a member or leader to indicate they are safe if they cannot attend a session. The only rigid requirements are confidentiality, reporting of child abuse, no abuse in the group, and no use of chemicals before the sessions.

Member Ownership

A self-help group belongs to its members. The host organization acts only in a supportive role to provide the sponsor, a meeting place, a monthly list of names and phone numbers of group members, and advocacy services. Each woman's style of work in and out of the self-help group depends on how she chooses to help herself. Within the sessions, she may utilize active silence as a form of participation, problem-solve, vent, be a helper, and/or be helped. Outside the group, networking is encouraged through use of the phone list. Family and Children's Service programs including advocacy, individual/family therapy, family life education, and/or outside support; Alcoholics Anonymous, Alanon, The Domestic Abuse Project, and Parents Anonymous are often suggested as optional supplements to group participation.

Mutuality Through Peer Support

A key ingredient to the effectiveness of the self-help model is the primacy of peer interaction.

> Mutuality is an important concept. . . . The members have an equality of status and are expected to give help as well as receive it. . . . The group emphasizes the power of the members to assist each other rather than depend on the help of professionals. The dual role of members include a combination of teaching and learning. (Olson & Shapiro, 1979, p. 13)

The commonality of the women's experiences and feelings provides the foundation for this mutuality. The women support each other by providing empathy, comfort, hope, a modeling of skills, information, resources, humor, a sharing of their own stories, and often availability outside the group. The opportunity to provide as well as receive support does not depend on the duration of a member's participation in the group. Nearly every woman finds ways to give as well as receive from the onset of her involvement in this "mutual help system" (Golan, 1981).

Dual Facilitators

Chairperson. A unique aspect of the therapeutic self-help model is the joint leadership of a professional (the "sponsor") and an indigenous person (the "chairperson"). The roles and interactions of these two women provide a critical foundation upon which the strength of the group is built.

The chairperson, herself a woman who is or has been in an abusive relationship, takes primary responsibility for facilitating the group. A volunteer for this position, the chairperson goes through a leadership training program and continues her education about group process and violence issues in meetings with the professional. In addition to leading the meeting, the chairperson serves as the primary contact for the women between sessions. She continues work on her own issues by participating as a group member during the meetings when she chooses. At such time the sponsor or another group member assumes the chairperson's tasks.

Sponsor. The professional or sponsor takes on many roles, the thrust of which are supportive rather than authoritative. To qualify as a sponsor, a professional must understand the dynamics of group process, the self-help model, and women in abusive relationships; be able to use herself appropriately during the meetings; be capable of giving the group power rather than holding an authoritative role; and be willing to develop a multifaceted relationship with the chairperson.

This professional acts as consultant, supporter, protector, liason, advocate, and model. As a consultant to both the group and the chairperson, the sponsor teaches, lends her skills during difficult group situations, provides resource material, takes responsibility for phone contact with new members, and maintains the phone list. As a support person the professional encourages members to make use of the group in appropriate ways; nurtures the growth of the group, the chairperson, and the members; and responds to the needs of the chairperson during meetings outside the group. In her protector role, the sponsor focuses on both the individuals and the group. She insures that group members can express their individuality and differences, while she simultaneously guards the group's life by setting limits about abusive interactions and by representing and symbolizing the "group as a whole" over a period of time. As a liason, the professional publicizes the group, serves as a link to other organizations (e.g., governmental agencies, the Battered Women's Consortium), takes responsibility for reporting child abuse, and makes referrals. As an advocate, she maintains up-to-date information about laws relating to partner violence, works on legislation that would benefit this population, educates the community about partner violence, and works with individual women as they deal with the systems necessary to ameliorate their situation. Finally, the sponsor serves as a model through her respectfulness, assertiveness, honesty, clear communication, and ability to relate with both openness and limits.

CHARACTERISTICS THAT CREATE DIFFICULTIES FOR WOMEN WHO ARE IN ABUSIVE RELATIONSHIPS

Women in abusive relationships are found in all socioeconomic levels, all educational and age groups, and from all races. The acts of violence against them, rather than any of their own behavior or characteristics, constitute the criteria that determine whether they are appropriate for the group. However, certain characteristics generally present in women in abusive relationships often create difficulties for them. Emphasis must be made that these traits do not cause the abuse and may indeed be a result of the violence.

Isolation

Isolation from friends, family and the community both result from the violence and make women susceptible to ongoing abuse. Brygger, quoted by Davidson (1978), says

> A battered woman tends to isolate herself with the help of the husband himself. He doesn't want her to give time to friends, neighbors, relatives, outside activities. . . . He wants all the attention himself. So she begins to rely on him for all *her* needs. . . . which he then discovers is too heavy a responsibility. . . . He beats her. (p. 56)

Once the battering has occurred, women continue to seclude themselves emotionally and/or physically because of their shame and fear.

Hopelessness/Helplessness/Sense of Powerlessness

Women who have been abused frequently "fail to perceive their options, see themselves as powerless to change their lives, and receive intermittent negative reinforcement" (Brygger, 1983). They appear overwhelmed with the obstacles, hopeless about doing anything to improve their situation.

> The battered wife has been at the mercy of someone else's mood fluctuation and predictable or unpredictable temper to the point where she feels she has no control over her own life. . . . The locus of control is not within herself. . . . It seems as if whatever happens is *done to her.* (Davidson, 1978, p. 57)

Hopeless about helping themselves, the women paradoxically hold unrealistic hopes that their partners will change.

Dependency

The dependency of women in abusive relationships can be misconstrued as masochism or as acceptance of their situation. Neither is accurate. The women do not enjoy the violence or wish to give in to it. Yet the pervasive and multifaceted dependence creates great obstacles.

The women often are dependent on others for their identity, defining themselves by their relationship to their partner. They often judge whether their behavior is acceptable by whether their partners approve. The dependence may take on a caretaking pattern as a woman "is willing to mother the emotionally immature (partner), sacrifice for him (her), and not expose him (her) no matter how unrealistic the demands" (Davidson, 1978, p. 63). The dependency pattern fosters a fear of being alone, which often is evidenced by hysterical or obsessive type responses when the women deal with a changing relationship.

Just as the locus of identity is outside the women, so is the locus of control. Since the women feel out of control, they have difficulty taking responsibility for their own actions, focusing on their own feelings, or even talking about themselves. Both the blame and responsibility for change may rest with the partner in their mind.

The dependence includes an economic facet. Women in this society are often not self-supporting, earning a fraction of what their male partners do. For women in abusive relationships, economic hardship creates a situation in which they often must choose to stay in a violent relationship or to leave themselves open to the whims of the many governmental, social service, and legal systems set up to "serve" them and their children.

Finally, the dependence often involves a chemical addiction. A large percentage of the women are either dealing with their own chemical, food, or relationship dependency and/or are coping with their partner's addictions.

Low Self-Esteem

For most of the women, low self-esteem predates their involvement in their current relationship. A majority have experienced incest, sexual assault, child abuse, and/or had parents in abusive relationships. They may have learned to equate love and abuse as children. Many were reared in emotionally neglectful homes, deprived of nurturing. The women may believe they deserve to be abused and may not be aware that any other form of relationship is possible.

Once in a violent relationship as an adult, the women may become ambivalent—hating the abuse but craving the attachment. The women's esteem spirals downward as they perceive themselves as failures. The combination of isolation and dependence hinder their finding self-worth in facets of their lives other than their relationship. The guilt about being/ staying with their partner and the overwhelming shame that arises out of the belief that they must be "bad people" result from low self-esteem and also add to it.

Lack of Information

The women lack knowledge in many critical areas. They are not informed or are misinformed about abusive relationships, how they are defined, the various types, and actions that might offer protection. They are missing information about healthy relationships, having had few healthy role models. Knowledge about sexuality, feelings, and addiction often appear limited. Myths, inappropriate family rules, and social pressures fuel the misinformation that many women hold as they enter the group.

Skill Deficits

Women in violent relationships often have not learned relationship-enhancing skills. They may not have been taught an assertive (as opposed to aggressive or passive) communication style. Hence, they do not handle their own anger well, know how to get their needs met, or problem-solve difficult situations. The women have not learned about psychological boundaries. They often trust too quickly or not at all. They may be either overly responsible or overly withdrawn, incapable in either instance of intimacy.

Having lacked adequate role models, the women have failed to discover ways to enhance their own self-esteem, to break their isolation, and to take and keep their own personal power. Even if they have learned these skills, they may have been unable to incorporate and practice them in their daily lives.

The above characteristics are present to varying degrees in most women in violent relationships. Yet these women often have deep strengths: caring, integrity, gentleness, and a courage to change. The characteristics mentioned above in no way represent the cause of the violence these women experience but rather affect the way they deal with violence.

HOW THE THERAPEUTIC SELF-HELP MODEL EMPOWERS AND FOSTERS CHANGE

The characteristics of the therapeutic self-help group model make it a particularly appropriate vehicle for meeting the needs of women in violent relationships. The form and function of this model act in a healing manner by doing the following:

Providing Hope

> The installation and maintenance of hope is crucial. . . . ; not only is hope required to keep the patient in therapy so that other curative factors may take effect, but faith in a treatment mode can itself be therapeutically effective. (Yalom, 1975, p. 6)

The therapeutic self-help group model offers immediate hope to the members. This group provides hope to women by its very existence. Many callers, having felt hopeless and helpless for years, are buoyed up by the fact that a service exists for them. Often immobilized and isolated, the women express relief that joining the group is so simple.

The open-ended and ongoing nature of the group make it possible for women at different stages of their work to participate together. This in turn facilitates hope for women at their first session. They hear success stories of changed patterns, practical protection plans, and improved self-esteem. They see women who have helped themselves through separation or through developing improved relationships. They hear women acknowledge similar experiences and feelings. The offers of encouragement and the presence of empowered members are critical factors that entice newer members to return.

Requiring Women to Take Responsibility for Self

While each woman's victimization is acknowledged as she tells her story, her sense of powerlessness begins to be altered immediately upon contact with this group. The focus on *self*-help remains the core of every facet of the group.

Even before the women join the group, the minimal entry requirements encourage self-responsibility. In the pregroup phone contact, the sponsor describes the group and then asks, "Might the group be right for you?" That the women determine when they enter and leave the group without any imposed definition of "being finished" continues to facilitate their sense of responsibility. At the beginning of each session each participant must determine if she wants group time during the session and must request it. First-time members are given much leeway and often decide to take time once the session is under way.

The member ownership quality of the group fosters self-responsibility by allowing each woman to participate in her own way. The group accepts and even validates active silence as a way of learning. Whereas some members remain silent for long periods, others have more active styles that include consistently taking their share of time or doing much of their work through verbal interactions with others who are taking time.

The content as well as the style for a woman's participation rests with her. Women may join the group when first battered, after long experience with being abused, or with the violence in their background. After a protection plan is developed by those with current abuse, the members may talk about any aspect of their lives, e.g., the abuse, their families of origin, sexuality, careers, friendships, or addictions.

As the women work, they may talk about their victimization. Their perspectives are validated. However, they are not treated as victims and in turn are encouraged not to act like victims. "Victims" do not make choices or protect themselves.

As Gottleib, Burden, McCormick, and Nicarthy note, the group process itself facilitates this alteration in attitude.

> Many abused women have been brainwashed into believing that they must obey their husband or boyfriend, that they somehow deserve to be abused, or that they cannot or should not leave the man, yet will become outraged when other women in the group say that they themselves have no right to safety from abuse. . . . She begins to see that she herself can claim rights she believes others should exercise. (p. 88)

Each member makes decisions about her life after the facilitators and other group members make certain she has knowledge of the necessary resources. Members discover that different solutions are appropriate for different persons.

Women gradually transfer their ability to be self-responsible within the group to their life outside the meetings. Their locus of control begins to change as they become proactive rather than reactive. They learn they can take responsiblity for protecting themselves even though they are not responsible for their partner's abusive behavior. They discover they have options about their sense of identity, self-esteem, sexuality, communication style, and the way they spend their time. They learn that they cannot control others or all aspects of their own lives but can feel new power in making the choices open to them.

Accepting/Building on Women's Strengths/Experiences

The self-help model ameliorates the conditions of the women in abusive relationships by accepting each member's personal experiences and strengths and by utilizing a process that makes use of and validates a feminine work style. Gilligan (1982) has emphasized the need for attachment in women's development. Greenspan (1983) applies this notion to women seeking help: "Women in emotional distress do not need distant, male-style experts. . . . [Needed are] an ability to listen, to intuit, empathize with and understand another person's experience—and to communicate that to her" (p. 239).

Women are encouraged to make attachments in the self-help model. They get affective needs met by nurturing and being nurtured, by being givers as well as takers. A nonhierarchical, nonpaternalistic, interactive process results from the peer focus of this group. Connecting and caring, rather than detachment, become the foundation upon which change occurs. "The essence of the process is mutuality and reciprocity" (Silverman, 1980, p. 10).

Each woman's personal experience, as well as her feminine style, is supported. Not only does each woman tell her story, she also learns that her experience is shared by others. Women who feel violated by the name-calling of their partner are affirmed as they learn that verbal abuse is one form of violence. Women who describe themselves as "crazy" because they remain in the relationship hear the struggles of their peers. Women's shame is reduced by the group's acceptance as they reveal histories that may include prostitution, incest, and abusiveness. Members point out strengths and constructive behavior to others who may not see them in themselves.

Intuition and "irrationality" in addition to logic are encouraged and trusted. Most women discover they must utilize these traits as they work on being cognizant of the early cues in their relationship that signal approach of violence. A stomach ache or a sense that "something is wrong" are as critical to a woman's protection plan as is her awareness of her partner's squinted eyes or clenched fists.

An outcome of the focus on a feminine work style and experience is acceptance of a spiral work process. Although the members do become empowered, their process is not a linear one. Rather, the members will cycle and recycle through a series of feelings, behaviors, and issues. This process is understood as a feminine and human one. When members moan that "nothing has changed," others point out that they are grappling with the same issue but from a different perspective. The welcoming back of a "graduate" attests to the support for the belief that growth happens in spirals and cycles rather than by moving from a beginning to an end.

Fostering Interdependence

The self-help group provides a model of interdependence, as opposed to either dependence or isolation. Women are joined to each other through their common background, issues, and womanhood. Though these common factors remain always apparent, the uniqueness of each woman is also supported. Through the simultaneous focus on differences and similarities, the women feel both separate and part of a whole. They develop a sense of interdependence.

The sense of interdependence requires a balance. Women who fear independence discover their own strengths through the group interaction. By observing other women, they learn that being strong does not mean being alone; being alone does not mean being lonely; and being autonomous does not mean being without support. Women who fear dependence learn that there is strength and comfort in numbers and that being in a group does not mean losing one's identity.

Some women make close friends within the group, perhaps learning to trust women for the first time. As interaction takes place, women are encouraged to maintain appropriate boundaries: neither opening up so quickly that they become frightened nor remaining so closed that they are not vulnerable. For members who never had close female friends, new relationships can provide a reworking of the latency "chum" stage and can help remove the fear of leaning on another.

One of the modes through which the group fosters interdependence is by modeling and teaching networking. Participants discover that there is strength in asking for help and in joining together. Newer members learn from older members how to get their needs met by asking for rides, sharing babysitting, and utilizing the phone list. The members network with other agencies and systems as well as with individuals within the group. Health services, advocacy services, the police, courts, and feminist groups can meet the needs of many members in a healthy way.

Women learn they can be in a relationship that is neither smothering nor abandoning. Without being either dependent or totally alone, women can receive acknowledgment, acceptance, and approval. There is a healthy middle ground between enmeshment and isolation.

Mobilizing Anger

Given the group support, empathy, safety, and the ground rules of no abuse in the group, members gradually feel free to be in touch with their own anger. Anger, always an issue for the abused as well as the abuser, may have caused depression, immobilization, or poor relationships. The rage that formerly might have caused abuse of self or partner becomes mobilized to provide energy for self-protection and a sense of empowerment.

Anger is not simply talked about in the group. When an intragroup difficulty arises, members are encouraged to express their anger within the group. They are guided in working out conflicts through assertive communication and problem-solving skills. Fear of anger diminishes as members discover they will not be abandoned or despised when they are angry.

A powerful moment in the group occurred when a member, a very angry person herself, moved close to and touched another as the latter was screaming in anger. The self-esteem of both was enhanced. That there can be anger without violence and hurt is learned.

Providing a Healthy System

Satir (1972) has described the four key factors in a healthy family as promotion of positive self-worth, open communication, clear rules, and a link to society. The four characteristics of the therapeutic self-help model offer these qualities, which the members may not have experienced in their families of origin.

The lack of entry requirements assumes an acceptance of the women as they are. No judgments are passed. This open system both welcomes new members and remains available to members' return. The women can be sure they will not meet with the rejection many experienced in their families.

The member ownership provides a system where each member can act as an individual and still feel part of a group. Women discover flexibility and consistency, not rigidity or unpredictability. The group rules provide limits, which in turn offer the members a sense of structure and protection. The limit-setting is done in a nurturing rather than a punishing manner. Individuality must co-exist with regard for others in a healthy system, yet most of the members have experienced neither. It is a relief, then, for women to be stopped from abusing others within the group and then to be taught other ways to handle their anger. Likewise, mothers in the group have shown cooperation and felt respected when asked to report their child abuse with the sponsor. The member ownership, finally, provides for development of rituals, an ingredient of a healthy system. Group sayings (e.g., "Don't go to the source of the pain for comfort") develop over the years. Potluck dinners have become annual.

The mutual support system provides attention for each person. Many women feel undeserving of this attention, having been told they were unacceptable for so many years. Yet they learn to relish the support, often expressing their "child" self in the group. Women ask to be held, to be listened to, and to be allowed to simply cry or be angry as they learn to trust the acceptance. They also discover that others may not agree with them or may not respond to a request but that rejection and abandonment do not accompany these refusals. Finally, the mutual support system provides encouragement for each individual. Within this framework, the members begin believing they can be different from one another without being better or worse than another.

The dual facilitation provides a demystification of authority figures. The leaders in this group model provide a supportive role, facilitating the process rather than dominating it. These "authorities" are nurturing teachers, protectors, enhancers, and congruent models who attempt to act in accordance with their beliefs. In this group model, the leaders are not the enemy and are not to be feared. Humanness and femaleness are accentuated as both the chairperson and the sponsor share their foibles, act with humor, behave tenderly and with understanding, and share their roles with others. The sponsor attempts to meet the needs of the members, referring to other systems to aid in shelter, legal advice, and therapy. The members themselves develop many leader skills as they begin to trust the facilitators and see their skills as important for any woman. Women become empowered as they benefit from their place in this healthy system.

Providing Knowledge and Skills

Women who attend the Group for Women in Abusive Relationships increase their awareness and build skills from their work with each other, with the sponsor and chairperson, and from the group process itself. From the other members and the two facilitators, women learn about the abuse cycle, how to make a protection plan, anger management, healthy sexuality, working with the legal system, and referral sources. Each new member is given a booklet about violent relationships. Most of the women attend a separate seven-week educational series about abuse offered by Family and Children's Service.

Through the interaction within the group, skills improve. Members are encouraged to utilize good communication patterns: speaking for themselves, identifying feelings and separating those from thoughts, and using an assertive style. Within the group the members also develop problem-solving and goal-setting skills. They learn how to utilize the special resources of the women within the group: asking those expert in finances about money management, turning to health specialists appropriately, and getting support from Alcoholics Anonymous members about addictions. More generally, members discover how to blend thinking and feeling, love and work, and the practical and the theoretical. They feel "freed up by (this) raised consciousness, not weighed down by the burden of the personal-political pain (they) carry" (Greenspan, 1983, pp. 249–250). The skills, gradually transferred to life outside the sessions, empower by increasing each woman's alternatives.

Being Holistic

Although this self-help group cannot meet all the needs of its members, it does address the whole person through both its content and the process. Discussions are not limited to the narrow confines of abusive incidents and protection plans. Rather, women deal with the issues that feed into and result from their life situation: finances, medical concerns, child care, dilemmas around legal issues, and housing. One woman discusses how she was fired from her professional job once her supervisor discovered she had been battered. Another member shares with the group her discovery of a housing fund. A third woman describes her new awareness of the impact of her religious upbringing on her attitudes toward violence. Larger perspectives become entwined with individual issues as the women recognize the impact of political, social, and cultural systems on their own concerns. The women gain a holistic view of the causes and effects of violence.

The process of the self-help group involves the whole person. Each woman can be both giver and taker, healer and healed, teacher and student. Women do not need to compartmentalize; they may focus on their past, present, or future. They may work from their "parent," "child," or "adult"; from an emphasis on thinking or venting; and from their logical or intuitive strengths. As all these facets are acknowledged and supported, women become integrated and feel whole.

Changing Self-Image: From Victim to Survivor

During their initial involvement in the self-help group, women are encouraged to acknowledge their victimization. Many fight against the group's unyielding belief that no person is responsible for someone else's violence. Acknowledging this belief makes the members feel out of control, for if they are not responsible for their partner's anger, they know they cannot change their partner's behavior. However, once women understand their lack of responsibility for their partner, they begin to recognize they can change their *own* behavior. With this transition women mobilize their energy, move out of their shame, see the realities more clearly, and focus on themselves rather than on how to control their partner.

Acknowledging one's victimization is quite different than having a victim identity. The former creates proactivity; the latter fosters continued passivity. The philosophy of this self-help group involves the notion that labels can become self-perpetuating. The sponsor helps women see themselves as "women in abusive relationships" rather than "battered women." Rather than taking on an ongoing self-image of "victim," women begin to understand that their victimization experiences need not define them. Women can become "survivors."

SUMMARY

The routes through which the therapeutic self-help model aids women in abusive relationships have been detailed. Behaviors, thoughts, and feelings alter as the group impacts the members via its form and its content. The women develop hope, become self-responsible, increase their awareness of and build on their strengths, become interdependent as they develop individual and system networks, familiarize themselves with and utilize their anger, learn about healthy interaction within a healthy system, develop skills to enhance their lives, and develop a sense of themselves as whole persons. The process of the self-help group itself addresses the needs of women in abusive relationships. In so doing, the therapeutic self-help model heals and empowers.

REFERENCES

Brygger, M. P. (1983, January 10). Talk to Region 11 Battered Women's Consortium, Minneapolis, MN.

Davidson, T. (1978). *Conjugal crime: Understanding and changing the wifebeating pattern.* New York: Hawthorn Books.

Gilligan, C. (1982). *In a different voice.* Cambridge, MA: Harvard University Press.

Golan, N. (1981). *Passing through transitions: A guide for practitioners.* New York: The Free Press.

Gottleib, N., Burden, D., McCormick, R., & Nicarthy, G. (1983). The distinctive attributes of feminist groups. In B. G. Reed & C. D. Garvin (Eds.), *Groupwork with women—Groupwork with men.* New York: The Haworth Press.

Greenspan, M. (1983). *A new approach to women and therapy.* New York: McGraw Hill.

Hartman, S. (1983). A self-help group for women in abusive relationships. In B. G. Reed & C. D. Garvin (Eds.), *Groupwork with women—Groupwork with men.* New York: The Haworth Press.

Olson, C. M., & Shapiro, M. (1979). *A combined therapeutic and self-help approach in working with former and current prostitutes.* Unpublished paper, Family and Children's Service, Minneapolis, MN.

Satir, V. (1972). *Peoplemaking.* Palo Alto, CA: Science and Behavior Books, Inc.

Silverman, P. R. (1980). *Mutual help groups: Organization and development.* Beverly Hills, CA: Sage Publications.

Yalom, I. D. (1975). *The theory and practice of group psychotherapy.* New York: Basic Books.

■ 7
Self-Help Groups with Agoraphobic Women

KATHLEEN A. BREHONY

> My three sisters are sitting
> on rocks of black obsidian
> For the first time, in this light
> I can see who they are.
>
> ADRIENNE RICH (1969)

OVERVIEW

Self-help groups for agoraphobic women are a new and, as yet, relatively unexplored approach to treatment for this clinically significant problem. While empirical evidence supporting self-help paradigms is in short supply, there are a number of compelling observations and theoretical foundations that support group approaches including therapy, consciousness-raising (CR), and self-help.

The lack of a robust empirical database prohibits this chapter from becoming "Self-Help Groups for Agoraphobia: A Review of Literature," and so, instead, I embark here on a more complex coalescence of theory,

---

This chapter is dedicated to the self-help group from whom I have learned fundamental truths about agoraphobia, caring, and friendship.

clinical observations, and views of agoraphobic women who have participated in self-help programs. To this end, it appears necessary to incorporate the following issues: (1) clinical descriptions of agoraphobia, (2) presentation of a feminist/clinical theory of agoraphobia, (3) healing components of group treatment (both self-help and therapy groups), and (4) conclusions and future of self-help groups with agoraphobia.

SCOPE AND DEFINITION OF THE PROBLEM

Agoraphobia is the most pervasive and serious phobic response seen by clinicians. The disorder accounts for approximately 50 to 60% of all phobic problems (Marks, 1969). Although many people interpret agoraphobia to mean "fear of open spaces," the term, from the Greek, actually translates to "fear of the marketplace," and even that fails to evoke the complexity of fears characteristic of agoraphobia. For example, agoraphobics report not only fear of "the marketplace" and other public places but also a generalized fear and avoidance response to leaving a place of refuge (almost without exception the home) and entering into the outside world. The phobic individual recognizes the irrationality of her avoidance behavior, yet continues to avoid fear-provoking situations that elicit high levels of anxiety and panic attacks. The concomitant physiological symptoms of anxiety (e.g., hyperventilation, tachycardia, tremor, sweating) usually accompany acute phobic reactions, although there is a great deal of individual variation as to which physiological symptoms dominate.

Marks (1970) observed that agoraphobic individuals have fears not only of going out into open spaces but also of being in closed spaces and of shopping, traveling, and entering social situations, especially when alone. There is much fear generalization to additional stimuli throughout the course of the disorder, and numerous other symptoms commonly are present, including panic attacks, "fear of fear," fear of fainting, tension, dizziness, frequent depression, depersonalization, obsessions, and numerous stress-related physical complaints.

Brehony, Geller, Benson, and Solomon (1979) observed that the mean duration of symptoms was about 19 years. Individuals with these fears generally develop extreme dependence upon others to take care of them in phobic situations and report that they feel unhappy, frightened, and lacking in confidence in their own abilities to handle themselves in panic situations. In sum, agoraphobia is a constricting, serious psychological/behavioral problem that disrupts all areas of an individual's life for a very long period of time (sometimes an entire lifetime).

The observation that most agoraphobics are women (Brehony, Geller,

Benson, & Solomon, 1979; Marks, 1970; Marks & Herst, 1969; Roberts, 1964) is extremely important. Fodor (1974) noted that 85% of agoraphobics seen by clinicians are female (studies indicate percentages that range from 64 to 100%).

A large-scale epidemiological study conducted by the National Institute of Health (Regier, Myers, Kramer, Robins, Blazer, Hough, Eaton, & Locker, 1984) concluded that anxiety disorders (including panic disorders, obsessive-compulsive disorders, and agoraphobia) were among the most common disorders. Approximately 8% of the people surveyed suffered from a clinically significant anxiety disorder. This study confirmed the widely held observation that women were more likely than men to confirm suffering high levels of anxiety and phobic avoidance. The marked predominance of women among agoraphobics is startling in view of the absence of such clear sex differences in most other "neurotic" disorders (Hare, 1965; Marks & Gelder, 1965). The possibility that women admit more fears than men does exist (Katkin & Hoffman, 1976), but this does not explain adequately the differential sex ratios for the various phobic disorders.

FEMININE SEX-ROLE STEREOTYPES AND AGORAPHOBIA

Fodor (1974) suggested that phobic symptoms, particularly those of agoraphobia, are associated with extreme helplessness and dependency and appear related to social expectations for women. Additionally, she noted that interpersonal "trapped-ness"—the feeling of being dominated with no outlet for assertive behavior—may further enhance the development of agoraphobia. Fodor also suggested that the agoraphobic response is an extreme and exaggerated extension of the stereotypic feminine role. Seidenberg and DeCrow (1983) view agoraphobia as "a paradigm for the historical intimidation and oppression of women. The self-hate, self-limitation, self-abnegation and self-punishment of agoraphobia is a caricature of centuries of childhood instructions to women" (p. 6).

The empirical literature supporting the hypothesized relationship between sex-role stereotypes and symptoms of agoraphobia has not matured to the point of allowing for unequivocal conclusions. There are many women who rigidly conform to sex-role stereotypes who do not manifest the clinical symptoms of agoraphobia. It is likely that other physiological, family system, behavioral, and emotional variables in complex interplay affect agoraphobic symptoms. Nonetheless, logical inferences from an understanding of the sex-role expectations for women's behavior and clinical observations of agoraphobics support the general view that the cultural expectations for women's behavior (e.g., dependency, escape from frightening situations, low assertiveness) and the symptoms of agoraphobia do not qualitatively differ.

Fodor (1974) noted the following:

> Many women have been trained for adulthood as child women. Under the realistic stresses of adult life and marriage these "stereotypic" emotional, passive, helpless women become anxious, wish to flee, dream of being more independent or of rescue or escape. For some the emotional stress is too great and phobia provides another solution. (p. 133)

Coming from a vantage point of history and philosophy, Janeway (1980) suggested that agoraphobia "is a kind of retreat into paralysis for those whose mistrust of life is pervasive but who can find no support that will settle the question of what to mistrust—oneself or the surrounding circumstances" (p. 169).

GROUP THERAPY FOR AGORAPHOBIA

There is little empirical literature describing self-help groups for agoraphobics, although there are some data regarding group treatment (therapist-facilitated) and some self-help programs that involve a spouse, partner, or friend (Mathews, Gelder, & Johnston, 1981).

One of the major functions of any therapeutic intervention for agoraphobia is exposure to the feared stimulus. That is to say, the state of the art of the clinical literature indicates that in vivo (in real life) or imaginal (e.g., imagery or hypnosis) confrontation with the feared stimulus must take place in order for extinction of the conditioned fear to occur.

Group in vivo exposure has been an effective procedure that may enhance cost-effectiveness as well as provide additional therapeutic advantages over individual in vivo exposure sessions. Watson, Mullet, and Pillay (1973) found significant improvement for agoraphobics treated by in vivo exposure groups. Similarly, Hand, Lamontagne, and Marks (1974) compared structured versus unstructured group in vivo exposure with agoraphobic subjects. Members of structured groups practiced together, whereas members of the unstructured groups practiced exposure alone. Data immediately following treatment showed group exposure to be as effective as individual exposure for both structured and unstructured groups. However, six-month follow-up results suggested that symptomatic improvement was enhanced for the members of the structured group. Additionally, it was noted that structured groups showed greater social cohesion and had fewer drop-outs and relapses. Moreover, Hand et al. (1976) observed that both group conditions appeared to increase social skills and assertiveness in group members. Teasdale, Walsh, Lancashire, and Mathews (1977) replicated the Hand et al. study but omitted the unstructured comparison group. Data showed that immediate effects of treatment were similar to the Hand et al. results. However, while improvement was maintained for the six-month follow-up, no further treatment gains were made during this period of time.

Hafner and Marks (1976) randomly assigned 57 agoraphobic subjects to an individual or group in vivo exposure treatment condition. Both interventions included four three-hour sessions of in vivo exposure delivered during a two-week period. Results showed no significant between-group differences. Additionally, and contrary to expectations, the group-treated subjects experienced more panic attacks during the treatment process than did subjects treated individually. Emmelkamp and Emmelkamp-Benner (1975) treated agoraphobics individually or in groups with instructions to turn back upon experiencing uncomfortable anxiety and to self-record the duration of time spent with the feared stimulus. Results showed no between-group differences, indicating the group procedure to be as effective as the individual procedures.

A more recent study (Silon, 1984) evaluated a group treatment program that incorporated education, therapy, and social models (based on Adlerian principles of social interest, responsibility, encouragement, and purposive behavior). The results indicated that clients who accepted responsibility for making changes in their lifestyle also reported diminished symptoms and an enhanced ability to reduce anticipatory anxiety. However, this study did not compare the group treatment approach to the same approach conducted with individual clients.

Although the data seem to indicate that group treatment is as successful as individual treatment (and sometimes more effective), there are a number of methodological constraints that prevent firm conclusions. First of all, clinical outcome research has many difficult design issues to overcome including the accuracy of measurement, the desynchrony of responses (e.g., physiological, behavioral, and self-report of improvement do not necessarily co-vary), maintaining the integrity of the independent variable (e.g., subjects in studies of treatment for agoraphobia often are a heterogenous group in that some are taking antianxiety medication and others are not, etc.), and sampling bias. Additionally, there are no studies in the literature that have directly compared group self-help approaches to therapist-directed group treatment. Nonetheless, it is possible to draw upon what we do know about group approaches, theory, and anecdotal evidence about the efficacy of self-help groups for agoraphobia.

We do understand that group procedures may offer additional important therapeutic ingredients not found in individual therapy. For example, Yalom (1975) pointed out that group process can foster the instillation of hope, impart information, and provide an opportunity to recognize that others are experiencing similar problems. Group members may develop a sense of altruism by sharing experiences and helping others, resulting in enhanced self-esteem and feelings of self-worth. Group cohesion can offer important feedback and reinforcement components not available in individual therapy. Finally, groups may allow for the observation of coping models that can effectively motivate and teach other group members. Additionally, group approaches have an enhanced cost-benefit ratio for treatment, thus allowing important growth opportunities for women who are economically disadvantaged.

Although there are no hard data on self-help groups for agoraphobic women, there is some knowledge. This author and her colleagues conducted group therapy with 12 severely agoraphobic women for a period of two months in 1980 (weekly group sessions). Following the formal "group therapy" we invited the members to participate in a modified self-help group for eight months. I delineate the self-help group as "modified" because a therapist was present, though she served more as a facilitator than a therapist. During the course of this program we learned a great deal about the critical variables associated with growth and change among the group members. There appeared to be a number of consistent and important components to successful reduction of agoraphobic symptoms. These are likely to remain the salient treatment variables regardless of whether a group is conducted as group therapy or as a true self-help group initiated and conducted by agoraphobic women who are not trained as therapists or counselors.

FACTORS IMPORTANT FOR REDUCING AGORAPHOBIC SYMPTOMS

Awareness of Others Sharing the Same Problem

For many years agoraphobia has been a "closet" disorder. Until relatively recently discussion of this problem was relegated to a few lines in abnormal psychology textbooks. In the past five or six years, however, it has become a frequently discussed topic on television talk shows and in magazines aimed at the general public and women's market. Many women refer themselves to treatment having correctly diagnosed themselves after reading a magazine or seeing a discussion on "Phil Donahue." Scores of women have told me that they had been trying to explain to their doctors for years how they felt, and now they could name it (many reported that they felt that their doctors could benefit enormously by reading McCall's). Even this vicarious support group (reading about or viewing on television another woman who voiced the same fears) may serve to reduce the sense of being alone. After all, as one woman explained, "Even little kids can go into a grocery store. I have felt so alone, like I was completely crazy, and ashamed to tell anyone about how I felt."

Janeway (1980) describes how the culturally disempowered (like women, especially agoraphobic women) come to accept the notion that they exist as "solitary freaks" unable to cope with the world or even simple tasks in any normal, productive fashion. Group experiences with other women with similar problems demand a personal paradigm shift. It no longer becomes possible to believe that one is entirely alone when confronted by flesh-and-blood evidence affirming one's experiences, as is the case in a group.

Personal is Political

Group process allows the sharing of nonagoraphobic experiences—experiences related to being a woman living in a fundamentally misogynist world. For years, agoraphobic women have been asked to view their fears and inability to confront these as personal weaknesses or resulting from a "neurotic personality." Groups foster the awareness that women, all women, share certain similar conditioning histories. It is this history, the ways women are taught to view themselves as dependent, helpless, and "rescuable," that provides the social backdrop for the agoraphobic avoidance behaviors to be played out. This consciousness-raising aspect of group experience appeared to be a critical component for growth and change. Kravetz (1980) noted that "Through sharing, CR groups help women understand and deal with personal problems as they are related to their sex-role conditioning and experiences with sex-role bias and discrimination. Through this process, personal attitudes, behavior, roles and relationships, as well as social policies and practices, become targets for change" (p. 269).

To indict cultural prescriptions for women's behavior is not to say that agoraphobic women are not ultimately responsible for making changes in their lives. Many nonfeminist therapists have criticized this aspect of feminist therapy by arguing that this is "blamecasting" and reduces the personal responsibility for change. It is quite possible to hold these sociocultural insights and still believe that no one but ourselves can be responsible for implementing change in our lives.

While the major process in the consciousness-raising aspect of our group was the sharing of personal experiences, the women also opted to include literature, films, music, and speakers as part of their learning. None of these directly addressed the issue of agoraphobia. For example, one speaker who addressed the group on several occasions was a specialist in continuing education at a local college whose expertise included women's literature. Group members read novels (e.g., by Charlotte Perkins Gilman, Toni Morrison, and Carol Gilligan, among others). Anecdotal evidence in the form of responses of the group indicated that these group activities formed common bonds among the group. They became critical and important learning opportunities that were far more robust by being shared and discussed.

Facilitating the Recognition and Assertive Expression of Feelings (Especially Anger)

Agoraphobic women often have a very difficult time in the correct labeling of feelings. Ever vigilant for the physiological symptoms of a panic attack, they tend to perceive all forms of arousal as a significant predictor of impending panic. They easily misattribute anger to anxiety. Groups offer unique opportunities to challenge these misattributions and give feedback for the accurate labeling of feelings.

Many women in our group reported that once they felt like they had "permission" to label their feelings as anger, "everything began to fall into place." The group emphasized that recognizing anger and learning productive and assertive methods of expressing these feelings was better than just "carrying it around." The group provided a gentle, nurturant environment in which members could experiment with new behaviors through role-playing and discussion of alternatives.

Social Support for In Vivo Exposure

Insight is not enough in overcoming agoraphobia. These individuals must behaviorally confront the situations and feelings that terrify them. From a behavioral perspective, exposure to the feared situations causes "extinction" of the conditioned response; from the psychoanalytic perspective, "catharsis." Our group preferred to think in humanistic terms and reported that confronting anxiety-provoking situations allowed them to feel "courageous." The literature has consistently demonstrated that exposure is an imperative treatment component. Experience in the self-help group has shown that agoraphobic women can demonstrate enormous courage in confronting their fears if given encouragement and support. The group evolved several subgroups that they labeled "buddy systems." For example, one woman in the group who could drive near her home but could not eat out in a restaurant paired up with another woman who found restaurants to be no problem but could not drive. This particular buddy system created opportunities for the woman who feared driving to drive the other to a restaurant for lunch. They recognized the need to confront the fears and organized strategies so that they could confront them together.

Management of Panic

As part of a larger goal of empowerment, it is important that the agoraphobic woman learn that there are a number of things she can do to control panic attacks. Without the knowledge that she has some control over these terrifying feelings it is unreasonable to ask her to confront the feared situations.

A number of researchers (e.g., Ley, 1985) have suggested that panic attacks are brought on by "overbreathing" or hyperventilation. Data indicates that rather than panic causing hyperventilation, it may be the other way around. According to this theory, overbreathing results in a depletion of carbon dioxide, thus causing the pH level in the blood to be out of balance, resulting in a state of alkalosis. The body literally feels like it is suffocating, and, naturally, the fight or flight response ensues. Thus, learning to control breathing is one way for the agoraphobic woman to take control.

The three panic management techniques that this self-help group utilized were (1) diaphragmatic breathing: taking a deep breath, holding it to the count of five, and slow exhaling; (2) Staying in the present: anxiety is almost always a "what if," experience and this is particularly true of agoraphobic panic (e.g., "what if it gets worse, and I faint, die, embarrass myself"); noticing the stimuli present in the environment (e.g., taste, touch, sight etc.) is important in remaining present-centered; (3) Stop negative thoughts: thought-stopping techniques were very helpful to a number of the group members; one woman noted that she "pretended it was somebody else's voice telling me that I better run because I would faint. I called her the 'old nag' and just told her I wasn't listening anymore."

Ellis (1962) and Beck and Emery (1985), among others, have described the cognitive issues and "automatic thinking" of agoraphobia. The first sign of panic elicits the "catastrophizing" thoughts of the worst possible outcome (e.g., I will die, I will go insane or out of control).

The group spent significant time on discussing and challenging these irrational thoughts. One unplanned but very effective therapeutic ingredient was humor. The cognitive factors of agoraphobia seemed to be fertile ground for these women to demonstrate gentle humor in taking these irrational thoughts to their most absurd. Because everyone in the group was "in the same boat" (e.g., experienced panic attacks) there was no defensiveness about humorous approaches to challenging these cognitive belief systems.

Management of Anticipatory Anxiety

Along with the irrational belief systems and "automatic thinking" relative to the experience of panic attacks, the agoraphobic engages in catastrophic thinking prior to finding herself in a fear-eliciting situation. Following classic patterns of approach/avoidance the anxiety mounts as the dreaded event draws near. One woman in our support group began worrying about having to "be the center of attention" at her daughter's wedding while this event was still eight months in the future. Social support and feedback from the group was critical in her finding new ways of thinking about her fear.

Coping with Depression

Agoraphobia is rarely seen as an isolated set of phobias that exist in an otherwise psychologically healthy person (Chambless, 1982). A number of research studies have shown that severely agoraphobic individuals have been found to have higher scores on a number of psychometric measures of depression (e.g., Chambless, 1981; Emmelkamp and Cohen-Kettenis, 1975). Chambless (1982) suggests this might reflect the effects of a restricted lifestyle and lowered self-esteem. Whiteford and Evans (1984) observed that agoraphobics (both male and female) evaluated on a dexamethasone suppression test (proposed to be a state-dependent biological marker of depression) scored higher than other patients with nonaffective psychiatric disorders though lower than patients with major depression.

Although the discussion of the etiology of depression in agoraphobia is not resolved, it is a general clinical obserservation that agoraphobic individuals report high levels of depression. Our support group directly addressed the issue of depression. Again, social support, a feeling of belonginess, and other characteristics of group experience appeared to have strong therapeutic properties for depression.

A number of process and content variables seem important for any group approach aimed at recovery for agoraphobic women. It is important to note that it may well be that for agoraphobic women who function at a high level, the participation in a grass-roots self-help group would offer all the therapy that is needed. The data and the symptoms themselves speak clearly to the idea that agoraphobia is highly related to sex-role issues and that the consciousness-raising that takes place in women coming together and sharing their experiences is powerful medicine. In *Powers of the weak,* Janeway (1980) reminds us that people sharing with each other "find out that they are not lonely sufferers, but patients with a common complaint. The powerful may find it odd that a shared experience of weakness can strengthen the weak; but out of the sharing comes an ability to trust those who have been caught in the same bind as oneself" (pp. 169–170).

Traditional therapy has emphasized adjustment rather than change in agoraphobia (as with most other "mental illnesses"). Group process brings this question—of adjustment or change—into broad light.

On the other hand, women with more severe agoraphobic symptoms may not be good candidates for such a group, since some of them literally could not get out of the house to attend the group experience. Self-help groups would have to incorporate outreach activities to pull in the least functioning women.

One can imagine a continuum of change opportunities that, perhaps, would include other more "traditional" forms of treatment, including individual and group therapy. Such an approach, however, might be best structured to lead to participation in a self-help group with the emphasis on additional changes such as consciousness-raising, self-esteem building, and the development of strong networks of friends.

The process variables associated with self-help for agoraphobic women include many that are consistent with the literature of group process. Notable among these are social support, reinforcement, feelings of belonging-ness, opportunities to nurture and be nurtured, and an increased awareness of one's worth as an individual and as a woman. The content variables of exposure to feared situations, education about anxiety states and panic attacks and how to control these, accurate attribution of feelings, and the development of assertive strategies for the expression of feelings are also of significance.

Our experience with a self-help group for agoraphobic women has been challenging and rewarding. Future research should be directed at the exploration of the efficacy of self-help and other group approaches for agoraphobic women. Kravetz (1980) noted that "the results of such investigations would provide the basis for appropriate linkages and referrals between professionals and nonprofessionals serving women. Once the relative utility of various help-giving systems is established, women will be able to choose among systems and approaches, using them separately or in conjunction with one another, depending on their particular preferences" (p. 280).

Agoraphobic women can and will find their own empowerment and affirmation. It is likely to be found in self-help groups, CR groups, therapy groups, in the office of a feminist professional therapist or counselor, in the poetry of Adrienne Rich, in the writing of Alice Walker, and in thousands of other ways in which women's voices rise together.

REFERENCES

Beck, A.T., & Emery, G. (1985). *Anxiety disorders and phobias*. New York: Basic Books, Inc.

Brehony, K.A., Geller, E.S., Benson, B., & Solomon, L.J. (1979). *Epidemiological data about agoraphobia: An American sample*. Unpublished manuscript, Virginia Polytechnic Institute, Blacksburg, VA.

Chambless, D.L. (1981). *Factors associated with the severity of agoraphobia*. Unpublished research, University of Georgia, Athens, GA.

Chambless, D.L. (1982). Characteristics of agoraphobics. In D.L. Chambless & A.J. Goldstein (Eds.), *Agoraphobia: Multiple perspectives on theory and treatment*. New York: John Wiley & Sons.

Ellis, A. (1962). *Reason and emotion in psychotherapy*. New York: Lyle Stuart.

Emmelkamp, P.M.G., & Cohen-Kettenis, P.J. (1975). Relationship of locus of control to phobic anxiety and depression. *Psychological Reports, 36*(2), 390.

Emmelkamp, P.M.G., & Emmelkamp-Benner, A. (1975). Effects of historically portrayed modeling and group treatment on self-observation: A comparison with agoraphobics. *Behavior Research and Therapy, 13*, 135–139.

Fodor, I.G. (1974). The phobic syndrome in women: Implications for treatment. In V. Franks & V. Burtle (Eds.), *Women in therapy: New psychotherapies for a changing society*. New York: Brunner/Mazel.

Hafner, R.J., & Marks, I.M. (1976). Exposure in vivo of agoraphobics: Contribution of diazepam, group exposure and anxiety evocation. *Psychological Medicine, 6*, 71–88.

Hand, I., Lamontagne, Y., & Marks, I.M. (1974). Group exposure (flooding) in vivo for agoraphobics. *British Journal of Psychiatry, 124*, 588–602.

Hare, E.H. (1965). *Triennial statistical report, 1961–1963*. Bethlem Royal and Maudsley Hospital.

Janeway, E. (1980). *Powers of the weak*. New York: Alfred A. Knopf.

Katkin, E.S., & Hoffman, L.S. (1976). Sex differences in self-report of fear: A psychophysiological assessment. *Journal of Abnormal Psychology, 85*, 607–610.

Kravetz, D. (1980). Consciousness-raising and self-help. In A.M. Brodsky & R. Hare-Mustin (Eds.), *Women and psychotherapy: An assessment of research and practice*. New York: Guilford Press.

Ley, R. (1985). Blood, breath, and fears: A hyperventilation theory of panic attacks and agoraphobia. *Clinical Psychology Review, 5*(4), 271–285.

Marks, I.M. (1969). *Fears and phobias*. New York: Academic Press.

Marks, I.M. (1970). Agoraphobic syndrome: Phobic anxiety state. *Archives of General Psychiatry, 23*(6), 538–553.

Marks, I.M., & Gelder, M.G. (1965). A controlled retrospect study of behavior therapy in phobic patients. *British Journal of Psychiatry, 111*(476), 561–573.

Marks, I.M., & Herst, E.R. (1969). A survey of 1,200 agoraphobics in Britain: Features associated with treatment and ability to work. *Social Psychiatry, 5*(1), 16–24.

Mathews, A.M., Gelder, M.G., & Johnston, D.W. (1981). *Agoraphobia: Nature and treatment*. New York: Guilford Press.

Regier, D.A., Myers, J.K., Kramer, M., Robins, L.N., Blazer, D.G., Hough, R.L., Eaton, W.W., & Locke, B.Z. (1984). The NIMH epidemiologic catchment area program. *Archives of General Psychiatry, 41*(10), 934–941.

Rich, A. (1969). "Women." In *Leaflets: Poems 1965–1968*. New York: Norton.

Roberts, A.H. (1964). Housebound housewives—A follow-up study of phobic anxiety states. *British Journal of Psychiatry, 110*(465), 191–197.

Seidenberg, R., & DeCrow, K. (1983). *Panic and protest in agoraphobia: Women who marry houses*. New York: McGraw-Hill.

Silon, B. (1984). Agoraphobia: The loss of social responsibility. *Individual Psychology: Journal of Adlerian Theory, Research and Practice, 40*(2), 133–140.

Teasdale, J.D., Walsh, P.A., Lancashire, M., & Mathews, A.M. (1977). Group exposure for agoraphobics: A replication study. *British Journal of Psychiatry, 130*, 186–193.

Watson, J.P., Mullett, G.E., & Pillay, H. (1973). The effects of prolonged exposure to phobic situations upon agoraphobic patients treated in groups. *Behavior Research and Therapy, 11*(4), 531–545.

Whiteford, H.A., & Evans, L. (1984). Agoraphobia and the dexamethasone suppression test: Atypical depression? *Australian, New Zealand Journal of Psychiatry, 18*(4), 374–377.

Yalom, I. (1975). *The theory and practice of group psychotheraphy*. New York: Basic Books.

■ three
GROUP TECHNIQUES AND ISSUES

■ 8
Woman Therapist as Group Model in Homogeneous and Mixed Cultural Groups

CLAIRE M. BRODY

In all-women therapeutic or support groups, each member is able to measure her individual adaptation against models provided by the other members. A group member may learn—often faster than in dyad communication—that feelings are realistically related to unsatisfyng life roles. The client in a therapy group benefits from the many-faceted reflected images of herself, derived from the responses of the other women and those of the therapist-leader, that accelerate the process of change. Similarly, the woman therapist in her own support group benefits from learning to be more authentic as an equal with women colleagues, and this can enable her to be more helpful with clients who struggle with similar problems. When a woman therapist can accept herself more fully as a leader, she can be a peer more easily.

In this chapter, the literature review will focus first on the dynamics of the therapist–client relationship and then on the female therapist as model

This chapter is an expanded version of a paper, "Women therapist as group model and group participant" published in *Psychotherapy in Private Practice*, 3(1), 1985. It also includes some material incorporated in an article "White therapist and female minority clients: Gender and culture issues" published in *Psychotherapy*, 24(1), 1987.

Special thanks are extended here to Marilyn McGirr, Frances K. Trotman, and Carolynn Hillman for their editorial assistance with this chapter.

for her clients in both homogeneous and mixed racial treatment groups. Finally, as counterpoint for understanding the dynamics of all-women groups (both culturally homogeneous and heterogeneous), the functioning of an ongoing women therapists' group will be described.

CLIENT-THERAPIST RELATIONSHIP

Kravetz (1976) and Walker (Chapter 1, *this volume*) state that in all-women groups, as opposed to mixed gender groups, there is greater possibility of developing closeness to other women and less of the game-playing often evidenced in the mixed-sex groups. Also, the women's group is less distracted by competitiveness than a mixed gender group would be. Because they may deliberately cultivate passivity in childhood even when it destroys competence, women who attempt to break out of the helpless female role often experience rage as a result of the role conflict (Mundy, 1975). In women's groups the tears of rage can be mobilized into structured action for change, through the empathy of the other women.

In considering various types of alternative models of client/therapist relationships that aim to be nonsexist and nonhierarachical, Schur (1983) points out that groups can run the gamut from women's consciousness-raising (CR) ones to a variety of humanistic, nontraditional therapies. Rather than focus attention on intrapsychic conflicts as the source of women's stress as has been done traditionally, a woman therapist with groups of women can work to redefine as social system deficiencies the conditions previously viewed as personal symptoms. In feminist-oriented group therapy, a goal particular to women is often to use the group experience to get rid of dependence, to share uniquely female experiences with other women, and for the therapist to help the clients change the political and social environment if they wish to (Rohrbaugh, 1979).

Chesler, writing in 1973, said that marriage and psychotherapy as institutions were similar in that both were unequal relationships. She also said that both experiences tended to isolate women from one another. However, the climate for and attitude of women seeking therapy in the mid-1980s has changed significantly. A women's group with a female leader can provide a forum for counteracting isolation and helplessness. As Bernardez (1983) states, "women in leadership roles ... may also serve to enhance the groups' desire to transform itself and achieve a higher integration. The specific ingredients that women and other minorities have to offer are linked with aspects that are devalued by the dominated culture but that paradoxically must be integrated to achieve increasing harmony and creativity (p. 48).

THERAPIST AS MODEL

An examination of the client/therapist relationship in groups must include the therapist as model. Bernardez (1983) says that although women in leadership roles may be castigated for their positions of power, this can also serve to enhance each group member's desire to transform herself. Dickstein (1982) reports on a study with college women in same-sex groups with a female therapist. The women develop more accurate perceptions of others' beliefs and define new ideals for themselves consonant with the goals of independence and equality. Earlier researchers (Ables & Brandesma, 1977) proposed the therapist as model through providing helpful comments; Lieberman, Yalom, and Miles (1973) said the therapist can offer her own problem-solving strategies or behavioral traits.

Lewis, Davis, and Lesmeister (1983) point out that an explicit communication of the therapist's values, methods, and goals may have the advantage of helping the client form more accurate expectations of the therapy process. In a study designed to measure the effect of "pretherapy information" about a therapist's feminist value orientation, it was determined that while this may be an ethically sound procedure, as was suggested by Hare-Mustin, Marecek, Kaplan, and Liss-Levenson (1979), such explicit presentation may be disadvantageous and confusing to the client. This therapist prefers to provide this orientation in the feminist milieu of the therapeutic relationship. As Lewis et al. (1983) suggest, a client is then more likely to "project" her own version of a feminist's values onto the therapist, which in turn can be a fruitful focus of exploration.

Dimidjian's (1983) article, "Seeing Me, Defining What It Means To Be Me, Describing What I Want To Be" offers a very original description of the impact of a woman therapist on her client. In the therapeutic relationship, the therapist assists each woman in validating her dream of feminine adulthood. Implicit in this is also the modeling role of the female therapist for the women in groups. Basing her formulation on the work of six female therapists, Dimidjian describes a process of "relational bonding" that enables the clients to model their development on that of the therapist by sharing *her* prior insights, while they are helped to articulate and define their own goals.

Daley and Koppenaal (1981), describing a short-term (15 week) group modality for women, discuss the role of modeling in the changes achieved. Prior to this, Brodsky (1977), Halas (1973), and Lynch (1974) described women's groups as providing greater opportunity for both role modeling and empathy around sex-role conflicts. Daley and Koppenaal found that groups composed mostly of women in their 30s focused more on the needs of that age group's developmental life stage and expectations: intrapersonal need for self-definition, power, and identity apart from both their families of origin and their current families. Most conflicts expressed were concerned with change and independence. These authors recommend that women's groups be homogeneous for adult developmental life stage in order to focus on relevant issues. They also propose a time-limited structure for such groups.

Kazdin's (1976) findings imply that treatment effectiveness is increased when the therapist models assertive behavior during therapy sessions, and the woman client is exposed to a competent model who can report reward for assertive behavior. This is in contrast to the fact that in their prior histories women were more often punished or ignored when assertive. [See Linehan (1984) and Chapter 11, *this volume.*]

There are two particularly significant personality components for the therapist to model for women in groups. The first is competency. Blechman (1984) suggests behavioral intervention to narrow the gap between the competency of dysfunctional women and more competent ones. Blechman hypothesizes that if problem-solving skills are related to the development of competency in women, physical and psychological well-being improve as competency grows. According to Imes and Clance (1984), who have written about the latent imposter feelings in women, a major goal of therapy with women is empowerment—helping women develop a solid, realistic sense of their capabilities in reaction to earlier family dynamics and societal expectations. A group therapy milieu seems the ideal place for competency disorders to be treated.

The second personality variable the therapist can model is a capacity for intimacy. Hagen (1983) says that in general, all-women groups appear to begin working on intimacy and interpersonal issues earlier than groups that include men. At the same time, conflict issues may not surface until members get to know one another and feel a degree of trust and safety. Here again, issues of conflict, competition, and confrontation are avoided, because women consider these issues more characteristic of male-dominated hierarchies. A woman therapist modeling an egalitarian relationship in groups composed only of women helps the group participants to "create strategies of survival and liberation somewhere between subordination and rebellion" (Kahn, 1981). In fact, the egalitarian structure of these women's groups may allow more democratic models of leadership to emerge in the client members. An increase in member assertiveness and individuality may also encourage inclinations to deal wtih conflict issues. For women who have been socialized to suppress anger and rebelious feelings, the group is a place to try on new modalities of behavior. It has been stated elsewhere (Brody, 1984; Kaslow, Cooper, & Linsenberg, 1979) that a therapist who reveals herself authentically and who is willing to share her feelings and experiences can facilitate therapeutic progress. There is risk-taking implicit in this but also the much greater possibility that clients will take license to do the same. A traditional, neutral stance too often carries with it a distance-making threat that ultimately can be fatal to the therapeutic alliance.

WORKING WITH CULTURALLY HOMOGENEOUS GROUPS

The author meets with small groups of women clients once a week for one and a half hours. The goal is to provide an arena for clients to share conflicts and aspirations and to explore new levels of relationships. In this setting the leader-therapist often plays the role of peer model, i.e., an equal participant member of the group. As such, she discloses and shares her own values about work, marriage, and personal life when these are relevant to what is being shared by the other women and if the conflicts are ones with which she has struggled and been more successful. At these times it is made clear that her own goals may be very different from the clients'. The therapist states that *her* current attitudes and functioning capacity are the result of her own evolution as a woman, reflecting many shifts over the years. She models an openness to change, an acceptance of differences and defiances, and an expectation that each woman can achieve her own goals—economically, occupationally, interpersonally—and is *worthy of success*. She abhors sexist language and terminology (e.g., members of the group are enjoined to refer to each other as women—not girls), and the stereotyping implications of "analytic verbal shorthand" (e.g., "transference," "preoedipal") are discussed (see Brown, 1984a, p. 74).

The groups to be described in this section are all composed of white, middle class women and are small: between four and seven women. The age range within each group is often wide: from mid-20s to 50s. The group members are married or divorced (none are single), probably an artifact of the suburban population from which they are drawn. One or two women in each group have no children. Educational level ranges from high school completion to graduate degrees; most of the women have had some college or specialized vocational training beyond high school. Three different groups of women will be described briefly: the first, a group of agoraphobic women; the second, a group of women with physical problems; a third group has sexual abuse as a significant background variable in each member's life.

The three groups varied in cohesiveness and capacity to develop closeness with one another. The therapist questioned from time to time whether a particular group would have been more stable if it were more homogeneous for developmental life stage, as Daley and Koppenaal (1981) suggested. Perhaps when there is significant attrition it is related to Walker's theory (Chapter 1, *this volume*) that women in the middle phase of a group's development perceive the therapist as less omnipotent. Although they are more likely to confront their feelings of anger and rage, they may be unable to work through their ambivalence about dependence and independence. Divorced women seem to have a greater propensity for dropping out of each of these groups. Perhaps the instability in their earlier marital relationships is reflected in their erratic affiliation to the group. These are all questions that could be explored in greater depth, perhaps more empirically in future research. [Huston (1986) makes a plea for more controlled research studies about women's groups in a recent special volume of *Psychotherapy* on gender issues.]

Among six women in the first group there were three who suffered from the same kind of agoraphobic syndrome described so well by Brehony (1983) and Rothblum (1983). These women were passive, shy, dependent, fearful, and nonassertive, exhibiting characteristics of the feminine sex-role stereotype. In their married lives, they had suffered from intermittent "fear of fear," panic, dizziness, and a variety of similar stress-related complaints. Fodor (1974) has pointed out the relationship of phobias to dependency, and, for women, dependency is often culturally molded. Modelling assertiveness and power over their lives, the therapist *and* group members provide ongoing antidotes to this kind of fear and dependency.

In the second group of women, there was a focus on physical problems as these intruded on otherwise relatively competent lives. This group of five women included one who had developed diabetes in her late 20s and another who was infected by the acquired immune deficiency syndrome (AIDS) virus through sexual contact with a spouse who subsequently died of the disease. The issues of vulnerability, neediness, and dependence were thrown into stark relief. Women as a group can be more nurturing, can easily identify with fears of abandonment and helpless rage, and, because many have played this role from childhood, can be supportive without expectation of reward. However, being able to give *and* get from one another in the group can become a new component of their lives. As Walker mentions (Chapter 1, *this volume*), women's groups—as compared with mixed sex groups—allow women to become more dependent in the *group* but also allow them to develop an active support system inside and outside the group that is different from the quality of dependence that may have demeaned them in the past.

In the third small group of women three members discovered they had had some experience with sexual abuse and one had a child who was abused by a relative. To find that this closely guarded secret was matched so easily by others was in itself therapeutic. For each to then be able to search out the thread of connection to her own history by identifying with the woman's abused child in the context of a supportive peer group enhanced their insight. Here the female therapist modeled trust, acceptance of differences, and hope. The positive aspects of learning and sharing were also mirrored. The therapist helped them focus more clearly their vulnerability to society's definition of their worth and desirability. Further, in modeling competence, the therapist represented the opposite of the female child still present in the adult selves of many of these women with abuse histories.

Women who have learned (usually from mothers) to doubt their competency in adolescence often marry dominating husbands. They then feel dominated with no outlet for assertiveness, hence trapped. In the group, this can change: the therapist's model of strength, self-sufficiency, and competence appear to be as important as the new socialization process in the group. There is acceptance of the women's weaknesses at the same time that the therapist and group members model a more desirable and rewarding autonomous role. They are no longer singular anomalies in the eyes of either their peers or the therapist, and they can gradually relinquish the need for helplessness in their life arena. Brehony (1983) and Rothblum (1983) also suggested this.

SOCIOCULTURAL VARIABLES IN MIXED CULTURAL GROUPS

In addition to insights obtained from working with culturally homogeneous groups, this author has found in her work with culturally heterogeneous groups that a primary factor is the style and gender of the therapist; these are perhaps of even greater importance than race. The reader should keep in mind that these observations are offered by a white middle class therapist. It would be important to compare and evaluate the references and hypotheses provided by Trotman and Gallagher (Chapter 9, *this volume*). They stress the importance of race to the overt and covert goals of the group members and the way race acts to mediate the interactional process within groups.

It is this author's point of view that the white feminist therapist's stance as an understanding authority may contradict earlier experienced attitudes and ultimately become a model for self-esteem. The personality of the therapist and the *meaning* of race and ethnic origin to the particular therapist appear to be important variables for success with minority clients. Contrary to reports of previous researchers, e.g., Rosen and Frank (1962), this author has found that black women do not automatically bring to therapy predisposing attitudes of resentful anxiety and projected self-hate.

Hall and Maloney, (1983), summarizing studies of interracial therapy in the 1960s and 1970s, remind us that in many of these earlier studies, realities of treatment may not have been accurately depicted: therapists often were not professionals; clients were not always mental health clients (college students often were recruited as subjects); sometimes only initial interviews were examined; and therapists were usually male, with female clients. Findings in those studies must therefore be viewed as inconclusive, since race in psychotherapy can be assumed to interact with many other variables to affect treatment outcome. Hall and Maloney (1983) suggest that psychotherapy in its traditional sense is often a form of social control with a goal of perpetuating majority culture norms; if so, it could contribute to conflicts in minority persons rather than alleviate them. For this reason, they hypothesize that therapists who have dominant personalities may be more effective with culturally similar than with culturally different clients. It is the author's opinion that dominance as a personality trait is not necessarily a disservice in cross-cultural therapy, depending on the characterological needs of a particular minority woman, in a dyad or a group. Jackson (1983), for example, points to threats to repressed wishes, impulses and drives, and the need to protect these primitive impulses as inhibiting personality traits for change in clients. A therapist's knowledge of self and of the culture of the client would be positive balancing factors; dominance or lack of it could be another significant variable.

Fleming's (1983) recent research suggests that black *and* white women who work have similar positions in society in regard to sex-role pressures and motivational patterns. This is contrary to Horner's (1968) earlier findings that the motive to avoid success may be associated with the middle class status of *white* women; it was a lesser motive for comparable populations of black women, who were seen as more achievement-orientated than their white counterparts. Likewise, Malson's (1983) research confirms that sex-role ideology for black women may be different now than in past eras; an integration of nontraditional (employment) and traditional (homemaking and childrearing) components. Statements by women studied supported the idea that black women in this decade want to do both; when women express a desire to work, it implies that working is part of their roles as wives and mothers. One implication for future sex roles of black women is that these two roles do not necessarily interfere but in fact can support one another.

As a white feminist therapist working with minorities, personal attitudes and values are brought to bear and need to be acknowledged. However, there is little in recent literature to either verify or refute this author's experiences with female minority clients in groups. In one recent article Greene (1985) says "understanding and evaluating the meaning of certain practices or attitudes remains difficult even when the patient and therapist share many similar values.... It is more difficult ... when their cultural values and experiences cause them to view their world in very different ways" (p. 389). It should be noted that there are several other writers who also reflect Greene's skepticism about the ultimate efficacy of a white therapist working with mixed racial groups (Comas-Diaz & Minrath, 1985; Davis, 1979; Nayman, 1983).

Trotman (1984), in her earlier writing, explained that black women have stereotypically not been acknowledged for their academic achievement or intellectual contributions to our culture. She says this may ultimately affect a black woman's perception of herself and her capabilities and result in an entrenched experience of intellectual phoniness. Also, some successful black women point to self-esteem, a networking system, finding mentors, and *successful role models* as key factors in counteracting the tendency to identify with the downtrodden and to feel like imposters when they are, in fact, successful.

Evans (1985) is one writer who provides significant variation from stereotypical thinking about the treatment of black clients by white therapists. She emphasizes that too often false information about minorities may inadvertently be put forth as "new knowledge," as when Boyd-Franklin & Hines (1982) suggest that black families require a "more active therapist," implying that black families need an approach uniquely different from families of other races. Shapiro (1974) provides evidence that therapists working intensely with white families are also required to be very active and that their personal affective reaction to patients is a most important variable.

Smith and Stewart (1983) state, "Where we study black women and take account of the social context, we can begin to specify how racism and sexism provide contexts for each other" (p. 12). Even though some of the stereotypes about personal qualities and social stereotypes may be different, individual processess involved in stereotyping and prejudice are involved in comparable ways in the development and maintenance of sexism and racism. One of the stereotypes about black women that Reid (1984) highlights is the one that states that black women have not been supportive of women's liberation causes. Although studies as far back as 1972 indicated that black women were *twice as supportive* (emphasis added) as white women, Reid says massive participation in such groups was avoided for some very good reasons, e.g., mistrust of white women's motives and objectives. Black women were, in fact, reaching for espoused goals of feminism, as well as offering themselves as models to young women of both races.

The importance of the therapist's understanding of the culture and values of a population different from her own can be illustrated by reviewing current literature on Hispanic women. Delgado (1983), mentioning reports by Hynes and Werbin (1977) and Menikoff (1979), among others, says that female Hispanic therapy groups are more common than Hispanic male or mixed gender groups. In fact, females usually outnumber males in mixed groups. He points out a number of cultural and socioeconomic reasons for this. It is related first to female Hispanics having been acculturated to accede to male authority for direction and support; the therapist, especially if male, has this stereotype projected on him. If the leader is female, however, the perception of her role as expert/authority may come about more slowly, but as group leader she is expected to share a great deal of herself in the group process. If this does not happen, the group is seen as less effective. Delgado (1983) says, "The ability to shift in roles from authority to peer *places prodigious demands upon the group leader* (emphasis added)."

Tylim (1982) explains that Hispanics in groups unveil an "idealizing transference" toward their male or female leader that is related to the high respect and admiration they hold for parental or authoritarian objects. These clients, therefore, reproduce an earlier developmental state of object relations. He also explains, referring to Winnicott's (1953) and Kohut's (1971) theories, that the (group) therapist becomes the stand-in for the original parental (and sibling) idealized objects. It is important to note that groups Tylim studied were conducted in Spanish, were of mixed gender, had male and female co-therapists, and were short-term. Tylim also states that this idealization—a variation of *respeto*—is a combination of fear and esteem for the male parent, along with an idealization of the female parent that is culturally syntonic for the Hispanic client. However, this idealization of the therapist appears to be the opposite of what this author fosters in her feminist-oriented, all-women, cross-cultural groups; a more egalitarian relationship is the goal, even though it may be more difficult for the Hispanic woman to accept it.

Helping minority women work for change in their societal milieu is an important goal of individual or group treatment, but the therapist must also be aware of the clients' real life needs, including whether they want to be politically active or not and whether such political activity is the most relevant current barrier to changing their lives. In order to do this, the therapist must take into account not only the individual client's political perspective but also the multiple variables that are part of the minority person's history. Rawlings and Carter (1977) have also made this point.

Chesler (1973) has noted that a black or Puerto Rican working woman has experienced sexism in her life quite differently from a white woman. She may *not* have been dependent on a man or yearned for independence. She may have worked outside the home and had more psychological and economic mobility than her white female counterpart. In fact, Chesler states, the black or Puerto Rican woman may want nothing more than to be *able* to stay home with children and have a man care for her. This is not to say that some white women may not have had the same yearnings; it is only to stress that for a black woman, going to work can be tied more closely to the need for economic survival and the different early family experience she has had, with a female parent modeling the necessity of independence for survival.

Helms (1979) reports on black women who have traditionally served the mutual role of wife, mother, and worker. Many of these women have learned to acquire self-esteem by performing satisfactorily in the role of mother *and* provider. However, as Helms points out, black women now outnumber black men to such an extent that many may never have the opportunity to fulfill the wife role or will be mothers only if they are willing to be single heads of household. Many will live out their lives without either husband or children, so a significant number of black women will need self-definitions different from ones their mothers used. Helms, like Chesler, points to the need to differentiate between discrimination problems of white compared to black women. White women's problems are more often based on socioeconomic status and sex, whereas the black women's problems stem from these factors as well as the additional cultural and racial strictures. For a mixed racial group to be effective these sociocultural variables must be understood and confronted explicitly, by *both* therapist and group members.

Kupers (1981), in writing about therapy in the public sector, says, "Whenever a member of a dominant group treats a member of a dominated group the isolation of transference and countertransference distortions from all the other complications of relationships is a difficult task" (p. 135). While one could agree that most white people in this society have a distorted perspective on race whether this is a conscious feeling or not, it is only by being open to the possibility of subtle racial biases and distortions that there can be the possibility of constructive interracial therapy. Jones and Korchin (1982) say that a cross-cultural perspective fosters a greater sensitivity to the role that values play in the study of any ethnic group. Sue (1981) explains the much higher rate of attrition through early termination of non-white counseling clientele by pointing to the "inappropriateness of interpersonal interaction" between (some) clients and counselors in cross-cultural dyads.

There is no doubt that class-bound and culture-bound values still persist and can be transmitted and adversely affect treatment. In the group setting, variables that interfere with credibility and trustworthiness can be recognized, accepted, and changed. Sue points to racial and attitudinal similarity–dissimilarity as two most important factors, *along with* degree of racial/ethnic consciousness, counselor style, and counselor experience. Block (1981) also emphasizes that black clients tend to present their ego strengths and symptoms differently. Nevertheless, she acknowledges that disclosure in treatment is related to trust and the degree to which client and therapist—as well as group mates—perceive themselves as similar to and acceptable to each other. An extensive review of the literature on race effects in psychotherapy (Abramowitz & Murray, 1983) is inconclusive regarding the greater importance of racial similarity over attitudinal similarity. While Sue was referring to white therapist–black client dyads, these observations seem particularly relevant for mixed racial groups as well.

WORKING WITH MIXED RACIAL GROUPS

For the past 10 years, the author has been working with clients of diverse ethnic, racial, and socioeconomic backgrounds in a variety of settings, including university counseling centers and community clinics, as well as private practice. Clients are seen individually as well as mixed racial groups. Minority clients come to private practice from the same referral sources as white clients. It is mostly an upper lower and lower middle class clientele, and the minority women are usually single, often divorced, and may or may not have children. These groups, too, have a wide age range.

Just as in the homogeneous groups mentioned earlier, what the author models best is someone who can be assertive, accept competence, take risks, and be open to both stereotyped and nonstereotyped life styles and interests. She shares her own experiences of bias and discrimination on the basis of gender and religion, in schooling and work, while continuing to model optimism and a persistent drive for achievement. It is important that there be a clearly stated trust in the client's ability to get what *she* wants, even though her ultimate goals may be different from the therapist's.

In this therapy practice an eclectic, problem-oriented, and realistic approach has been effective with minority clients in mixed racial groups. To illustrate, one black woman client working in a women's group about a year felt trapped in a relationship with a verbally and physically abusive spouse. A traditional psychodynamic group approach might have allowed this client to stay in this risky situation while working through the transferential and parataxic implications of her relationship with the therapist. However, this author encouraged this client, in a fairly directive way, to leave her spouse and consider her options from a safer distance.

Mindful of the feminist stance that a woman is not responsible for being physically abused, it is especially important for a white woman therapist in a cross-cultural therapeutic setting to contradict the view that women are "naturally" masochistic (Caplan, 1984). It is not sufficient to say that the client's behavior—like the relationship to an abusive spouse—is inherently self-punishing, reflecting a low self-image. An alternative explanation is that it could be behavior based on guilt about prematurely independent or sexually defiant behavior and needs to be distinguished from behavior related to underdeveloped or distorted relationships with earlier parenting people.

The author tries to be authentic with all clients. Authentic, as used in this context implies the therapist's selective sharing of her personality, lifestyle, and experiences with the client; using herself as a model when this is relevant and can be helpful (see Brody, 1984). Trained in a psychoanalytic frame, she has evolved an eclectic style, more active than passive, more direct than indirect. With minority women, in particular, the goal is to bypass defensive posturing and to reach for trust as early in the first few encounters as possible. One way this is done is to discuss the issue of racial or ethnic differences between therapist and group members. It is sometimes suggested by the therapist as a theme for the first one or two sessions of a new group; this encourages early confrontation with an issue that carries the potential for inhibiting communication and closeness. The possibility is left open for any group member to shift to a culturally homogeneous group or therapist if she covertly or overtly expresses discomfort with the group's cultural heterogeneity. The option is rarely taken.

The therapist, in implicit and explicit sharing of her own educational and family experiences where this is relevant, models a woman who has both the earmarks of success and a respect for the possibility that the clients can achieve it too. The therapist dissociates herself from a variety of negative or ambivalent forces that may have operated before, especially for the minority clients. For example, she might say to one client in the group, "I don't agree with your mother that you were not smart enough to go to college; or that it is more important to find a job and be able to support yourself and a family right after high school." Similar to Evans (1985) who was cited earlier, it has been this author's conviction that a therapist who lacks optimism and hope about black clients' growth potential can greatly impede treatment success. Chessick (1971) said this too, noting that psychotherapists, whatever their color, who do not succeed in helping minorities, essentially lack "the stuff" out of which conviction and hope are born: broad knowledge and appreciation of different cultures and the histories of the people being helped. All of this is especially relevant to working with minority women in groups.

In mixed racial groups, minority women tend to protect themselves carefully from criticism, even though they may hear comparable life events described by non-minority members. However, minority women can perceive the female therapist transferentially as an idealized parent who protects them from competitive and overbearing siblings. Although the therapist is seen initially as the mother who was revered but to whom they could not talk, ultimately she becomes the dominant adult whom they can turn to with trust and aspire to be like.

As the therapist accepts criticism, anger, and contradiction from the group members, the minority client begins to feel license to do the same; the group becomes the second chance family for learning new ways to cope with competition or defiance. A black woman in one group projected an image of her office colleagues who rejected and demeaned her onto her group co-members. She could then turn to the therapist for help in more accurately defining her self-worth, as she was not able to do with her office boss and as she could not do before that with a parent.

Since there is less game-playing and more possibility for minority women to develop closeness and trust in the all-women groups, the empathy of the other women about a variety of issues related to role conflicts can mobilize frustration and rage into structured action for change. The white women group members most often support the positive life drives of the minority women. They identify easily with the oppressed status. They also take a cue from the therapist's response that models equality and peerlike respect for all group members. In a mixed racial group, black women are forced to deal with their fears and distortions about acceptance; in the group, there is less possibility of escaping or denying their own responsibility for negative responses. Multiple mirrors are a good antidote for distorted perceptions (Brody, 1984). To date, there is a paucity of literature on mixed cultural groups and their effects on minority and black women when the therapist is a white woman. There also needs to be further discussion of the effects on *white* women of being in a mixed cultural group. It would be important for other therapists to confirm or refute this author's experience, as well as the different theories presented by Nayman (1983), Comas-Diaz and Minrath (1985), and Trotman and Gallagher (Chapter 9, *this volume*).

THERAPIST AS GROUP PARTICIPANT IN A THERAPISTS' GROUP

In addition to working with women as a group therapist, about eight years ago the author helped organize a group of women therapists in the county where she practices. She was motivated by Clance and Imes' (1978) paper on the imposter phenomenon. At last someone put a label on and confirmed what she personally had experienced at various crossroads in her life and what still plagued her periodically in her work as a teacher and therapist. What she wanted from this group was validation of experiences she had thought were unique; to confirm that her work was competent, helpful, and worthy of respect. In this peer group setting, the author could also explore and find acceptance for nontraditional approaches.

The group consists of 10 to 14 women therapists, ranging in age from their 30s to 60s and has met at least once a month. The members' backgrounds are in psychology, social work, psychiatry, and education. All have postdegree therapy training. The group is less concerned about issues and definitions of feminist therapy training, than about defining themselves individually, as therapists who happen to be women.

There are few references in the literature to similar groups of women therapists, to date. In one, Radoc, Masnick, and Hauser (1977) reported a study on a group of women mental health professionals who met as equals to focus on an intellectual task in a sharing way. They stated that the therapist group members developed a sense of the import of their work on their self-images.

In a more recent citation referring to a therapists' support group, Friedman (1984) described a study group of three therapists who met regularly to talk of their own personality conflicts and lives in relation to understanding the dynamics of cases with which they were involved. This group's democratic leadership model appeared to be structured similarly to the therapists' group to be discussed here. In another peer group consultation team described by Rabi, Lehr, and Hayner (1984), it is suggested that group members should have an equal level of competence, although anxiety and competitive strivings will need to be confronted. Lerman (1984) implies that women therapists have a special need for emotionally supportive professional networks because of the emotional demands made by clients. The single, female, feminist, and heterosexual therapist practicing alone in her home appears to be the most vulnerable, according to Lerman.

The lesbian feminist therapist copes with a different set of variables (Brown, 1984b).

As is suggested in these papers, in the therapists' group, we share and explore the pieces of our lives that have shaped us as women. As a group we have come to question traditional theories about women and how best to treat women's disorders. For example, in this group this author has refined a treatment methodology (Brody, 1984) that includes making values known within a psychoanalytic/humanistic frame. With this group of peers, as in client groups, the benefits of autonomy over the kind of dependency that perpetuates women's stereotype are modeled by the women therapists with each other. One of us is an expert sex therapist; another developed a modality for working with dreams in group therapy. In each case, we respect each other's competence and creativity. We do this by demonstrating, explicating, and refining the wide variety of treatment styles we use in our work with women. We read, discuss, and find relevance in the current literature of psychotherapy with women.

In the women therapists' group, just as in the client groups, we would like to know what variables of member selection might account for the attrition of certain members and not others. Was the disaffection of one member related to her difficulty in expressing anger or competitive strivings with peers? A feeling of inadequacy because of few earmarks of achievement (academic degrees)? Here, too, modeling is in operation. Although the group is essentially leaderless, at each monthly meeting a hierarchy of skills in certain specialties of therapy emerges. Women professionals, like their clients, need to feel closeness, trust, and acceptance within the group, and some peers provide it better than others; none of us has fully worked through all the nuances of parataxic distortions from our past.

Rothblum, Green, and Collins (1983) point out that professional women are significantly more at risk for depression and suicide than their non-professional female counterparts. They have more often encountered prejudice and sexism in training for their work. In addition, they have had the stress of simultaneously pursuing nontraditional sex roles regarding work, marital relationships, and motherhood. Davis (1984) also emphasized the constant tradeoffs between the roles of mother, wife, and therapist that occur for women at different stages of their professional and family life. While these issues form significant recurring themes in the women therapists' group, there is now an ongoing opportunity for support, feedback, and coping with these problems. The group acts as an antidote for the kind of depression that all therapists experience who work in relative isolation from peer interaction, and an additional advantage is the sharing of professional conflicts unique to women therapists, such as their recurring, irrational feelings of incompetence—the "imposter phenomenon."

CONCLUSIONS

Whether it is within the framework of a group of white middle class women, mixed racial groups, or a group of women therapists, groups offer support for women who want to help others while advancing their understanding of themselves. When the woman therapist knows herself better, her motivations, her left-over insecurities, and her parataxic distortions, she can be a more effective professional for her women clients.

The therapist who aims to be an authentic model needs to create an environment in which women clients can learn to come to terms with their competencies and independence in the matrix of a variety of new role options open to them. A feminist therapist is interested in social networks, as these reinforce or counteract pathology, with emphasis on personal and social responsibility for change. A feminist therapist believes in an egalitarian relationship between therapist and clients, and expects to be viewed as a role model for women in a group. A feminist therapist may make her values explicit; she may consider disclosure important for clients validating their own, often accurate perceptions.

In a women's group, validation of competency is, overall, a slow process spread over countless separate interactions between women in many different phases of acquiring it. The myriad reflecting mirrors are part of the facilitating process, as is also the input of nurturing peers and nurturing authority. But these carers are different from developmentally earlier ones, in that their opinions are viewed as more honest, trustworthy, and consistent. There are fewer double messages.

An eclectic, problem-orientated approach and an active, rather than passive, style has been found to be effective with minority clients. The therapist models assertion, competence, risk-taking, and an optimistic and persistent drive for achievement; she conveys trust that the minority clients can get what *they* want even though their ultimate goals may be different from the therapist's.

The therapist is, at the same time, both peer and model in the group. She may tell of her own recurring imposter feelings, but she also models competencies, self-respect, and achievement, while remaining caring and accepting of clients' slips on the upward climb. If she is to affect the women's acceptance of their real, not imposed, selves then the therapist must be able to come to terms with her own entitlements to power and achievement, with *her own* competencies.

An interesting question that needs to be explored further is the possible relationship between the personality of the therapist working with a group of women and the degree of stereotyping to which a particular therapist is prone, which in turn affects her interrelationships in the group. It could be said that the ability of the therapist to help women become self-actualized may be more related to personality variables and the matching of these between therapist and clients, than just to the gender or cultural likeness of the therapist and clients. Personality characteristics that appear to carry the most weight are functions of whether or not the therapist feels bound by cultural traditions and values, and the degree of structure—referred to as instrumentality—the therapist requires. That is, of course, in addition to variables associated with the quality of the clients' early relationships with parents, the clients' current developmental level, and, most important, the therapist's sensitivity to value systems regarding gender and culture issues.

REFERENCES

Ables, B. S., & Brandesma, J. M. (1977). *Therapy for couples.* San Francisco: Jossey-Bass.

Abramowitz, S. I., & Murray, J. (1983). Race effects in psychotherapy. In J. Murray & P. R. Abramson, *Bias in psychotherapy* (pp. 215–255). New York: Praeger.

Bernardez, T. (1983). Women in authority: Psychodynamics and interactional aspects. *Social Work with Groups, 6*(3–4), 43–49.

Blechman, E. (Ed.), (1984). *Behavior modification with women.* New York: The Guilford Press.

Block, C. B. (1981). Black Americans and the cross-cultural counseling and psychotherapy experience. In A. J. Marsella & P. Pederson (Eds.), *Cross-cultural counseling and psychotherapy.* New York: Pergamon Press.

Boyd-Franklin, N., & Hines, P. M. (1982). Black families. In M. McGoldrick, J. Pearce, & J. Giordano (Eds.), *Ethnicity and family therapy.* New York: Guilford Press.

Brehony, K. A. (1983). Women and agoraphobia. In V. Franks & E. D. Rothblum, *The feminine sex-role stereotype: Effects on mental health.* New York: Springer.

Brodsky, A. (1977). Therapeutic aspects of consciousness-raising groups. In E. L. Rawlings & D. K. Carter (Eds.), *Psychotherapy for women: Treatment towards equality.* Springfield, IL: Charles C Thomas.

Brody, C. M. (1984). Authenticity in feminist therapy. In C. M. Brody (Ed.), *Women therapists working with women: New theory and process of feminist therapy.* New York: Springer.

Brown, L. S. (1984a). Finding new language: Getting beyond analytic verbal shorthand in feminist therapy. *Women and Therapy, 3*(1), 73–80.

Brown, L. S. (1984b). The lesbian feminist therapist in private practice and her community. *Psychotherapy in Private Practice, 2*(4), 9–16.

Caplan, P. J. (1984). The myth of women's masochism. *American Psychologist, 39*(2), 130–139.

Chesler, P. (1973). *Women and Madness.* New York: Avon Books.

Chessick, R. (1971). *Why psychotherapists fail.* New York: Science House.

Clance, P., & Imes, S. (1978). The imposter phenomenon in high-achieving women: Dynamics and therapeutic interventions. *Psychotherapy: Theory, Research and Practice, 15*(3), 241–247.

Comas-Diaz, L., & Minrath, M. (1985). Psychotherapy with ethnic minority borderline clients. *Psychotherapy, 22*(2), 418–426.

Daley, B. S., & Koppenaal, G. S. (1981). The treatment of women in short-term women's groups. In S. H. Budman (Ed.), *Forms of brief therapy.* New York: The Guilford Press.

Davis, L. (1979). Racial composition of groups. *Social Work, 24*(3), 208–213.

Davis, B. (1984). Wife, mother, therapist . . . Which comes first? *Psychotherapy in Private Practice, 2*(4), 17–24.

Delgado, M. (1983). Hispanics and psychotherapeutic groups. *International Journal of Group Psychotherapy, 33*(4), 507–520.

Dickstein, L. (1982). Women university students and inequality. *Women and Therapy, 1*(1), 83–88.

Dimidjian, V. J. (1983). Seeing me, being me, becoming the me I want to be: The import of the dream in identity formation during women's early years. *Women and Therapy, 2*(4), 33–48.

Evans, D. A. (1985). Psychotherapy and black patients: Problems of training, trainees and trainers. *Psychotherapy, 22*(2), 457–460

Fleming, J. (1983). Sex differences in the educational and occupational goals of black students: Continued inquiry into the black matriarchy theory. In M. Horner, C. C. Nadelson, & M. T. Notman, *The challenge of change.* New York: Plenum Press.

Fodor, I. G. (1974). The phobic syndrome in women: Implications for treatment. In V. Franks & V. Burtle (Eds.), *Women in Therapy: New psychotherapies for changing society.* New York: Brunner/Mazel.

Friedman, C. (1984). Study group 1: A tale of three therapists. *Journal of Strategic and Systemic Therapies, 3*(2), 63–65.

Greene, B. A. (1985). Considerations in the treatment of black patients by white therapists. *Psychotherapy, 22*(2), 389–393.

Hagen, B. H. (1983). Managing conflicts in all-women groups. *Social Work with Groups, 6,* 95–104.

Halas, C. (1973). All women's groups: A view from inside. *Personnel and Guidance Journal, 52*(1), 91–95.

Hall, G. C. N., & Maloney, H. N. (1983). Cultural control in psychotherapy with minority clients. *Psychotherapy: Theory, Research and Practice, 20*(2), 131–142.

Hare-Mustin, R. T., Marecek, J., Kaplan, A. G., & Liss-Levenson, N. (1979). Rights of clients, responsibilities of therapists. *American Psychologist, 34*(1), 3–16.

Helms, J. (1979). Black women. *Counseling Psychologist, 8*(1), 40–41.

Horner, M. S. (1968). Sex differences in achievement motivation and performance in competitive and noncompetitive situations. (Doctoral dissertation, University of Michigan, 1968). *Dissertation Abstracts International, 30,* 407B. (University Microfilm No. 6912135).

Huston, K. (1986). A critical assessment of the efficacy of women's groups. *Psychotherapy, 23*(2), 283–290.

Hynes, K., & Werbin, J. (1977). Group psychotherapy for Spanish-speaking women. *Psychiatric Annals, 7*(12), 52–63.

Imes, S., & Clance, P. R. (1984). Treatment of the imposter phenomenon in high-achieving women. In C. M. Brody (Ed.), *Women therapists working with women: New theory and process of feminist therapy.* New York: Springer.

Jackson, A. (1983). Treatment issues for black patients. *Psychotherapy: Theory, Research and Practice, 20*(2), 143–151.

Jones, E. E., & Korchin, S. T. (1982). *Minority mental health.* New York: Praeger.

Kahn, D. G. (1981, June 19). Paper presented at Fifth Bershire Conference on the History of Women, Bunting Institute of Radcliffe College. *The New York Times,* p. B4.

Kaslow, F., Cooper, B., & Linsenberg, M. (1979). Family therapist authenticity as a key factor in outcome. *International Journal of Family Therapy, 1*(2), 184–199.

Kazdin, A. E. (1976). Effects of covert modelling: Multiple model reinforcement on assertive behavior. *Behavior Therapy, 7*(2), 211–222.

Kohut, H. (1971). *The analysis of the self.* New York: International Universities Press.

Kravetz, D. F. (1976). Consciousness-raising groups and group psychotherapy: Alternative mental health resources for women. *Psychotherapy: Theory, Research and Practice, 13*(1), 66–71.

Kupers, T. (1981). *Public therapy: The practice of psychotherapy in the mental health clinic.* New York: Macmillan.

Lerman, H. (1984). The solo heterosexual woman in practice. *Psychotherapy in Private Practice, 2*(4), 3–8.

Lewis, K. N., Davis, C. S., & Lesmeister, R. (1983). Pretherapy information: An investigation of client responses. *Journal of Counseling Psychology, 30*(1), 108–112.

Lieberman, M. L., Yalom, I. D., & Miles, M. B. (1973). *Encounter groups: First facts.* New York: Basic Books.

Linehan, M. M. (1984). Interpersonal effectiveness in assertive situations. In E. A. Blechman (Ed.), *Behavior modification with women.* New York: Guilford Press.

Lynch, C. (1974). Women's groups. *Family Therapy, 1*,(3) 223–228.

Malson, M. R. (1983). Black women and sex roles: Social context for a new ideology. *Journal of Social Issues, 39*(3), 101–113.

Menikoff, A. (1979). Long term group psychotherapy of Puerto Rican women: Ethnicity as a clinical support. *Group, 3*(3), 172–180.

Mundy, J. (1975). Women in rage. In R. K. Unger & E. L. Denmark, *Women: Dependent or independent variable?*. New York: Psychological Dimensions, Inc.

Nayman, R. L. (1983). Group work with black women: Some issues and guidelines. *Journal for Specialists in Group Work, 8*(1), 31–38.

Rabi, J. S., Lehr, M. L., & Hayner, M. L. (1984). Study group II. The peer consultation team: An alternative. *Journal of Strategic and Systemic Therapies, 3*(2), 61–71.

Radoc, C. G., Masnick, B. R., & Hauser, B. B. (1977). Issues in feminist therapy: The work of a woman's study group. *Social Work, 22*(6), 507–509.

Rawlings, E. I., & Carter, D. K. (1977). *Psychotherapy for women: Treatment toward equality.* Springfield, IL: Charles C Thomas.

Reid, P. (1984). Feminism vesus minority group identity: Not for black women only. *Sex Roles, 10,* 247–255.

Rohrbaugh, J. B. (1979). *Women: Psychology's puzzle.* New York: Basic Books.

Rosen, H., & Frank, J. D. (1962). Negroes in psychotherapy: *American Journal of Psychiatry, 119,* 456–460.

Rothblum, E. D. (1983). Sex role steretypes and depression in women. In V. Franks & E. D. Rothblum (Eds.), *The stereotyping of women: Its effects on mental health.* New York: Springer.

Rothblum, E. D. Green, L., & Collins, R. L. (1983). A therapy group for depressed women. In R. A. Rosenbaum (Ed.), *Varieties of short-term therapy groups.* New York: McGraw-Hill.

Schur, E. M. (1983). *Labeling women deviant.* Philadelphia: Temple University Press.

Shapiro, R. (1974). Therapist attitudes and premature termination in family and individual therapy. *Journal of Nervous and Mental Diseases, 159*(2), 101–107.

Smith, A., & Stewart, A. J. (1983). Approaches to studying racism and sexism in black women's lives. *Journal of Social Issues, 39*(3), 1–15.

Sue, D. (1981). *Counseling the culturally different: Theory and practice.* New York: John Wiley.

Trotman, F. K. (1984). Psychotherapy with black women and the dual effects of racism and sexism. In C. M. Brody (Ed.), *Women therapists working with women: New theory and process of feminist therapy.* New York: Springer.

Tylim, I. (1982). Group psychotherapy with Hispanic patients: The psychodynamics of idealization. *International Journal of Group Psychotherapy, 32*(3), 339–350.

Winnicott, D. W. (1953). Transitional objects and transitional phenomena. *International Journal of Psycho-Analysis, 34,* 89–97.

■ 9
Group Therapy with Black Women

FRANCES K. TROTMAN and ABISOLA H. GALLAGHER

So much is said and written about the negative side of black life in general and black women in particular that we hope to share with the reader (as black women often do in black women's groups) some of the positive aspects of black womanhood. In this chapter, we will discuss differences between black and white women and the different therapeutic milieu provided black women as they relate in (1) an integrated male/female group, (2) an integrated women's group, (3) an all black, mixed sex group, and (4) a black women's group. We will point out the uniquely therapeutic effects of a black women's group, and we will add to previously presented insights (Trotman, 1984) concerning effective selection and preparation of therapists to treat the special needs of black women.

DIFFERENCES BETWEEN BLACK AND WHITE WOMEN

Do black women have special needs? There is often the well-meaning assumption, sometimes explicit and often implicit, that black women are like all other women and can therefore be treated as such. There are, however, areas contributing uniquely to the development of the black woman that have implications for therapy in general and group therapy in particular that must be considered. Staples (1981) believes that it is impossible to state that the black woman is just like the women of other races. Her history is different from that of the prototypical white woman, and her present-day behavioral patterns have evolved out of her historical experiences. Mays (1985) agrees that "the process of slavery and its debilitating effects on the development of self-identity imposed on the Black American present a unique psychological development which is not comparable with any other group lacking such an experience" (p. 385).

To begin to look at differences between black and white women of the United States, Williams and Trotman (1984) examined four areas that contribute to the uniqueness of the black female experience: (1) physical characteristics; (2) historical/social/cultural dynamics; (3) emotional/intellectual characteristics; and (4) sex roles and male/female relationships. Gunnar Myrdal in *An American Dilemma* (1944) over 40 years ago attributed skin color and identifiability as the basis of racism and discrimination against blacks in the United States. In addition to skin color, there are characteristic features (nose, lips, hair texture, etc.) that distinguish the black person. Physical differences are the basis of initial and ongoing differences in the treatment of all blacks by both white men and white women as well as other blacks (male and female). The general perception of blackness based on physical characteristics is a basis of treatment by whites, resulting in discrimination in all institutions (education, social interaction, legal treatment, politics, employment, religion, marriage, etc.). The physical characteristics that distinguish the black woman are also often the basis of adverse treatment by other blacks in the family and in the black community. Intragroup verbal, social, and physical rejection is often based on such factors as skin color, facial features, and hair texture. The fact that there are distinguishing physical characteristics of the black woman that result in such psychologically destructive behavior by others is an aspect of her psychological life that must be considered in the organization, composition, and direction of groups that address black women.

The black woman's African origins contribute cultural as well as physical characteristics to her experience. An oral rather than a literary tradition, polyrhythmic musical influences, Black English, an extended family, the central role of religion, as well as different values, priorities, and attitudes are all African and slavery influences that have been perpetuated across centuries in the United States by racism and isolation. Because the major impact of culture on personality has to do with the behaviors of others towards an individual and the individual's observations and resulting patterns of behavior and responses towards people and objects (Linton, 1945; Nigel, 1976), the black female's perception of self may depend on the degree to which she has experienced segregated schools, colleges, and neighborhoods or whether she has had the opportunity to experience acceptance and rejection by *both* blacks and whites. All of the cultural influences on the black woman—rural versus urban, northern versus southern, West Indian versus Carribean versus African versus American, etc.—cannot begin to be addressed in this chapter. A knowledge of these differences and that these differences profoundly affect and distinguish the psychological life of the black woman is, however, crucial to the successful psychotherapeutic conduct of a group for black women. Bulhan (1985) examines the ethnocentric basis of the history of psychological assessment, theories, and research findings central to the teachings of psychotherapy, and concurs that "mental health professionals who seek to work with blacks must learn their history, culture, communication patterns, hurts, strengths and aspirations as they experience and define them not as professionals assume them to be" (p. 176).

The distinguishing emotional and intellectual characteristics of the black woman must also be considered by the professional who is to work with her in a group. Differences in the incidence of broken homes, female-headed households, poverty, extended family traditions, and the experience of strong female role models (who from the very beginning were viewed as sources of labor valued for the amount of work they could perform) have helped to lead to the "black superwoman" image with its concomitant expectation that the black woman must "do all" and "be all," often ignoring her individual needs. Alice Walker, reporting to Bradley (1984), underscores this subtle difference in emotional and intellectual outlook by pointing out that "white feminism teaches white women that they are capable, whereas my [Black] tradition assumes I'm capable" (p. 36). Staples (1981) goes on to say that because of their history, black women are "more aggressive and independent than white women" (p. 31), and Ladner (1971) posits that black female strength has been confused with dominance, whereas Staples (1981) asserts that any inordinate powers that black women possess are owed to white United States' racist employment barriers. The net effect of this phenomenon, he believes, is not black female dominance but greater economic deprivation for families deprived of the father's income. Smith (1982) found that "whereas black young women formulated their work commitments on a socialized sense of family economic responsibility, white women more often indicated that they desired to work for self-fullfillment" (p. 282). All of these views point out the often subtle but important differences that distinguish the black woman's intellectual or emotional point of view. The group leader's awareness of these differences facilitates the optimum growth experience for the black women in group therapy.

The final difference between black and white women that we consider relevant to the optimum conduct of black women's group psychotherapy is that of black male/female relationships and roles. Thomas and Dansby

(1985) believe that "black professional women with advanced degrees have competently balanced the work role (with its racial and sexual discrimination) and the home role" (p. 405). The authors go on to state that "with the increased participation of white married women in the labor force, there is much they can learn from the experience of well-educated black women" (p. 405). According to Thomas and Neal (1978), black male-female interaction is much more egalitarian than that of white couples. Proportionately more black women have always worked outside the home than white women. Historically, the slave woman was first a full-time worker for her owner and only incidentally a wife, mother, and homemaker. The slave woman learned that her potential as a woman was the same as her man's. She developed the qualities of hard work, perseverance, self-reliance, tenacity, resistance, and sexual equality (Hooks, 1982).

The black woman has never expected a man to take care of her. Yet "black women view their familial responsibilities in a very stereotypically female manner" (Helms, 1979, p. 40). At the same time, black women outnumber black men to such an extent that many may never have the opportunity to fulfill the wife role. Many will accomplish the mother role only if they are willing to be single heads of household, and many will live out their lives with neither husband nor children (Jackson, 1976).

The white feminist is often puzzled by the black woman's apparent lack of commitment to "the cause" and may not realize that the black American woman's experience of racism may result in a black woman's perception of whiteness, not sex, as the major factor preventing equity.

Indeed, Hooks (1982) reports that "in the 19th and early 20th century America few if any similiarities could be found between the life experiences" (p. 122) of black and white women. "Although they were both subjected to sexist victimization, as victims of racism, black women were subjected to oppression no white woman was forced to endure" (p. 122). In fact, "white racial imperialism granted all white women, however victimized by sexist oppression they might be, the right to assume the role of oppressor in relationship to black women and black men" (p. 123).

The group therapist must closely consider the physical, historical, and emotional context in which group therapy takes place for the black female group member. As the examples above suggest, there are often subtle but significant differences between the black and white female that could affect the therapeutic experience. The therapist must also be "aware that all Black women are not alike and that the nature of the problems that they bring to counseling may differ depending upon such factors as socioeconomic status, family size, age, and marital or relationship status" (Helms, 1979, p. 41).

BLACK WOMEN AND THE GROUP EXPERIENCE

In addition to the differences that distinguish black women from other women and each other, another aspect of the therapeutic experience to be considered for the potential black female group member is the sexual and racial composition of the group. Whether she is a black woman in an integrated male/female group, in an integrated women's group, in a black male/female group, or in a black women's group can present very different types of experiences for the black woman. However, despite the information available to guide practitioners in composing treatment groups (Yalom, 1975), very little exists that addresses the issue of race in composing groups.

The race of the group members and leaders is always important even when race per se is unrelated to the goal of the members. Despite the best of intentions, race, covertly, if not overtly, acts to mediate the interactional processes within groups. Social, psychological, and therapeutic evidence indicates that the racial composition of the group influences the communication and interactions that take place in the group. (Katz & Benjamin, 1960; Shaw, 1976). Race consistently influences the interactional process. Race is notably more important in some groups than others. As a general rule, it appears that race becomes more important as an issue as the intimacy of the group increases (Davis, 1979).

RACIALLY MIXED GENDER GROUP

For a heterogeneous male/female group, blacks have been found to prefer racial compositions in which they are approximately one-half of the population. In contrast, whites in the same situation appear to prefer compositions in which blacks are approximately 20% or less of the total population (Davis & Burnstein, 1981). Davis (1980) believes that whites, because of their customary numerical racial dominance, may feel themselves to be psychologically outnumbered in groups where blacks are present in numbers greater than 20%.

As far as the black woman is concerned, there may be some disadvantages to her membership in an integrated rather that an all-black group, which must be overcome if she is to have a successful group experience. The possibility, for example, that the black female group participant might become a peripheral member of the group and less engaged in its communication network poses a group management issue for the leader (Nayman, 1983, p. 34).

The black woman may be very reluctant to address the very issues that cause her the most psychic pain, e.g., intrafamilial and intragroup issues concerning skin color or black male/female relationships, in front of white group members or leaders. She may well believe that these are intragroup issues that one does not discuss in "mixed company." We have found in our work with the black woman in all kinds of groups that she is more likely to take responsibility for, support, and protect the black man in a mixed race group than she would be in an all-black group, where she could feel free to confront problems with him. The black woman will also not bring up issues of skin color, facial features, or hair texture in a mixed group, whereas in an all-black group, these issues are of paramount concern and importance. The role of the black woman and the issue of the black matriarchy is another issue of vital importance to the black woman that is less likely to be addressed in a heterogeneous group.

In a mixed race group, the black woman is more likely to address the issue of American racism, and a large percentage of her "floor time" is spent "educating" white members about racism and discrimination. In an all-black group, there appears to be no need to mention racism, and more time can be spent by each person in taking responsibility for coping with her situation rather than assessing blame for it.

The behavior of the black female participant in a heterogeneous group is likely to also be influenced by one or more of the following characteristics, which Cheek (1977) states distinguish the black client from the white client:

1. Bi-dialectical, which means having a knowledge of standard English as well as a familiarity with or emphasis upon Black language or non-standard English
2. Cultural paranoia, a general distrust of Whites until proven otherwise
3. Preoccupation with race and its importance
4. Seething aggression and pent up anger and rage
5. Lack of loyalty to white institutions or organizations
6. Conflict in whether to talk "white" or "black"
7. Alertness to preferential treatment given to whites
8. Ability to fake it with white people and not reveal self
9. Sensitivity to nonverbal cues such as body posturing, manner of walk, use of eyes, sucking of teeth, and facial expressions
10. Suspiciousness and unconvinced attitude concerning patriotism, authority, the value of law and hard work

INTEGRATED WOMEN'S GROUP

The black woman in an integrated women's group may be in a somewhat better position than in a group in which men are also present. In the all-women group, the black woman at least shares with her white sisters the bonds of oppression by white males, but the black female is still unlikely to attack the black male or bring up negative issues concerning him, and the above mentioned problems hindering her full participation in the heterogeneous group still hold for the mixed race women's group. Hooks (1982) believes that "racism is the barrier that prevents positive communication" (p. 152), and Jones (1980) has stated that "it is to the average white person's most basic, intimately personal advantage not to truly understand the black person's condition" (p. 420). "Ethnocentrism—feelings of racial superiority—is a formidable obstacle in helping process with minorities" (Nayman, 1983, p. 33), and much work is needed to overcome it in order to optimize the healing process of group therapy.

Buber (1958) has described the healing process as one in which one person aids another to establish a better identity. If one allows the other person to be different and still accepts and confirms her, then the first person will have helped her to realize herself as she could not have done alone. This is the core goal to be achieved in each interracial group. When this goal is achieved, when blacks and whites are able to accept and confirm one another in their differentness, each feels stronger, more individual, yet closer to the other because of their differences. Comas-Diaz and Minrath (1985) suggest that "introducing the topic of ethnicity and race (color) as themes related to trust is of the utmost importance in the solidification of a working alliance" (p. 426). "Being black holds such a central place to the identity of blacks that to not discuss it is to deny a significant part of the client's self-image" (Thomas & Dansby, 1985, p. 401). Ibrahim (1985) adds that effectiveness in cross-cultural counseling is determined by how well the helper understands and accepts the world view of the client" (p. 322).

Because black men and women of the United States share much of the same world view through their shared history of slavery, discrimination, and oppression, an all-black male/female group can provide a valuable experience for the black woman, a place where she can deal with fundamental issues below the symptomatic surface. We have observed a tendency, however, for black women to defer to black men in such groups and to not show the full force and splendor of the qualities that are so evident in the black woman's group—her assertiveness, independence, power, and sense of responsibility. This deferential behavior is often an attempt on the part of the black woman to either bolster and support her black man against the burden of discrimination and oppression that she perceives as weighing heavily on him, or it is sometimes an effort to not contribute further to the myth of the black matriarchy (see Staples, 1981). One disadvantage, therefore, for the black woman in a mixed sex black group is that she is often not fully participating in or acknowledged for her powerful personhood.

BLACK WOMEN'S GROUP

As the reader may have inferred, it is in the black women's group that we believe the black woman can experience a safe environment in which she can speak expressively and directly about issues of vital importance to her mental health, while developing and modeling her unique style in the intimacy and love of her black sisters.

Much has been said and written about black rhythm and expressiveness (see Pasteur & Toldsen, 1982). In a black woman's group, the black women can free the reins of their natural expressiveness.

> Black language is direct, creative, intelligent communication between black people based on a shared reality, awareness, understanding which generates interaction; it ... places a premium on imagistic renderings and concretizations of abstractions, poetic usages ... idiosyncrasies—those individualized stylistic nuances (such as violation of structured syntax)—which nevertheless hit "home" and evoke truth; it is an idiom of integrated insight, a knowledge emanating from a juxtaposition of feeling and fact (Fabio, 1972, pp. 182–211).

It is through the full expression of her depth of feelings, naturalistic attitudes, distinctive stylistic renderings, poetic and prosaic vernacular, and expressive movements that the black woman experiences her self-fulfillment. "Being natural ... is fundamental to optimal mental health and is the mark of the Black/African heritage." (Pasteur & Toldsen, 1982, p. 265). The black woman's group provides an environment in which even upper middle-class professional black women can "let down dey hair" and "get down" to the curative feelings, attitudes, style, prose, and movements of the "Black Experience," often at a noise and activity level that is rare for white or integrated groups.

Many of the issues addressed in black women's groups are also rare topics for white or integrated groups. The "hurtful" issues such as the effects of skin color, hair texture, etc. or interactions among blacks, the relationship of black men and women, bourgeois blacks, house niggers, welfare, or the role of the black church are issues of great importance to black women and are explored most readily in black women's groups. The black woman seems to be best able to express some of the truest sources of her pain only in the safety and intimacy of her black sisters. The black women's group can provide a safe setting in which the black woman can begin to reexperience some of the painful and damaging incidents of childhood that are indirect results of racism but involve only other black people and are therefore inappropriate for discussion outside "the family" of blacks.

Racism as a shared experience of black women can be assumed, and there appears to be little need to discuss it in a black women's group. This frees the black woman to go on to the task of taking responsibility for her own life and developing coping strategies to deal with the effects of discrimination and oppression (Comer, 1980). The black woman can explore her options e.g., "Uncle Tomming" versus assertiveness as a reaction to racial oppression. She can make clear and conscious choices about her participation in the majority culture in view of the influence of the traditional Afro-American culture which includes the concept of we-ness (Nobles, 1980, p. 29), reflected in the strong extended family (Billingsley, 1968; White, 1980); a strong emphasis on spirituality (Nobles, 1980; White, 1980); a flexible concept of time (Nobles, 1980); a well-developed ability to use affect (Pasteur & Toldsen, 1982); and a general sensitivity to others (White, 1980). The black woman can then evaluate all variables within the context of her own set of personal and family experiences and endowments to gain a clearer sense of who she is in the world.

The black woman's group, therefore, provides the opportunity for the black woman to explore herself as a whole personal being, both black and woman. With other black women there is an immediate sense of sisterhood, a sense of belonging, a shared history, an opportunity for personal growth with support for (1) clarifying her identity as a person, as a woman, and as a black, while looking at how this affects her relationships; (2) identifying her concept and image of her self as a woman; and (3) dealing with roles that she plays and stereotypes that hamper her full expression of self.

Accordingly, the roles that the black woman plays can be enhanced, developed, and expanded through the role modeling of the group therapist and the other group members. As black women communicate honesty, sincerity, and love to each other, they also subtly and simultaneously identify the details and mechanisms of their successes, "thereby demystifying success and making it accessible to the [other] black female" group members (Trotman, 1984, p. 105).

A corollary of black women's success and achievement is often the imposter phenomenon (see Imes & Clance, 1984; Trotman, 1984).

> It is critical that the black woman suffering the imposter phenomenon feels safe enough and understood enough to share her feelings of fraudulence. A group experience with other achieving black women who risk exploring the commonality of fraudulent feelings is particularly therapeutic in such cases (Trotman, 1984, pp. 99–100).

SPECIAL NEEDS OF BLACK WOMEN IN GROUPS

A review of the literature (Copeland, 1977; Davis, 1985; Nayman, 1983; Nobles, 1976) supports the value of group therapy with black clients. Shipp (1983) indicates three important aspects of group work for black clients:

1. Psycholearning that occurs when members interact and evaluate their social microcosm. Within this sphere, members acquire an awareness of their universality—by sharing fears and fantasies they come to realize that they are not unique . . . [in addition] group work offers a new sense of hope to the member and sets the stage for behavior change.
2. Emphasis on interpersonal feedback and consensual validation, which in a group setting allows members to redefine social reality and test new definition with the other group members.
3. Individual members share in the responsibility for helping and guiding other group members.

Other facilitative factors in the group process include installation of hope, altruism, corrective recapitulation of the primary family group, imitative behavior, imparting of information, group cohesion, catharsis, and existential factors (Yalom, 1975). Nobles (1976) also suggests that group experiences highlight familial relationships that reinforce the values black clients place on family sharing and cooperation.

The positive aspects of group experiences can be undermined, however, by stereotypic and negative racial attitudes on the part of therapists, which can serve to delimit their work with black clients. These attitudes have particular consequences for the black female client because of the dual stigma of being black and a woman in a society that devalues both. Sue (1981) contends that as a white middle class activity, counseling embodies values, assumptions, and expectations at variance with Third World groups.

Thomas and Sillen (1972) suggest that racism in the mental health professions has a significant impact on black clients in that black clients are perceived as abnormal or pathogenic, often overdiagnosed in some categories and underdiagnosed in others. Black clients are sometimes perceived as unsuitable for long-term, insight-oriented treatment because of the perception that they are nonverbal, paranoid, and insufficiently psychological minded; this is reflected in a tendency toward concrete rather than abstract thought processes. Further, in working with clients from other cultures, there is a greater danger of mutual misunderstanding, less understanding of the other's culture and unique problems, a natural hostility that destroys rapport, greater negative transference toward the counselor, and the danger of confusing a client's appropriate cultural response with constructs of "neurotic transference" (Pedersen, 1976).

Research has consistently emphasized the need for therapists to be aware of the race and cultural differences of their clients and to be aware of their own biases. To address this issue, the American Psychological Association in 1973 developed a policy statement declaring it unethical to counsel a person of a different culture without expertise in the area (Korman, 1973). Race of therapist, the importance of cultural and social class of the therapist, the effect of therapist attitudes, same sex versus opposite sex of therapist, and the importance of role models was identified as significant in the psychotherapy process of black female clients (Trotman, 1984).

In view of salient issues mentioned above, Helms (1979) recommends several principles for therapists working with black women: (1) to be familiar with black history and contemporary politics as they affect black women; (2) be knowledgeable about myths, overgeneralizations, and stereotypes about black women; (3) believe that racially different is not necessarily "disadvantaged"; and (4) be willing to abandon middle-class values and moralistic judgments. Helms emphasizes that the therapists who intend to be successful in their work with black female clients must be aware that all black women are not alike and that the nature of their problems may differ depending upon such factors as social-economic status, family size, age, and marital or relationship status. (Note: We include in social-economic considerations factors such as whether clients are from an urban or rural setting, northern or southern, American citizen or foreign born, etc.).

Several specific guidelines have also been outlined to increase the effectiveness and relevance of group process for black female clients (Nayman, 1983). These guidelines include directives such as (1) be aware of your own race, social class, sex, and age biases; (2) be flexible in the design and implementation of group services and be prepared to adopt nontraditional roles (e.g., it may be useful to make personal telephone calls to prospective participants to follow up on general announcement of the program offerings); (3) if you are uncomfortable or fearful in approaching black women, do not attempt to relate to or serve them; your attitude will show and be interpreted as racist or uncaring; (4) do not exploit her strengths—help her to get in touch with her weaknesses and particular needs; (5) always consider the social ecology of the black client, that is, the functional and dysfunctional aspects of her environment and its influence on her; (6) anticipate that the period of testing the group leader may last longer with the black member than with the white member; establishing, nurturing, and maintaining trust with the black group member will be an ongoing group management issue for the group leader; (7) use a holistic approach in providing services for the black woman—spiritual, intellectual, family kin network, and community resources.

Keeping the aforementioned issues, recommendations, and guidelines in mind, a strong basis for therapeutic interventions with black female clients should, of course, also include acceptance of the client, genuineness, openness, and honesty on the part of the therapist. These factors are key in efforts to help women and blacks realize their human potential.

During the past 15 years there has been a significant increase in research on counseling effectiveness for women and minorities, with little attention given to the specific needs of black female clients. Copeland (1977) suggests that research of women tends to focus on the needs of women who are white and middle class, whereas research on blacks lump black men and women together. We have begun to address the differences between white and black women and have offered suggestions concerning the conduct of groups for black women, but additional research needs to be conducted on the influence of race on group composition and, specifically, on the experience and needs of black female clients in group psychotherapy.

REFERENCES

Billingsley, A. (1968). *Black families in white America.* Englewood Cliffs, NJ: Prentice Hall.

Bradley, D. (1984, January 8). Telling the black woman's story. *The New York Times Magazine*, pp. 24–37.

Buber, M. (1958). *I and thou.* New York: Scribner.

Bulhan, H. A. (1985). Black Americans and psychotherapy: An overview of research and theory. *Psychotherapy, 22*(2), 370–378.

Cheek, D. K. (1976). *Assertive black . . . puzzled white.* San Luis Obispo, CA: Impact.

Comas-Diaz, L., & Minrath, M. (1985). Psychotherapy with ethnic minority borderline clients. *Psychotherapy, 22*(2), 418–426.

Comer, J. P. (1980). White racism: Its root, form and function. In R. L. Jones (Ed.), *Black Psychology*(2nd ed.). New York: Harper & Row.

Copeland, E. (1977). Counseling black women with negative self-concepts. *Personnel and Guidance Journal, 55*(7), 397–400.

Davis, L. E. (1979). Racial composition of groups. *Social Work, 24*(3), 208–213.

Davis, L. (1980). When the majority is the psychological minority, *Group Psychotherapy, Psychodrama, and Sociometry, 33,* 179–184.

Davis, D. (1985). Group work practice with ethnic minorities of color. In M. Sundel, P. Glasser, R. Sarri, & R. Vinter (Eds.), *Individual change through small groups.* New York: The Free Press.

Davis, L. E., & Burnstein, E. (1981). Preference for racial composition of groups. *Journal of Psychology, 109,* 293–301.

Fabio, S. W. (1972). Blackness can: A quest for aesthetic. In A. Gayle (Ed.), *The black aesthetic,* New York: Anchor Books.

Helms, J. E. (1979). Black women. *The Counseling Psychologist, 8*(1), 40–41.

Hooks, B. (1982). *Ain't I a woman: Black women and feminism.* Boston: South End Press.

Ibrahim, F. A. (1985). Effectiveness in cross-cultural counseling and psychotherapy: A framework. *Psychotherapy, 22*(2), 321–323.

Imes, S., & Clance, P. R. (1984). Treatment of the Imposter Phenomenon in high achieving women. In C. M. Brody (Ed.), *Women therapists working with women: New theory and process of feminist therapy.* New York: Springer.

Jackson, A. M. (1976). Mental health delivery systems and the Black client. *The Journal of Afro-American Issues, 4,* 28–34.

Jones, R. L. (1980). *Black psychology* (2nd ed.). New York: Harper & Row.

Katz, I. & Benjamin, L. (1960). Effects of white authoritarianism in bi-racial work groups. *Journal of Abnormal and Social Psychology, 61,* 448–456.

Korman, M. (1973). *Levels and patterns of professional training in psychology,* Washington, DC: American Psychological Association.

Ladner, J. A. (1971). *Tomorrow's tomorrow.* New York: Anchor Books.

Linton, R. (1945). *The cultural background of personality.* New York: Appleton Century-Crofts.

Mays, V. (1985). The Black American and psychotherapy: The dilemma. *Psychotherapy, 22*(2), 379–388.

Myrdal, G. (1944). *An American dilemma: The negro problem and modern democracy.* New York: Harper.

Nayman, R. L. (1983). Group work with black women: Some issues and guidelines. *Journal for Specialists in Group Work, 3,* 31–38.

Nigel, C. (1976). *The human conspiracy.* New York: Viking Press.

Nobles, W. (1976). Extended self: Rethinking the so-called negro concept. *Journal of Black Psychology, 2*(2), 15–24.

Nobles, W. (1980). *African philosophy: Foundations for black psychology* (2nd ed.). New York: Harper & Row.

Pasteur, A. B., & Toldsen, I. L. (1982). *Roots of soul.* New York: Anchor Press.

Pedersen, P. B. (1976). The field of intercultural counseling. In P. Pedersen, W. Lonner, & J. Draguns (Eds.), *Counseling across cultures.* Honolulu: University Press of Hawaii.

Shaw, M. E. (1976). *Group dynamics: The psychology of small group behavior.* New York: McGraw Hill.

Shipp, P. (1983). Counseling Blacks: A group approach. *Personnel and Guidance Journal, 62*(2), 108–11.

Smith, E. J. (1982). The black female adolescent: A review of the educational, career and psychological literature. *Psychology of Women Quarterly, 7*(3), 261–287.

Staples, R. (1981). The myth of the black matriarchy. *The Black Scholar, 12*(6), 26–34.

Sue, D. W. (1981). *Counseling the culturally different: Theory and practice.* New York: John Wiley.

Thomas, M. B., & Dansby, P. G. (1985). Black clients: Family structures, therapeutic issues, and strengths. *Psychotherapy, 22*(2), 398–407.

Thomas, M. B., & Neal, P. A. (1978). Collaborating careers: The differential effects of race. *Journal of Vocational Behavior, 12*(1), 33–42.

Thomas, A., & Sillen, S. (1972). *Racism and psychiatry.* New York: Brunner/Mazel.

Trotman, F. K. (1984). Psychotherapy with black women and the dual effects of racism and sexism. In C. M. Brody (Ed.), *Women therapists working with women: New theory and process of feminist therapy.* New York: Springer.

White, J. L. (1980). Towards a black psychology. In R. L. Jones (Ed.), *Black psychology* (2nd ed.). New York: Harper & Row.

Williams, B., & Trotman, F. K. (1984, April). *Black women: The original superwomen.* Paper presented at Annual Meeting, New York State Psychological Association, New York.

Yalom, I. D. (1975). *Theory and practice of group psychotherapy* (2nd ed.). New York: Basic Books.

■ 10
Feminism and Systems Theory: Its Impact on Lesbian and Heterosexual Couples

BARBARA R. ROTHBERG and VIVIAN UBELL

As couples therapists we often experience a situation similar to the one we encounter when we run groups. The need to focus on process rather than content and the need to deal with the dyad in its relationship with the therapist are elements of the couples therapy. In addition, as systems therapists we deal with the couple as a system that interacts with larger systems. Thus, when we sit with a couple, we are often working with their extended family systems, friendship systems, societal systems, etc.

All therapists struggle with value issues in treatment. As feminists we feel committed to transmitting these values through our work. As we have tried to integrate feminist and systems approaches, we have been forced to explore our values, options, and treatment techniques. As feminists, we work with both lesbian and heterosexual couples and have had the opportunity to understand the similarities and differences in the two systems. In this chapter, we will explore the interrelationship between our systems and feminist perspectives, the dilemmas in trying to join these views, and how we intervene in the treatment process.

The authors contributed equally in preparation of this paper.

REVIEW OF THE LITERATURE

There has been little exchange between practitioners of family systems and feminist therapy. The differences in the orientations are clearcut. Feminist therapy is based on a linear cause and effect model, whereas family systems therapy views problems as circular or systemic. For the feminist therapist the target of change is the individual in society as well as the society itself. For the systems therapist, as well as the group therapist, the targets of change are the interactions and relationships that are usually the foci of the problem.

Hare-Mustin (1978) reports that traditional sex-roles are unwittingly reinforced by therapists who work on the assumption "that traditional roles are the basis for healthy functioning" (p. 184). She makes the case that family therapists should examine their own biases and describes how feminist principles can easily become assimilated into family treatment. This is also applicable for group therapists.

Libow, Raskin, and Caust (1982) present a comprehensive analysis of feminist and family therapy perspectives. In the family therapy movement, male pioneers did research that pointed to the "bad" mother. In contrast, feminist therapy was pioneered by political feminists who emphasized society's attitudes toward women rather than stressing individual psychopathology as contributing factors to women's problems.

The two orientations differ in regard to insight. According to Libow et al. (1982), in feminist therapy understanding and insight are the goals. In family therapy, behavioral change in the interaction between members of the system is a primary goal. An even greater difference lies in the acceptable strategies for effecting change. Whereas feminist therapy stresses the importance of open, honest, and direct communication, family therapy uses a wide variety of techniques that are often manipulative and even paradoxical. In this sense, feminist therapy and group therapy are more aligned.

Though they originate from different frameworks, there are some similarities between the two approaches. The social context in which people function is primary to each. Both use modeling as an important tool and in assessing change and both value observable, concrete, and behavioral differences.

DEFINING FEMINIST THERAPY

Feminist therapists, whether working with individuals, couples, or groups, are concerned with addressing women's psychological development in a way that validates their feelings and experiences, that recognizes the society's impact on women, and allows for their own life experiences when relevant. Historically, women have been blamed and diagnosed as pathological when they chose nontraditional paths in life. Feminist therapists recognize the need to counter these traditions and formulate a new psychology.

For the purposes of this chapter, feminist therapy is defined as a therapeutic orientation that involves breaking away from gender stereotypes, opening options, and viewing sex roles as fluid. In treatment, Libow et al. (1982) state the goal is to "free clients from destructive and unnecessary limitations on their personal choices, self expression and self concepts, limits which were originally derived from now outmoded sex role constraints as well as an oppressive social structure (p. 6). Additionally, in working therapeutically with lesbians, feminists maintain a woman-identified orientation that assumes an understanding of society's view of homosexuality as well as an acceptance on the part of the therapist that it is healthy for women to maintain primary relationships with one another.

SYSTEMS THERAPY AND FEMINISM

A system is an organization of elements that are related to each other in a consistent way. The system tries to maintain a homeostatic balance, keeping the status quo of organization, interactions, and boundaries. Any force from outside or inside the system activates it to try to restore homeostasis.

In a couple or a group system within this framework, people organize their relationships in consistent ways, affecting each other in a circular rather than a linear fashion. For example, Joanne and Susan are together for three years and come into therapy because "Susan is a nag" and "Joanne withdraws." In a linear view, it is said, Joanne withdraws, therefore Susan nags, or vice versa, thereby assigning the fault to one person. With circular causality, we look at the interrelationship and do not assign fault: Susan nags because Joanne withdraws and Joanne withdraws because Susan nags.

The fluidity or rigidity of the system, its degree of control and steadiness, is determined by rules, mores, traditions, sex roles, etc. A system also has a spatial structure (where the couple lives, where a group meets, how often couples see relatives, etc.) and a temporal process and function (how communications are made, who makes decisions, etc.). In viewing the world systemically, coupling is one of the many systems in which an individual operates. As systemic therapists, we intervene with the couple system while remembering the relative strength and power of other systems that impact on the couple. For example, if Joanne works long hours at a job, then her work system may have a stronger impact on the couple system than Susan's does.

Since each element of a system is interrelated, a change in any one part of the system will affect change in the rest of it. If Joanne stops withdrawing, Susan will stop nagging, or if Susan stops nagging, Joanne will stop withdrawing. The therapist, in order to avoid enmeshment in the system, must decide where to impact upon it. The couple's definition of the problem is not accepted in that it is almost always linear in nature; it places blame on only one part of the system rather than looking at the interrelationship. For example, Joanne comes into therapy and states "We'll be fine if you just get her to stop nagging."

As therapists, we want to impact on, rather than become enmeshed in the system. However, by virtue of the therapist's interrelationship with the system, we influence it by becoming yet another part of the interlocking gears. We would argue that all therapists bring a piece of their own value systems to therapy, even if only reflected in when they say "yes, go on" or "uh huh." Because we subscribe to a feminist view of the world, our feminism does have an effect on the therapeutic process whether we declare it overtly or covertly to the couple. Thus, feminist underpinnings are operative even though they sometimes are not evident. When the treatment goals are achieved, the feminism seems clearer.

The dilemma is that an overt feminist position may in fact drive one person, and hence the couple, out of treatment. If neither member of the couple is committed to feminism, this certainly is so. This issue is particularly true in the early stages in treatment when the therapist does not have a strong enough alliance with both members to perhaps introduce feminist principles more directly and safely. In the middle phase, there may be more leeway.

If the therapist is female and assumes a feminist position, the less feminist member of the couple, generally the male in a heterosexual couple, may feel a coalition between his mate and the therapist. This alliance may overtly exert enough pressure to push the resistant member to change but leave him feeling alienated and unheard. Passive aggressive moves on his part to reestablish a homeostatic balance are not uncommon at this point.

With lesbian couples, even if one member is more resistant to feminist principles than the other, the nature of the feminist therapy rhetoric and the positive value of a feminist consciousness for both members of the couple make it safe for the therapist to declare herself openly as a feminist.

TECHNIQUES

The concepts of resistance and joining are relevant at this point. If one person brings the couple into treatment with the accusatory stance of "it's all your fault," the accused often feels defensive and resistant. Unlike other theoretical orientations to treatment where resistance is analyzed, interpreted, or, at times, confronted, in a systemic model, resistance is often joined. Therapeutically, identifying or predicting the possible negative consequences of change for the system or warning against change allows the resistant person to, in fact, feel supported and ultimately more open to the possibility of change. In addressing the issue of changing the system, rather than the person, the resistant member needs to be joined with as strongly as, or perhaps more strongly than, the member who is pushing for change. Otherwise, the resistant member is ultimately successful in maintaining a homeostatic balance. Thus, the therapist looks at the point of resistance as a place of primary intervention. In other words, the therapist may appear more aligned with the resistance—often an antifeminist position—although, in fact, the ultimate goal of the therapist is to produce change that supports feminist ideals. In joining resistance the therapist often uses skills that may seem manipulative in order to join with the male partner, knowing that in her trusting relationship with the woman she will ultimately create change and role flexibility.

Change, for our purposes, is defined as new behavior in the system. If change occurs in a piece of the system and the feedback loop reinforces the change, then the change becomes stabilized into the system. Often the behavioral change precedes an individual's sense of feeling different.

To give an example, Jan and Peter, who have been married for 10 years, come into therapy with Jan's complaint that Peter never shares his feelings and that Jan wants more communication in the relationship. Peter and Jan have already begun to make some feminist structural changes in the relationship, such as sharing childcare, but it is evident that Jan is the one who is pushing for change and that Peter reluctantly gives in to her demands. His withholding of feelings seems to be a passive aggressive way to express power and anger. The therapist, joining with Peter and establishing an initial alliance, would make a strong move by praising him for his willingness to come into treatment. The therapist could acknowledge Jan's need more subtly by telling her that "communication is important and a desirable goal for both of them; that while they've done without it for 10 years, they may need to do without it for sometime longer. Change doesn't occur quickly, and this shift will be difficult for both of you." Such an approach reassures Peter that the therapist will not be demanding rapid change for which he is not ready. In addition, the therapist immediately identifies the issue that a change in one part of the system implies change for the whole system. If Peter is to become more open with his feelings, Jan may have to be put on "hold" for a while. The therapist, as a feminist, feels strongly that Jan's demands to have a more feeling and sharing relationship are valid.

The therapist is sincere in stating that change will be difficult for both of them. If Peter begins to share his feelings, Jan may discover feelings of weakness or distress that she has never heard and that she finds uncomfortable. She then may experience feelings of anger or resentment. She may also discover her strength in the relationship in a new way that is both frightening and liberating. In assuming a cautious position regarding change, the therapist does not duplicate Jan's role in pushing for Peter's feelings.

We should note here that the above example assumes Jan's desire for the relationship and her willingness to wait for Peter to change as well as her willingness to look at her part in the system that keeps Peter from sharing her feelings. If she wanted out of the relationship, we would support that option.

The techniques of joining resistance with lesbian couples are similar even though the issue of hiding one's feminism becomes irrelevant. If one partner in a lesbian couple is more resistant to change, you may have to use maneuvers similar to those described above with Jan and Peter.

We would also like to note that there are some instances where our feminism supercedes our systems approach. For example, with a battered or abused woman, we would push first for the woman's safety and address the systemic piece only after her safety was insured.

In addition to joining resistance, the systemic therapist utilizes reframing as a central concept to produce change. Often, at first glance, reframing may appear to be sarcastic, unfair, or nonfeminist. In fact, reframing is often done to create a crisis and to promote change by pinpointing another side of the issue or by relabeling the behavior in terms of its positive connotation in the system. The couple will see the problem in a new way and hence begin to change their thinking about the problem. To return to our example, we can reframe Peter's behavior by stating "he's being helpful to Jan by protecting her from ever having to know his negative feelings towards her." This reframing of his negative behavior of withholding into a positive framework of protection often brings about a powerful move in the system towards change. Peter feels supported and yet indignant because in fact he doesn't want to be protective. Jan counters—"I don't want to be protected"—and begins, in fact, to reassure Peter that she does want to hear his feelings. This often will bring both members of the couple more directly into the arena of dealing with their real feelings.

Another concept employed by the therapist is rebalancing. If the system is out of balance in that one person holds too much power or one member is too distant, the therapist needs to help move the system to a more balanced position. The options might be to lessen the power of one or to enhance that of the other, or both. Rebalancing the system also helps the person who seems powerless to recognize the power inherent in his or her position. Nancy and Margaret have been lovers for the past six years. Nancy seems to be the powerful member of the couple, and Margaret states that she finds it hard to win any battles with Nancy. On closer examination, however, we discover that Margaret is depressed, and her depression is very powerful in the couple system, allowing Margaret to win battles without overtly fighting them. As Madanes (1981) points out, this is maintaining power through the one-down position. If she can be made to see the power of her depression, the system becomes more balanced, and the therapist can then help her to begin to fight more openly.

As stated earlier, another concept used by the systemic therapist is that of negative consequence of change wherein the therapist explores the possible problems that may occur once change is accomplished. If changes did occur, what new problems might arise? For example, Rosemary and Lorraine are lovers. They enter therapy with the presenting problem of Rosemary being a workaholic who does not come home until late. In exploring this dynamic, it becomes apparent that there are many serious issues that are masked by Rosemary's late hours. If Rosemary were to change her hours, the couple would be confronted with having to deal with the reality of their poor communication, lack of sexual desire, different interests, etc.

A related technique is exploring the system to its extreme to help the members verbalize their fears and fantasies. Often if the dreaded is aired, the fear of those consequences is diminished and change can occur.

Tasks are another tool for the therapist to help produce change in the system. If the couple can experience doing something different and get positive reinforcement for doing so, then the difference can be incorporated into the system on a permanent basis. Tasks can be very helpful in modeling new role behavior by creating a less sexist familial structure, facilitating communication, etc.

Circular questioning is the final concept we will describe. In circular questioning, one partner is asked about the other partner's perception of the system and vice versa. This technique offers the therapist information about how well each member understands the other's perceptions, how far apart the members are in their views of the problem, and where the resistance lies.

LESBIAN AND HETEROSEXUAL COUPLES

As couples therapists we see presenting problems recur thematically. With both lesbian and heterosexual couples we encounter problems of distance, closeness, intimacy, and power as primary concerns. For example, in heterosexual couples, the issues of power and control often are evident. We see the controlling husband and the passive wife or the domineering wife and the acquiescing husband. In lesbian couples, as feminism becomes integrated into relationships there is often a hope and expectation of an equal power base; however, power struggles arise. These struggles are often similar to, though perhaps more covert, than those that occur in heterosexual couples. Decisions about vacations, spending money, and how often to see relatives are almost universal problems. Issues of dependency, sex, and dealing with families of origin and children are also frequent complaints. In lesbian couples, fusion (a symbiotic merging of lovers) presents itself as a problem distinct from heterosexual couples. We believe the prevalence of fusion is due to society's discrimination and the position of lesbians as a minority rather than to individual pathology, lack of ego boundaries, or narcissism. We will now address ourselves to the major differences in dealing with lesbian and heterosexual couples in treatment. Many of the differences described here apply as well to lesbian versus heterosexual groups.

Because couples function as a system, many of the issues of lesbian couples are similar to those of heterosexual couples, yet lesbian couples experience other issues due to their relationship to society and to the nature of female bonding. Dealing with one's family of origin is always basic in couple treatment. For lesbian couples this issue is often painful and unresolved. A lack of understanding and acceptance from both partners' parents or even worse, from one woman's parents, adds enormous stress to the relationship and can create an imbalance in the system. Some families "resolve" their problems when either the lesbian or her parents break off the relationship. This lack of relationship with the family of origin has an effect on the couple system, because the couple system then becomes the primary family for its members. When a relationship with parents is maintained, the issue becomes how the lesbian and her parents accept and deal with her lesbianism and her lover. As therapists dealing with lesbian couples, we need to be conscious of the special problems lesbians face in dealing with their parents in addition to the problems that all couples deal with regularly.

Society's view of homosexuality exerts pressure on lesbian relationships. As Potter and Darty (1981) point out, lesbians experience double jeopardy as women and as lesbians. Lowenstein (1980) reports that lesbians have to deal with the phenomenon of passing which adds the burden of double identity. In a couple, either woman may or may not choose to pass, often depending on her job, which causes tensions in the relationships. Lesbians are susceptible to society's pressures, particularly if they are politically active and have to deal with pressure and expectations from the lesbian subculture. Power, a conflict in so many relationships, exists somewhat differently in lesbian relationships because society's power ascribed to men is absent. It is often assumed, however, that because both members of the couple are women the power struggle will be eliminated. This is particularly a problem for women who have recently come out and have entered their first lesbian relationship. On several occasions in treatment, we have heard women say, "But I thought this wouldn't be a problem in a lesbian relationship." The disillusionment women experience needs to be addressed in therapy. Princess Charming is not a reality. The disillusioned lesbian is often angry at her partner for not living up to her expectations and for recreating the one-up–one-down power struggle maintained in heterosexual relationships. Here, a systems perspective becomes pertinent. Rather than exploring the linear or causal factors of the anger, as systems therapists we look at how each woman contributes to creating the power struggles, expectations, and possible myths that evolved. Although overtly a more equitable power relationship operates in a female relationship, we know as therapists that power is not only based on the inequality of men and women. It is also derived from class status, money, children, jobs, and personality factors.

Couple fusion, a symbiotic merging, which is occasionally a problem in heterosexual relationships, is more often a problem in lesbian relationships. In dealing with pressures from society and in an attempt to develop comfortable boundaries with other people, lesbian couples become more insulated. Lack of approval from family of origin and lack of rituals to celebrate relationships are two examples of the difficulties that lead lesbians to depend more on each other and act as two against an unaccepting world. The pressures lead to the formation of a closed system as a coping mechanism, which in turn creates other problems such as lack of individuation. One way to begin to balance the fusion and to help the couple understand the process is to encourage them to become part of a friendship group in order to gain peer support. This is helpful, but it may produce other problems. There is often a lack of boundaries between lesbian couples in friendships, in part due to the small size of the lesbian community; both partners often share the same friends, thereby resulting in competition and jealousy. This is contrary to the boundaries established by society for heterosexual couples in which bonding naturally occurs between same sex people. In dealing with lesbians as couples or in groups, we are often amazed by the degree of entwined interrelationships.

Another issue that presents itself differently in lesbian and heterosexual couples is that of dealing with children. Although increasingly lesbians are birthing their own children as well as adopting them, the majority of lesbian mothers are those who have been previously married. When a lesbian mother gets involved with a nonmother, many issues arise. The primary one of children accepting the new lover must first be addressed. Then coparenting needs to be explored. Time spent with children versus time spent alone usually is a problem. The exhusband—his involvement, or lack of involvement, either way—is always a problem. The strains of the reconstituted family need to be dealt with in all couples and become exacerbated for lesbian couples where there are few role models.

The major difference between a lesbian couple and a heterosexual couple in terms of parenting is that there is no role model for the lover of a lesbian mother. Heterosexual parental roles are defined by the sex role of the partners. A lesbian nonmother is clearly not the mom nor is she the dad. Most lesbian mothers do not want to be usurped as mothers, and the couple may experience competition in parenting.

COMPARISON OF TREATMENT APPROACHES

The following is an example of the difference in treatment approaches to work with the same problems. Martha and Max come into therapy after seven years of marriage. Martha says she feels that Max does not care about her and seems disinterested in sex. Martha wants more contact and often initiates sex. Max pulls away physically and says he does not like Martha approaching him all the time. He states that he just wants some space.

A lesbian couple, Linda and Lucy, enter therapy after a five-year relationship with the same complaint. Linda wants more sex than Lucy, and when she initiates contact, Lucy pulls away.

All individuals need to establish a comfortable balance between closeness and distance in their relationships. If the discrepancy between the partners is too great, problems ensue. In working with problems of distance and closeness, the basic tenet of "never pursue a distancer" is generally adhered to, because if you pursue a distancer they will move further away. Often the pursuer is seen as the "good" partner who wants more, and the distancer is seen as the "bad" one. By using a variety of techniques, we teach the pursuer to back off, then we enable the distancer to pursue, thereby rebalancing the system. Since traditionally women are seen as demanding too much from their relationships and we are determined not to maintain this myth, we will often choose techniques based on whether the pursuer is male or female. We do not want to put the woman in a position where once again she feels blamed for the imbalance in the system. In dealing with lesbian couples, there is more leeway in choosing techniques, as we do not have to protect a partner from sexist norms.

In the first case, the therapist begins to explore the distance/closeness dance that occurs between Martha and Max. If Martha's comfortable space is closer than Max's she will always pursue, and he will always distance (within the framework of circular causality, it does not matter which came first). If we push Martha to be more distanced, she will feel blamed. If we push Max towards a position of more intimacy he will move away and will experience the therapist as chasing him just as Martha does, and Max too will feel blamed. As systems therapists we would repeatedly reframe the problem to help Martha distance and Max pursue without either feeling blamed. For example, we might note that Martha's moving in closer helps Max avoid having to know the feeling of being "needy," which is scary for him, or we might comment to Max that he has been helpful to Martha in giving her the space to explore her assertiveness in meeting her sexual needs.

In the case of the lesbian couple, the therapist points out that Lucy is very helpful to Linda in always saying "no" to sex, because that allows Linda to look as though she is the "good" one in the couple system. Linda never has to confront her own ambivalence about sex. The therapist identifies the system: Linda can safely initiate sex daily knowing that Lucy won't comply. This move produces change in the system by redefining the pursuer and distancer. Linda is no longer seen as the "good" one.

If we assumed this same position with Martha and Max, Martha would feel misunderstood and probably angry that we did not trust her desire for more assertiveness in her sexuality. More importantly, however, from a feminist perspective it would leave Martha feeling blamed. The feminist issue is less toxic with a lesbian couple because of the fluidity of the roles.

CONCLUSION

For many of us as feminist therapists when the Women's Movement first impacted on our lives, we felt compelled to bring our enthusiasm about our feminism into the therapy arena. Now, as feminism has become more integrated into our lives and we see the complex struggles that couples experience, we realize that sometimes we have to guard our feminism, using it judiciously in the treatment process. Our priority, at times, must be the system, rather than the feminism, but the feminism is always present. Even when part of the system is put on hold, we never lose sight of the woman in the room or lose respect for her basic struggle. We are continuously challenged with the problems that arise in the integration of these approaches and are committed to working them through creatively, pushing the field to accept new dimensions in treatment.

REFERENCES

Hare-Mustin, R., (1978). A feminist approach to family therapy. *Family Process, 17*(2), 181–194.

Libow, J., Raskin, P., & Caust, B., (1982). Feminist and family systems therapy: Are they irreconcilable? *The American Journal of Family Therapy,10*(3), 3–12.

Lowenstein, S. F. (1980). Understanding lesbian women. *Social Casework, 61*(1), 29–38.

Madanes, C. (1981). *Strategic family therapy.* San Francisco: Jossey-Bass.

Potter, S., and Darty, T. (1981). Social work and the invisible minority: An exploration of lesbianism. *Social Work, 26*(3), 187–192.

SUGGESTED READINGS

Berger, R. (1982). The unseen minority: Older gays and lesbians. *Social Work, 27*(3), 236–242.

Caust, B., Libow, J., & Raskin, P. (1981). Challenges and promises of training women as family systems therapists. *Family Process, 20*(4), 439–448.

Dulaney, D., & Kelly, J. (1982). Improving services to gay and lesbian clients. *Social Work, 27*(2), 178–183.

Hall, M. (1978). Lesbian families: Cultural and clinical issues. *Social Work, 23*(5), 380–385.

Hershey, S., & Weiner, E. (1975). Dominance in marital decision making in women's liberation and non-women's liberation families. *Family Process, 14*(2), 223–233.

Joslyn, B. (1982). Shifting sex roles: The silence of the family therapy liberation. *Clinical Social Work Journal, 10*(1), 39–51.

Krestan, J., & Bepho, C. (1980). The problem of fusion in the lesbian relationship. *Family Process, 19*(3), 277–290.

Leader, A. (1979). The notion of responsibility in family therapy. *Social Casework, 60*(3), 131–137.

Nagy, B., & Spark, H., (1973). *Invisible loyalties.* New York: Harper & Row.

Paolino, T., & McCrady, B. (1978). Marriage and marital therapy. New York: Brunner/Mazel.

Peal, E. (1975). Normal sex roles: An historical analysis. *Family Process, 14*(3), 389–409.

Penn, P. (1982). Circular questioning. *Family Process, 21*(3), 267–280.

Peplan, L., Cochran S., Rook, K., & Padesky, C. (1978). Loving women: Attachment and autonomy in lesbian relationships. *Journal of Social Issues, 34*(3), 7–27.

Radov, C., Masnick, B., & Hauser, B. (1977). Issues in feminist therapy: The work of a women's study group. *Social Work, 22*(6), 507–509.

Rice, D., & Rice, J. (1977). Non-sexist marital therapy. *Journal of Marriage and Family Counseling, 3*(1), 3–9.

Thomas, S. (1977). Theory and practice in feminist therapy. *Social Work, 22*(6), 447–454.

■ 11
Dialectical Behavior Therapy in Groups: Treating Borderline Personality Disorders and Suicidal Behavior

MARSHA M. LINEHAN

This chapter focuses on group therapy for women diagnosed as Borderline Personality disorder. The treatment was originally designed for women who also have a concomitant pattern of serious suicidal behavior, including multiple instances of parasuicide (often referred to as suicide attempts but also including self-mutilative and other self-injurious behaviors). Suicidal behavior shares many characteristics of other escape behaviors. Thus, the treatment can also be used with nonsuicidal women who, nonetheless, deal with stressful situations by engaging in dysfunctional problem-solving and escape behaviors. The group treatment described here is part of a larger treatment program, Dialectical Behavior Therapy, developed for this population. Group treatment consists of skill-training in specified areas. It does not focus on the weekly individual crises in the lives of borderline suicidal women. The goal, instead, is to teach general problem-solving skills that can be used across many problematic life situations. Thus, at least with many, group skill-training is meant as ancillary to individual therapy or to another group therapy that can attend to the current life stresses typical of this population. In my work, the integration of the skills learned in group therapy is dealt with intensively in individual therapy.

Preparation of this chapter was funded by National Institute Grant MH34486.

To date, all published treatment approaches and accompanying theoretical perspectives on Borderline Personality disorder have arisen out of the psychoanalytic treatment community. Most notable are the approaches of Kernberg (1984), Masterson (1976), and Adler (1985). Each recommends long-term, intensive, individual psychotherapy. Also characteristic of the analytic approach is an acceptance of long-term inpatient treatment programs (McGlashan, 1986). In contrast, treatment approaches to suicidal individuals have often stressed a more time-limited crisis intervention approach to treatment (Hawton & Catalan, 1982). Hospitalization is usually short-term, intended to provide a safe atmosphere for the woman in crisis.

Dialectical Behavior Therapy is based on a biobehavioral perspective of the borderline personality disorder and suicidal behavior and, as one would expect, is quite different than the prevailing psychoanalytic approach. Although it includes many crisis intervention techniques, it is neither brief nor primarily supportive. The treatment views suicidal behavior, including parasuicide, and the impulsive and disruptive interpersonal behaviors typical of borderlines as problem-solving behaviors designed to cope with or ameliorate psychic distress and other problematic situations. The borderline, suicidal person is viewed as trapped in a rigid cognitive and emotional framework, unable to move to reconciliation and synthesis.

In what follows, I will first discuss the characteristics of borderline and suicidal women. An understanding of the typical behavior patterns of these women is essential to treating them. Often one's ability to predict ahead of time their emotional responses and behavior is important. Especially so because these women often have great difficulty communicating their concerns and feelings. Next, I will briefly describe the theoretical orientation underpinning Dialetical Behavior Therapy. It is this theoretical position that informs individual decisions in carrying out the treatment program. Finally, I will describe in detail the conduct of dialectical behavior therapy in a group setting.

BORDERLINE PERSONALITY DISORDER AND PARASUICIDAL BEHAVIOR

The Problem

Both Borderline Personality disorder and parasuicidal behavior are observed more often among women than men (American Psychiatric Association, 1980; Linehan, 1971). Gunderson (1984) estimated that up to 15% of individuals seeking professional mental health care can be diagnosed as borderline. The proportion among women is undoubtedly higher. Estimates of parasuicide in the general population range from a low of 1% (Dublin, 1963) to a high of 13% (Shneidman, 1971). The ratio of female to male parasuicides is estimated at between two and nine to one (Neuringer & Lettieri, 1982). Between 10 and 39% of parasuicides will be repeated within the next year (Hawton, 1979; Kennedy, 1972). Parasuicide is particularly prevalent among individuals diagnosed as Borderline Personality disorder. Gunderson (1984) has suggested that parasuicide may come closest to representing the "behavioral specialty" of this particular form of personality disorder. Likewise, a diagnosis of borderline personality is most frequent in samples of self-mutilative and parasuicidal individuals (Crumley, 1979; Graff & Mallin, 1967; Grunebaum & Klerman, 1967).

Behavioral Characteristics

Borderline Personality Disorder. A DSM-III diagnosis of Borderline Personality disorder requires the presence of five out of eight behavioral characteristics (American Psychiatric Association, 1980). These characteristics can be grouped into four categories. First, disturbance in emotional functioning is evidenced by emotional lability and/or problems with anger and anger expression. Second, interpersonal problems are evidenced by disruptive and chaotic relationships and excessive fear of being alone. Third, problems in self-schema are indicated by identity diffusion and/or a pervasive sense of emptiness. Finally, problems in impulse control and distress tolerance are evidenced by a pattern of extreme, problematic impulsive behavior and/or parasuicidal behaviors.

Parasuicide. Characteristics of individuals with Borderline Personality disorder are remarkably similar to those that have been identified as typical of suicidal individuals. The emotional picture of the parasuicide is one of chronic, aversive affective experiences. They appear to be more angry, hostile, and irritable (Crook, Raslin, & Davis, 1975; Richman & Charles, 1976) and more depressed (Warden & Sterling-Smith, 1973) than nonsuicidal psychiatric and nonpsychiatric individuals. They also report discomfort and anxiety when approaching people (Cantor, 1976). Parasuicides often have relationships characterized by hostility, demandingness, and conflict (Weissman, Fox, & Klerman, 1973), and they have weak social support systems compared to others (Linehan, 1981). Generally, they are unlikely to have the cognitive and interpersonal skills required to cope effectively with these stresses. They are characterized by cognitive rigidity (Levenson & Neuringer, 1971), dichotomous thinking (Neuringer, 1961), and poor interpersonal problem-solving (Goodstein, 1982). In our research, we have found that parasuicides more often than suicide ideators and nonsuicidal psychiatric patients, report interpersonal situations as their chief problem (Linehan, Chiles, Egan, Devine, Laffaw, & Egan, 1987) and exhibit a more passive problem-solving style (Linehan, Camper, Chiles, Strosahl, & Shearin, in press). In the face of these emotional and interpersonal difficulties, many parasuicides report that their behavior is designed to provide an escape from what, to them, seems like an intolerable and unsolvable life (Cantor, 1976).

BORDERLINE PARASUICIDAL WOMAN

Behavioral Syndromes

I have found it useful to identify some of the common behavioral patterns one is likely to encounter in conducting therapy with this group. Understanding and predicting these patterns is essential if treatment is to be successful. Although these patterns are common, they are by no means universal. Given that caveat, I have found it therapeutic in group meetings to discuss the syndromes. Generally, they strike a resonant chord with the women and help them achieve a better organization and understanding of their own behavior. Since the seeming inexplicable nature of their behavior is often an important issue, this is no small achievement when successful.

Emotional Vulnerability Syndrome.   Many borderlines are exquisitely sensitive to any kind of stimuli, but most especially to emotional stimuli. They seem unable to regulate incoming external and internal stimuli effectively. In addition, they appear to respond intensely to even low stimuli. These women cope with their sensitivity in various ways. Most common is the tendency to vacillate between simply shutting down, avoiding, and blocking all incoming stimuli and a pattern of intense overreaction. Some women describe this sensitivity in terms of feeling like they have no skin, as if their whole psyche is like an open wound that they are unable to protect. It is their inability to protect themselves and the resulting hopelessness engendered that makes them so interpersonally dependent at times. In turn, this dependency leads to intense responses to the threat of loss of interpersonally significant people. This can be a very important therapeutic issue. The group leader's absence, e.g., by going out of town, might be an occasion for extreme overreactions on the part of group members. Other members leaving the group can also have a similar, if attenuated, effect. Predicting and openly dealing with these issues is essential.

Self-Invalidating Syndrome. Emotionally labile, intense, and stimuli-sensitive temperamental characteristics can be especially deleterious if a woman lives in an environment that characteristically invalidates her experiences and difficulties. Even under the best of circumstance, learning emotional control and coping strategies can be extraordinarily difficult for the sensitive and vulnerable individual. If the family cannot understand the individual's inability to control his/her emotions and responds less sensitively to situations, the task becomes almost impossible. Families of borderlines and, consequently, they themselves are often unable to accept failure or any lack of success. Such nonperfection may be viewed as a personal failure due to lack of motivation, lack of discipline, not trying hard enough, etc. It is similar to the "you can pull yourself up by the bootstraps" approach, the Horatio Alger syndrome, and a belief system that anyone can make it if they only try hard enough. Great value is attributed to the state of being happy or at least to grinning in the face of adversity, to believing in one's own capacity to achieve any objective or at least to never "giving in" to hopelessness, and, most of all, to the power of a "positive mental attitude" in overcoming any difficulty.

This point of view may not be damaging and may even be useful to the person who is temperamentally suited to it and can learn attitude and emotional control. But, it vastly oversimplifies the situation in the case of the emotionally sensitive and vulnerable person. What other people succeed at—control of emotions and their expression—the borderline often can succeed at only sporadically. However, borderlines themselves too often adopt the same intolerant attitude. Self-hate and a feeling of being undeserving are often a result.

The intuitive knowledge that such an approach is oversimplified, however, also leads to vacillation between intolerance of self and intolerance of others, coupled with extreme anger at others' lack of empathy and understanding. An appreciation of this invalidating syndrome can make more understandable the borderline parasuicide's difficulties with any therapeutic approach that proposes that emotional happiness can come if one can only change one's attitudes. An oversimplified approach to behavior change will be met with hostility and rejected. The therapist's invalidation is sometimes so subtle, unrecognized by the therapist, that the resulting client anger and hostility may seem irrational or out of context. An oversimplified approach, in addition, will further entrench the client's continuing self-rejection.

Apparently Competent Woman Syndrome. Borderline women often appear very competent interpersonally and in other ways. In reality, they are. But, they also have areas of incompetency, which they often find extraordinarily difficult to communicate to others. The appearance of total competence can fool others into believing they are more competent than they actually are. In reality, however, they often need large amounts of encouragement, emotional support, advice, and help coping with situations that to them are unmanageable. An inability to integrate or synthesize the notions of both competence and incompetence, of needing and not needing help can lead to conflict and dysfunctional behaviors. Believing that they are competent to "succeed," they can experience intense guilt about their presumed lack of motivation when they fall short of objectives. At other times, they experience extreme anger at others for their lack of understanding and unrealistic expectations. Both experiences—intense guilt and intense anger—can lead to dysfunctional behaviors aimed at reducing the painful emotional states.

Learned Helplessness Syndrome. Co-existing with the apparently competent woman syndrome is the learned helplessness syndrome, its polar opposite. The defining characteristic of this syndrome is the tendency to approach problems passively and helplessly, rather than actively and competently. The borderline woman observes her frequent inability to interact successfully and is aware that she is often not only unhappy, hopeless, and unable to see the world from a positive point of view but is also unable to maintain an uncracked facade of happiness, hope, and untroubled calm. These observations can lead to the learned helplessness syndrome. The experience of failure despite one's best efforts is the precursor of such a syndrome. In addition, in an environment where difficulties are not recognized, the individual does not learn how to deal with problems effectively. Learning such coping strategies requires, at a minimum, the recognition of a problem. In an environment where difficulties are minimized, an individual learns to magnify them so that they will be taken seriously. It is this magnified view of difficulties and incompetence that further characterize the learned helplessness syndrome. The individual balances nonrecognition of inadequacy with extreme inadequacy and passiveness.

The individual and collective passivity of borderline and suicidal women poses a formidable roadblock for the group therapist. Breaking through it and generating active participation in the group is a continuing task. The mistake the therapist must avoid is that of continuing the oversimplification of the clients' difficulties. The easier the therapist makes progress sound, the more passive the group is likely to be. But by stressing the inherent difficulty, while at the same time requiring active progress nonetheless, active work can occur. The primary task of the therapist is to maintain patience while at the same time requiring movement on the part of the group. Dialectical Behavior Therapy rests on the assumption that change can only occur by active participation of the client. Such participation, however, is not often the expectation of the group members. Thus, a first task for the therapist is teaching the rules of this new therapeutic approach.

Crisis-of-the-Week Syndrome. Borderline and suicidal individuals are often in a state of perpetual crisis. Although suicidal and other dysfunctional behaviors are conceptualized in Dialectical Behavior Therapy as responses to problems in living, a more accurate statement might be that these behaviors are a response to a state of chronic, unrelenting, and overwhelming crisis. This chronic, unrelenting crisis is debilitating not because of the magnitude of any one stressful event, but instead by virtue of its chronic nature. For example, simultaneous loss of job, spouse, children, and concomitant serious illness would, theoretically, be easier to cope with than the same set of events experienced on a sequential basis. Repetitive stressful events, coupled with an inability to ever recover fully from any one stressful event, results in, as Berent (1981) suggests, "weakening of the spirit" and subsequent suicidal or other "emergency" behaviors. In a sense, the client can never return to a baseline of emotional functioning before the next blow hits.

From the theoretical perspective of Dialectical Behavior Therapy this inability to return to baseline may be a result of several factors. Inadequate interpersonal skills and inability to tolerate or reduce short-term stress are creative factors in building long-term stressful events. Equally inadequate social support networks may contribute to an inability to control negative environmental events. In turn, the absence of positive environmental supports further weakens the ability to develop needed capabilities. The resulting chronic, unrelenting nature of stressful events, combined with an initial low tolerance for such events and an inability to avoid such situations, lead almost inevitably to the experience of crisis events as overwhelming. It is this experience of being overwhelmed that is often the key in understanding the borderline woman's repetitive and seemingly determined tendency to parasuicide, threaten suicide, or engage in other impulsive, dysfunctional behaviors. Small events are the "straws that break the camel's back." Seemingly incomprehensible overreactions to apparently minor events, criticisms, losses, etc. become understandable when viewed against the backdrop of the helplessness in the face of chronic crises experienced by these women.

Inhibited Grieving Syndrome.   Balancing the tendency to be in perpetual crisis is the corresponding tendency to inhibit and block emotional experiences. Thus, the borderline woman often vacillates between intense overreaction and just as intense underreaction. One often finds a pattern of repetitive losses in the lives of these women, losses that have never been experienced adequately and integrated. It is as if these women inhibit the process of grieving. Such inhibition is understandable. We can only enter the grieving process if we are confident that it will someday, sometime end. We can "work through it," so to speak. It is not uncommon to hear these women say that they feel that if they ever do cry, they will never stop. Indeed, that is their common experience; the experience of not being able to control, or titrate, their own emotional experiences. In the face of such helplessness and lack of control, refusal to start the process is understandable. And perhaps wise. Thus, the task of the group therapist is to first help these women understand their inhibition and second offer realistic hope that they can indeed survive the process of grieving. Such realistic hope requires that the therapist both teach grieving skills and mobilize the group and herself to offer emotional support as well.

DIALECTICAL BEHAVIOR THERAPY

Dialectical Behavior Therapy has two overriding characteristics, a behavioral problem-solving focus and an emphasis on dialectical processes. The term dialectical is meant to convey the multiple tensions that co-exist and must be dealt with in doing therapy with severely suicidal and borderline patients. The overriding dialectic is that of the necessity of acceptance of the client as she is within the context of trying to teach her to change and be different than she is. The term behavior therapy is meant to convey the focus of the treatment on capability enhancement (skill-training), collaborative problem-solving (including functional analysis), contingency clarification, and the observable present.

The treatment is most closely related to cognitive-behavior therapies. However, there are substantial differences. The most notable ones are the emphasis on the relationship and the dialectical balance in Dialectical Behavior Therapy, as well as a belief, communicated to the client, that the emotional system is often the primary system and cannot always be readily accessed or changed by modifications in the cognitive system. In many respects, however, the treatment is similar to cognitive therapies. For example, several techniques used in Beck's cognitive therapy (Beck, Rush, Shaw, & Emery, 1979) are employed in Dialectical Behavior Therapy. Group therapy in Dialectical Behavior Therapy targets interpersonal effectiveness, emotional control, and distress tolerance in consecutive fashion. Interpersonal effectiveness training involves a mixed regimen of assertiveness, social skills, and interpersonal problem solving training. Emotional control training teaches a range of behavioral and cognitive strategies for reducing unwanted emotions. Distress tolerance training involves the systematic introduction to, and training in, self-observation, meditation, mindfulness, and various related techniques.

Dialectical Behavior Therapy Treatment Strategies

Dialectical Behavior Therapy is defined by a number of therapist strategies that guide the conduct of the therapy. Strategies are of three types: overriding strategies that apply to all aspects of therapeutic communication, basic strategies that are used to varying degrees in most sessions, and integrated strategies that are designed to deal with specific problematic situations that come up in the treatment of the borderline suicidal woman. The strategies are described below.

Overriding Strategies. 1. *Dialectical Strategies.* The essential component of the dialectic approach is the notion that all elements of reality are intimately interconnected. Constant change and, therefore, growth occur as a result of opposition between contradictory, but interacting forces (thesis and antithesis) and their continual reconciliation on a higher level (synthesis). From this perspective, every element in reality contains within it an opposing force, like two sides of a coin. The rigid adherence to either pole of the dialectic contributes to stagnation and inhibits change. The task of the therapist in Dialectical Behavior Therapy is to facilitate change by highlighting both aspects of the dialectical oppositions, and fostering their successive reconciliation and resolution at increasingly more functional levels for the individual client.

The dialectical focus in treatment involves two levels of therapeutic behavior. On the one hand, the therapist is always alert to the dialectical balance occurring within the treatment environment itself. Each group member, including the leader, is in a constant state of dialectical tension at many levels and in many directions. One tension is between each individual pair within the group, a tension that can become active at the moment of interaction between group members. Overlaying, so to speak, and influencing these two levels is a third dialectical tension between each individual and her individual environment, brought into the treatment situation via long-term memory and cognitive schemas. The group leader must be aware of the multiple tensions impinging on the therapy situation at any given time. Maintaining a therapeutic balance and moving the balance toward reconciliation and growth are the tasks of the group therapist.

The second level of focus is on teaching and modeling dialectical methods of reasoning in the individual case. The message communicated to the group is that "concerning every subject, opposite statements are possible." Thus, there is no absolute truth, and no rigid position is possible. The strategy involves direct teaching, questioning the individual group members to open up new avenues of thinking, offering alternative ways of thinking, and, most important, modeling dialectical thinking. Techniques include the use of paradox, story- and myth-telling, cognitive restructuring techniques (Goldfried, Decenteceo, & Weinberg, 1974), and the deliberate balancing of client extreme statements with the other extreme, while simultaneously taking the client's point of view.

2. *Irreverent Communication Strategy.* This strategy involves taking a very matter of fact attitude toward client's dysfunctional problem-solving attempts. Suicidal behaviors and other dysfunctional escape behaviors such as substance abuse, sexual promiscuity, terminating relationships, etc. are met by calmness and a clinically analytic attitude. Emotional reactions to such behaviors are at a minimum. As will be seen below in the validation strategies, however, use of this strategy is always employed in the context of the emotional validation strategies, where the client's suffering is never met with a matter of fact, indifferent attitude.

3. *Consultant Strategy.* This strategy requires that the group leader keep his/her role to that of a consultant to the client, rather than a consultant to other therapists that the client might have. If the client is in individual therapy independent of the group therapy, i.e., with another therapist in a different treatment setting, this policy generally involves limiting contact with the other therapist to those instances requested by the client. Although material taught in the group sessions can and usually should be shared with other therapists in contact with the client, the basic approach here is that the client is capable of performing this intermediary function between the different treating professionals. Thus, the group therapist does not play a parent role, assuming that the client is unable to communicate in a straightforward manner with each treatment agency. Difficulties that the individual experiences with other therapists can be dealt with in the group, if those difficulties are relevant to the skills being taught in the group. Thus, during the interpersonal effectiveness group, an individual might be helped to communicate more effectively with other professionals treating her. During the emotion control group, she might be helped to modulate her emotional reactions to these professionals. During distress tolerance groups she might be assisted in accepting and tolerating behaviors of other professionals that she finds difficult to understand or tolerate.

Basic Strategies. 1. *Validation Strategies.* Validation strategies are used in every group session in Dialectical Behavior Therapy. These strategies involve several components designed to help the client improve her sense of confidence in herself, decrease her need to look outside of herself for acceptance and validation, and let go of her often defensive and rigid hold on particular beliefs and emotional reactions. The first task in validation is helping group members identify their emotions, thoughts, and behavioral patterns. Secondly, the therapist communicates accurate empathy with a client's emotional tone, understanding of (though not necessarily agreement with) her beliefs, expectations, and assumptions, and clear observation of her behavioral patterns. Third, and most important, the therapist communicates that the client's behavior, emotional responses, and/or beliefs, assumptions, and expectancies are understandable and make sense in the context of her life. The therapist communicates clearly that all human reactions are caused, even though we often do not have access to the information needed to understand those causes.

This strategy is absolutely essential to Dialectical Behavior Therapy. It requires a nonjudgmental therapeutic attitude, where the therapist is constantly on the lookout for the essential validity of the client's responses. Thus, the therapist functions as the dialectical opposing pole to the self-invalidating environment experienced by the client. In the group sessions, this strategy means that the therapist always points out the truth inherent in client comments, even while simultaneously demonstrating the contradictory point of view. Conflict within the group and between individual group members and the therapist is dealt with by focusing on how both sides of the conflict can be validated, arriving at a resolution by integrating both points of view. Thus, conflict is resolved by a process of co-validation, rather than by invalidation of one side or the other.

2. *Relationship Strategies.* There are three types of relationship strategies: relationship enhancement, relationship problem-solving, and relationship generalization. Relationship enhancement requires that the therapist focus both on creating a positive therapist-group relationship and also on developing positive relationships and cohesion between group members. Therapists can convey expertness and credibility by sharing information about their background, training, and experience. Warmth and empathy are essential. At a minimum, this requires that the therapist express pleasure at seeing individual group members each week, keep track of at least major developments in their lives, and make every attempt to view and express life from the client's own point of view. Self-disclosure by therapists of current important events in their lives, especially if they influence in-session behavior, and of therapists' attempts to solve similar problems can be especially important in building a close therapist-group relationship. The attitude to be conveyed is that rather than being on a dif-

ferent life path altogether, the therapist is simply farther along on a life path in common with group members.

In our groups, we have used several strategies to induce group cohesiveness. First, we have a waiting room for group members where they collect before the group begins, an atmosphere conducive to conversation. One or two 15-minute breaks are given during each meeting and members generally congregate in the same waiting room. At the end of each session, group members are left alone for 10 to 15 minutes to "debrief." They are instructed to use this time any way they see fit so that they can leave the group feeling ready to face the next week. The clear message is that the group members, together, can help each other integrate the session and shift the emotional tone from the intensity generated by focus on life's problems to a lighter tone generated by self-directed conversation. There is respect for the enormous power in the group to heal each other. Finally, we encourage group members to bring snacks for the group, to give each other rides home, and, in general, to assist in problem-solving.

As with any treatment relationship, many problems will arise between both the group and the leader and between the individual group members. Problems between the group and therapist are discussed openly in group. In general, the therapist takes a problem-solving approach to such issues. It is essential that the therapist be prepared to change the structure, format, or other details of the group if necessary. Changes should be arrived at through a process of negotiation, with everyone encouraged to express openly their wishes and opposition to proposed solutions. It was this process that led to the development of our debriefing process and the institution of two breaks instead of one. In these situations, the leader should model the skills taught in the interpersonal effectiveness part of the group and encourage and reinforce group members' efforts to apply the same skills. In our groups, we have not dealt with individual conflict between group members or between individual participants and the leader during the group meeting itself. Instead, breaks and the 15 minutes before and after group are used for this purpose. However, the same strategies are used during these more private meetings. During the first year, time used for attending to group problem-solving has to be balanced with the need to attend to teaching the skills relevant to each group module. After the first year of therapy, however, more time can be spent practicing the skills within the context of the group process itself.

Relationship generalization strategies involve the attempt to relate problems encountered in the group to those encountered outside the group. Many opportunities are available. Tendencies to miss sessions, not do homework, avoid discussing problems, maintain privacy and distrust, feel ashamed, and react oversensitively to the therapist and other members, for example, are excellent opportunities for discussing how similar behavior patterns lead to difficulties outside of sessions.

3. *Problem-Solving Strategies.* Aversive life situations presented by the clients are treated by the therapist as problems that can be solved, even if the solution only means a new way of adapting to life as it is, i.e., problem acceptance rather than problem-solving and change. The first step in problem-solving requires the therapist to assist the client in identifying the problem causing distress. The second step in problem-solving, or addressing any new target behavior, is a thorough behavioral analysis of the problem. The therapist works with the group members in generating and evaluating hypotheses about variables influencing or controlling the problematic situation or behaviors in question. Finally, solutions must be actively generated by group members, evaluated, and tried. An important part of each group module is teaching these principles as they relate to the specific topic—interpersonal effectiveness, emotion control, distress tolerance—of the respective group module. In addition, problem-solving strategies form the backbone of the therapeutic response to client noncompliance, especially in carrying out homework assignments.

4. *Capability Enhancement Strategies.* The term skill or capability in Dialectical Behavior Therapy is used in its broadest sense, including those cognitive, affective, and overt behavioral (action) skills, together with their integration, that are necessary for effective performance. The first task in capability enhancement is response acquisition. Strategies here include task overview, instructions, and modeling. The first group sessions should provide a task overview, including precise information about what is to be learned as well as a clarification of the conceptual model within which the learning will take place. Instructions consist of verbal guidelines describing the response components to be learned. They can vary from general guidelines to very specific suggestions as to what the person should do or think. They can be presented in a didactic lecture format, they can be suggested as hypotheses to be considered as thesis and antithesis to be synthesized, or they can be drawn from the members utilizing a Socratic method of discourse. Modeling can then be provided by the therapist in the form of role-playing, self-disclosure, videos, storytelling, or focusing the members' attention on models in their natural environment or within the group.

Once information on a skill is acquired, the next task is response shaping and strengthening. Procedures here include behavioral rehearsal, response reinforcement, and feedback and coaching. For learning interpersonal skills, behavioral rehearsal can take place via role-playing between group members or between members and the therapist. If members are inhibited in role-playing, we have found it useful to go around the group, each member giving only one response in an interaction with the therapist. The task is to either advance a role-play dialogue with the therapist or give another example of using the particular skill under discussion. Emotion control skills can be practiced via developing imagined situations in the group. The difficulty of finding common situations to practice on, the reticence of this population to relax and enter imagined scenes in a group setting, and the difficulty of creating nonartificial practice situations, however, makes in-session rehearsal very difficult. In distress tolerance groups, meditation techniques can be practiced in group. The distress of sitting through long group sessions also offers an opportunity for practice.

After in-session practice exercises and during discussion of self-reported attempts to practice skills between sessions, the therapist must closely attend to the client's behavior and provide appropriate reinforcement, feedback, and coaching. Praise is one of the most powerful techniques in shaping and strengthening skilled behavior. Frequently, borderline and suicidal individuals have lived in environments that stress punishment over praise. They often expect negative, punishing feedback from the world in general and utilize self-punishing strategies almost exclusively in trying to shape their own behavior. Therapist praise can serve both to modify the patient's self-image in a positive manner as well as increase the frequency of skilled behavior. In response feedback and coaching, the therapist combines praise with gentle and flexible suggestions about alternate approaches to the situation.

Response transfer and generalization is facilitated primarily by the assignment of between-session homework that requires the practice of skills in the clients' natural environments. At the end of every session, the therapist suggests ways to practice the skills being learned. Homework recording pages are also given out, both as a reminder of the skill to be practiced and as a form to record the event so that it can be shared with the group the next week. At the beginning of each session, the first hour or so is spent going over each member's attempt to practice her skills during the preceding week.

Finally, it is important that the therapist manage the contingencies occuring in the therapy. The therapist must keep a close eye on individual participant's behavior and attempt to respond such that skilled behaviors are reinforced and nonskilled behaviors are not. The rules here, however, are not rigid. Room must be made for shaping and for letting warmth and caring, at times, supercede immediate behavioral consequences.

5. *Reality Testing/Contingency Clarification Strategies.* These strategies involve giving the client information about what she can reasonably expect from the therapist and group, information about the process and re-

quirements of the therapy, as well as information about factors known to influence behavior in general, and theories and data that might cast light on group members' particular behavior patterns. Essentially, these strategies require the therapist to assume the role of active teacher. They should always be employed when a group member is (a) violating the therapy contract or is threatening to (e.g., does not come to group meetings), (b) is threatening suicide or other dysfunctional behaviors, (c) appears to be making unrealistic demands or has unrealistic expectations of the therapist or group, or (d) is having difficulty using therapy appropriately, e.g., does not talk in sessions or characteristically does not attempt homework.

Integrated Strategies. Integrated strategies are simply combinations of basic strategies to deal with special problems likely to occur in treating borderline and parasuicidal women. The therapeutic situations include noncompliance, suicidal behavior and threats, and crises. A special problem in group skill-training is that of noncompliance with homework assignments. In our experience, it can take up to six months for clients to learn to actively practice skills during the week. Persistent use of problem-solving strategies, contingency management (attending every week to each individual and her progress in homework practice), attention to any relationship problems that may be interfering with group cooperation with treatment, and clarification of the importance of practice can be effective here if applied with vigor and without fail.

Session Format. In my current program, I offer the modules sequentially in eight-week blocks. Women stay in the program for at least one year and, therefore, participate in each module twice. After the one-year program, a continuing, supportive-expressive group therapy is available to help integrate and reinforce the continued application of newly learned skills. There are any number of formats for conducting skill-training groups. In my program, sessions meet for one three-hour session weekly. The first hour of each session is devoted to going over each group member's homework (and reasons why homework was not done). The remaining part of the session is devoted to presenting new material, behavior rehearsal, and discussing how the new skills might be used in each participant's daily life. One or two 15-minute breaks are planned.

Group Content. The content for each group by approximate week of presentation is listed in Tables 11.1–11.3 below. Much of the content for the interpersonal skills module (Table 11.1) is drawn from Linehan and Egan

TABLE 11.1 Interpersonal Skill Training

Week	Content
1	Introduction to the group: introductions, task overview, structure of the group, role of interpersonal problems in our lives
2	Determining priorities in interpersonal situations: analyzing the situation and what we want
3	The role of cognitive inhibition in interpersonal problems: thoughts that contribute to effectiveness, those that interfere, and how to challenge them
4–5	Skills useful in obtaining one's objective or goal in an interpersonal interaction: how to ask for what I want or need, say no clearly and resist pressure, stay focused, look confident
6	Skills useful in maintaining a good relationship during an interpersonal interaction or conflict: how to care skillfully, look interested, be nondemanding, be diplomatic
7	Skills useful in maintaining self-respect during interpersonal conflicts: general skills, how to ask for what I want or need with self-respect, say no and resist pressure with self-respect
8	Integration of skills and ending the group

TABLE 11.2 Emotion Regulation

Week	Content
1	Introduction to the group: introductions, task overview, structure of the group, role of unwanted emotions in our lives, myths about emotions
2	Understanding emotions: the role of prompting events, mental work (appraisal), body/chemical change, action tendencies, and automatic brain reactions in emotions; learning to observe and identify emotions
3–5	Steps for reducing intense emotions: reducing emotional vulnerability, observing and getting distance, experiencing the emotion (flooding, systematic desensitization), distraction techniques, problem solving the prompting event, leaving the situation
6–7	Steps for reducing intense emotions: challenging thoughts, assumptions and beliefs, confronting thinking in extremes, thinking either-or, thinking judgmentally, thinking magically, thinking rigid, cutting off one's nose to spite one's face
8	Integration of skills and ending the group

TABLE 11.3 Distress-Tolerance/Reality-Acceptance

Week	Content
1–4	Accepting reality: learning to self-observe via meditation, observing nonjudgmentally, practicing mindfulness, and entertaining the notion of a radical acceptance of reality
5–7	Tolerating distress: thinking tolerant, thinking future, diverting, focusing on the positive, finding meaning, blocking

(1979, 1983). Contents for all three modules (Tables 11.1, 11.2, and 11.3) are described fully in Linehan (1984).

REFERENCES

Adler, G. (1985). *Borderline psychopathology and its treatment.* New York: Aronson.

American Psychiatric Association. (1980). *Diagnostic and statistical manual of mental disorders* (3rd ed.). Washington, DC.

Beck, A. T., Rush, A. J., Shaw, B. F., & Emery, G. (1979). *Cognitive therapy of depression.* New York: The Guilford Press.

Berent, I. (1981). *The algebra of suicide.* New York: Human Sciences Press.

Cantor, P. C. (1976). Personality characteristics found amoung youthful female suicide attempters. *Journal of Abnormal Psychology, 85*(3), 324–329.

Crook, T., Raskin, A., & Davis, D. (1975). Factors associated with attempted suicide among hospitalized depressed patients. *Psychological Medicine, 5*(2), 381–388.

Crumley, F. (1979). Adolescent suicide attempts. *Journal of American Medical Association, 241,* 2404–2407.

Dublin, L. (1963). *Suicide: A sociological and statistical study.* New York: Ronald Press.

Goldfried, M. R., Decenteceo, E. T., & Weinberg, L. (1974). Systematic rational restructuring as a self-control technique. *Behavior Therapy, 5*(2), 247–254.

Goodstein, J. (1982). Cognitive characteristics of suicide attempters. (Doctoral dissertation, The Catholic University of America, 1982.) *Dissertation Abstracts International, 43,* 1613B.

Graff, H., & Mallin, R. (1967). This syndrome of the wrist cutter. *American Journal of Psychiatry, 124,* 74–79.

Grunebaum, H., & Klerman, G. (1967). Wrist slashing. *American Journal of Psychiatry, 124,* 524–534.

Gunderson, J. G. (1984). *Borderline personality disorder.* Washington, DC: American Psychiatric Press, Inc.

Hawton, K. (1979). Domiciliary and outpatient treatment following deliberate self-poisoning. In R. Farmer & S. R. Hirsch (Eds.), *The suicide syndrome*. London: Croom Helm.

Hawton, K., & Catalan, J. (1982). *Attempted suicide: A practical guide to its nature and management*. New York: Oxford University Press.

Kennedy, P. (1972). Efficacy of a regional poison treatment centre. *British Medical Journal, IV*, 255–257.

Kernberg, O. F. (1984). *Severe personality disorder*. London: Yale University Press.

Levenson, M., & Neuringer, C. (1971). Problem-solving behavior in suicidal adolescents. *Journal of Consulting and Clinical Psychology, 37*(3), 433–436.

Linehan, M. M. (1971). Towards a theory of sex differences in suicidal behavior. *Crisis Intervention, 3*, 93–101.

Linehan, M. M. (1981). A social-behavioral analysis of suicide and parasuicide: Implications for clinical assessment and treatment. In H. Glazer & J. F. Clarkin (Eds.), *Depression: Behavioral and directive intervention strategies*. New York: Garland Press.

Linehan, M. M. (1984). *Dialectical behavior therapy for treatment of parasuicidal women: Treatment manual*. University of Washington, Seattle, WA.

Linehan, M. M., Camper, P., Chiles, J. A., Strosahl, K., & Shearin, E. (in press). Interpersonal problem-solving and parasuicide. *Journal of Cognitive Research and Therapy*.

Linehan, M. M., Chiles, J. A., Devine, R. H., Luffaw, J. A., & Egan, K. A. (1987). Presenting problems of parasuicides versus suicide ideators and non-suicidal psychiatric patients. *Journal of Consulting and Clinical Psychology*.

Linehan, M. M., & Egan, K. (1979). Assertion training for women. In A. S. Bellack & M. Hersen (Eds.), *Research and practice in social skills training*. New York: Plenum.

Linehan, M. M., & Egan, K. J. (1983). *Succeeding socially*. London: Lifecycle Publications.

Masterson, J. F. (1976). *Psychotherapy of the borderline adult*. New York: Brunner-Mazel.

McGlashan, T. H. (1986). The chestnut lodge follow-up study. *Archives of General Psychiatry, 43*(1), 20–30.

Neuringer, C. (1961). Dichotomous evaluations in suicidal individuals. *Journal of Consulting Psychology, 25*, 445–449.

Neuringer, C., & Lettieri, D. J. (1982). *Suicidal women*. New York: Gardner Press, Inc.

Richman, J., & Charles, E. (1976). Patient dissatisfaction and attempted suicide. *Community Mental Health Journal, 12*(3), 301–305.

Shneidman, E. S. (1971, June). You and death. *Psychology Today*, pp. 43–45, 74–80.

Warden, J. W., & Sterling-Smith, R. S. (1973). Lethality patterns in multiple suicide attempts. *Life Threatening Behavior, 3*, 95–104.

Weissman, M., Fox, K., & Klerman, G. L. (1973). Hostility and depression associated with suicide attempts. *American Journal of Psychiatry, 130*(4), 450–455.

■ 12
Cognitive-Behavioral Group Therapy for Women

JANET L. WOLFE

The change in female roles in the past 15 years, along with the overrepresentation of women in certain psychological disorders, has pointed to a need for therapy approaches better geared to helping women with the practical and emotional problems they face as they attempt the transition into more effective functioning. Rational-emotive therapy (RET), along with other cognitive behavior therapies, provides an effective and well-defined self-help system for dealing with women's three biggest issues: (1) enhancing self-acceptance, (2) learning personal effectiveness skills, and (3) dealing with frustration and anger.

RET AND FEMINIST THERAPY

Leading rational-emotive therapists specializing in sex role issues include Oliver (1977); Russianoff (1982); Walen (1983); Wolfe (1975, 1980, 1985); and Zachary (1980). Working at the Institute for Rational-Emotive Therapy in New York City, the author has developed a broad spectrum program for women (Wolfe, 1985), including ongoing women's therapy groups; six-session groups in assertiveness, effectiveness, and sexuality; and one-day workshops dealing with self-acceptance, life-cycle change, habit control (weight, procrastination); and mother-daughter communications.

Institute staff have also done collaborative groups with various women's organizations, including the National Organization for Women (NOW) and a program to train minority women in the building trades.

RET teaches women how to define their problems, identify the variables that influence their present feelings and actions, and to alter both their behavior and the environment in positive ways. More than any other school of therapy, RET seems to come closest to meeting the criteria for effective feminist therapy: (1) it deals with the shoulds, musts, self-rating, and "love-slobbism" inherent in female sex role messages and provides a concrete method for disputing them; (2) it helps women to stop condemning themselves for their emotional disturbances and maladaptive behaviors; (3) it does not label assertiveness as masculine striving; (4) it encourages autonomy through client involvement in goal-setting and self-therapy; (5) it shows women how to stop depressing themselves about their frustrations with a society that is not sex-fair and how to fight determinedly for social systems change—a component often lacking in most therapies (Blechman, 1980).

KEY COMPONENTS IN RET WOMEN'S GROUPS

Before describing a case study, the general themes that occur in all types of RET women's groups will be outlined.

Consciousness-Raising

Whether a workshop or an ongoing therapy group, relevant sex-role socialization messages that interfere with women's self-actualization are identified and examined. These socialization messages are seen as a sort of "primordial soup" in which irrational beliefs abound.

In an ongoing group, these messages may get elicited in a go-around on early messages from parents ("Be sweet . . . don't act too smart") or from media images ("You must be thin, young, and beautiful to be worthwhile"). Members may from time to time be assigned feminist literature on marriage and other topics.

In a six-session sexuality group, an experiential exercise is done in which women call out names for women who are sexually active (slut, whore, tramp); names for men who are sexually active (Don Juan, swinger); names for women who are sexually selective (prude, uptight, dyke); and general "nasty names" for men (pussywhipped, faggot, mama's boy). The group then "analyzes" the data, drawing from it the insight that there is a highly prejudiced, double standard for men and women; that women are damned if they do and damned if they don't; that men are labeled "good" for the same acts for which women are labeled "bad"; and that the worst thing you can say to a man is to derogate him by associating him with womanhood (Walen & Wolfe, 1983).

Goal-Setting

Group members, collaborating with the therapist, learn to set their own goals, breaking them down into cognitive, emotive, and behavioral goals. They thereby receive practice in counteracting passivity and dependency, in defining their own life plans instead of waiting for white knights to come along and plan for them. The women may be asked to set up and review three-month plans, and to do time projections up to the age of 90.

Cognitive Restructuring

The core work in the groups is combatting the cognitive castigation that women usually impose on themselves. RET, a therapy approach developed over 30 years ago (Ellis, 1956), offers a well-defined personality theory and system of therapy. It provides an excellent means for carrying out the very important task of psyche-strengthening—helping women change an "I'm helpless and worthless" belief system to one of optimism and self-acceptance. RET also provides help with developing better coping responses to the "real world" by teaching women to strengthen frustration tolerance and, in particular, to handle their anxiety and rage.

Through mini-lectures and demonstrations on individual members, group members are taught Ellis's cognitive analysis system (Ellis, 1962; Ellis & Harper, 1975). The rationale for this approach, they are told, is that by learning to identify their irrational cognitions, they will develop the power to greatly modify their emotional and behavioral reactions. In RET, A stands for an Activating event (son gets bad conduct demerits in school). Point C is the dysfunctional Consequence (anxiety, depression, self-downing, anger). The focal point of cognitive therapy is B—the irrational Beliefs that the individual has about the event ("If my child fails, I'm a bad mother; if I'm a bad mother, I'm a hopeless failure and my kid will probably end up a failure as well"). Feeling inadequate and depressed, this mother will probably start interacting poorly with her child. Her impaired performance may then lead her on to more irrational beliefs ("I can't do anything right") and will enhance her feelings of anxiety and depression.

Group members are taught to keep records of key problem situations that occurred during the week and of their internal dialogues and self-talk that mediated their upset reactions. The bulk of the session time is spent in helping members identify irrational beliefs and teaching them to vigorously challenge or dispute their beliefs and replace them with more rational self-messages.

Whether the group is an ongoing one or a one-day workshop, the basic tenets of RET are taught and handouts such as a list of "Irrational beliefs that cause disturbance" (Ellis & Harper, 1975) are distributed. Members are taught to differentiate their dysfunctional emotional reactions (anxiety, depression, rage, guilt) from appropriate negative reactions (apprehension, sadness, annoyance, regret). They are taught the four common forms of irrational or self-defeating thinking that lead to psychological disturbance (Ellis & Bernard, 1985): (1) worthlessness ("I am a worthless person if I don't always perform well or am not approved of by all significant others"); (2) awfulizing ("It is awful, terrible, or horrible if I make a mistake or things do not go as I wish"); (3) I can't-stand-it-itis ("I can't stand the things that are happening to me; they must not happen!"); (4) allness or unrealistic overgeneralization ("Because I failed at the important task that I should not have failed at, I'll always fail and never succeed").

Beck's list of cognitive distortions (Burns, 1980) are sometimes given to clients as another way to help them identify and challenge irrational thinking.

A major cognitive focus is on self-acceptance and acceptance of the now; these are seen as crucial precursors to helping members change other attitudes or learn new skills. By self-acceptance we mean acceptance of oneself as a fallible human being, acceptance of one's partner or significant others, and acceptance of reality. Very commonly, women may be blaming themselves heavily or blaming others for not doing what they want them to do. The resultant emotions, whether anger or depression, are incompatible with good functioning. Once this nondemanding philosophy is accepted, group members can move forward far more efficiently.

Another very important cognitive focus is on changing dysfunctionally high levels of frustration and anger to more appropriate levels of annoyance or "rational anger." In a world that is not fair to women, women have two choices: to beome paralyzed with rage or to reduce it and determinedly set out to problem-solve and try to change what can be changed. A woman heatedly describing what a "male chauvinist bastard" her boss is, is first helped to "antiawfulize" and arrive at more rational counter-messages: "I don't like his behavior, but I can stand it; he is not a rotten condemnable person for acting in this poor way." Unlocked from her rage, she has more options available to her: to choose not to respond or to respond in a calm and assertive fashion, and then possibly go to the personnel department or to an organization designed to handle problems of sex discrimination and harassment.

To aid in the difficult task of changing long-practiced irrational cognitions, homework assignments are given, such as disputing the idea that everyone you are interested in must like you or visualizing, every time you get enraged, "stop demanding." Self-help forms may be given to members to help them more efficiently identify and dispute irrational beliefs related to specific situations. Bibliotherapy is also prescribed: for example, reading chapters on self-acceptance and frustration tolerance in *A guide to rational living* (Ellis & Harper, 1975). Or an "empty chair" technique may be assigned, in which the member first sits in one chair, voicing aloud her irrational self-talk, then moves to another empty chair opposite her and argues against her self-defeating beliefs. The process is repeated until the rational beliefs are stronger and more internalized.

Behavioral Techniques

RET is classified as a cognitive-behavioral approach. Because one way to feel better and to reinforce attitude change is to behave differently, group members are encouraged to practice new behaviors and challenge themselves with new behavioral risks both within the group sessions (e.g., asking for help or clarification) and in homework assignments. Perhaps the most important behavioral skill area is assertiveness training, to which as much as one-third to one-half of the session time may be devoted. Assertiveness training is seen as constituting a major remediation for females' passive and dependent behaviors. Assignments are given to help members combat their fears of taking risks and of being disapproved of by others, and to replace their habits of learned helplessness with ones designed to increase personal effectiveness.

Members are regularly encouraged to take risks and push themselves into previously avoided situations and behaviors, beginning with less anxiety-evoking ones first and working their way up to more difficult ones. These situations often are ones they can all identify with: asking questions of your gynecologist or car mechanic or seeking out the company of people you are intimidated by (without comparing yourself or putting yourself down). Frequently, members rehearse these situations in imagery, along with coping self-statements to counter anxiety or self-downing about failure or negative reactions.

Other behavioral techniques used regularly include the following: (1) making a contract with the group—for example, agreeing to make three positive statements about herself each session and participate in the discussion of another member's problems at least once per session; (2) to reinforce such assignments, *operant techniques* are sometimes used; for example, a woman may allow herself to do something she really loves to do (such as watching the evening news) only after she has fulfilled her assignment (talking to her boss about a raise; (3) shame-attacking exercises (doing some nonnormative social behavior, such as loudly calling out the stops on a bus, in order to help desensitize herself to her fears of social disapproval; (4) behavioral monitoring—keeping a record of target behaviors, such as the number of times per day that she thinks self-downing thoughts or asserts herself; and (5) practicing RET on a friend or relative as a way of helping strengthen her own rational thinking.

Emotive Techniques

Emotive techniques employed in the groups include (1) self-disclosure (telling the group the thing the member is most ashamed of, for example); (2) empathy or sharing personal feelings with other members; (3) rational-emotive imagery (closing one's eyes and imagining oneself in a situation feeling very upset e.g., being dumped by your lover), then working on reducing one's feelings of upset and changing them to more appropriate ones, such as disappointment or sadness). Usually this process is achieved by changing cognitions; the exercise is practiced twice a day for 10 minutes).

Therapist Role-Modeling

Because of the dearth of self-accepting and achieving female role models in women's lives, therapist modeling and self-disclosure can provide an important model of women who have overcome their programming and are successful at acting in self-reinforcing ways. For example, a client struggling to achieve greater autonomy from her husband may benefit from a description of how the therapist and her spouse handle their finances.

Participants as Role Models

Additional role-modeling is provided by encouraging group members to share how they achieved emotional or behavioral mastery of previous problem areas. This offers another source of effective role modeling and also helps the group members to give themselves credit for their successes as an antidote to their usual overfocusing on their flaws.

Use of Humor

Humor and a playful, belly-laughing atmosphere reinforce RET's emphasis on combatting misery by not taking life's inevitable hassles overly seriously.

Humor is also an efficient way of helping the women realize some of the absurdity of their socialization messages. The group members are never the butt of a joke, although their cognitive distortions may be.

Focus on Self-Nurturance

A large percentage of women have especially well-developed "flaw-detecting kits" and are practically addicted to self-downing (Russianoff, 1982). Women are regularly given assignments to write or recite to their mirror three positive traits or behaviors each day, or to "brag" aloud—first to the therapist and other group membes, and then to do so to others in their social environment. Another type of assignment may be a self-pleasuring assignment, designed to combat cognitively and behaviorally the "put others first" and "I must not be selfish" sex-role messages. These beliefs are especially strong in those who are deeply embedded in their roles as wives and mothers. Such women define their role as that of taking care of other people and have often grossly neglected the habit of doing nice things for themselves. Homework assignments such as taking time for a long bubble bath, buying oneself flowers, getting a massage, or having caviar and cognac in front of a fire by oneself are useful means for reinforcing the idea that "I have a right to do nice things for myself." At the same time, group members are learning to give themselves the kinds of stroking often expected only from males.

Encouragement of Female Friendships

Women frequently use the term "relationship" as synonymous with heterosexual sex-love relationships (e.g., "I haven't had a relationship for years!") and, in so doing, negate or minimize the value and importance of female friendships. Friendships with women are encouraged as fine ways for women to get caring, loving, sharing, support, intimacy, and nurturance into their lives—whether or not they are involved in a sex-love relationship. As women learn to value themselves, they learn to value other women, and as they learn to appreciate other women, they come to appreciate themselves more. Strong friendships often grow among the women in the groups and are greatly encouraged; they provide peer therapy for reinforcing rational thinking, as well as models for loving and energizing relationships that help wean women away from their conviction that the only valuable affectional relationships are with men.

TABLE 12.1 Case Study of Gena

Session no.	Key issues	Cognitive assignments	Behavioral assignments
1	23-year-old secretary. Massively self-downing. Two-year relationship with "inconsiderate, domineering man." Angry at self for staying in job with a volatile and critical boss.	Read at least half of (short) assertiveness book, *Project You: A Manual of Rational Assertiveness Training* (Paris & Casey, 1976). Dispute idea that "I must be a worthless person if people treat me so badly." Give self message that "I have the right to express my feelings and to ask for more respectful treatment."	After rehearsing first in group, request of lover that he call her in advance if he is going to be late.
2	Began report by comparing self negatively to other group members, announcing self as "the group failure." When reminded she was not supposed to be perfectly assertive in one week, it emerged that she had asserted herself with boss when she yelled at her, but did not "count" that.	Give self three positive messages each day. Dispute idea that "I cannot effectively respond" and "I am a weak, wimpy person." Continue reading book.	Listen to relaxation tape three times and use procedure before next assertiveness attempt with lover. Practice less-anxiety-potentiating situations (asking for $1 worth of gas in a gas station; saying "no" to an unreasonable request).
3	Completed relaxation practice and expressed to lover her frustration at his lateness and lack of responsiveness to her feelings. Got angry at his hostile response and wanted to break up but afraid of doing so.	(To counter escalation into rage when lover responded to badly): Tell self that "he is not a rotten person for behaving badly—just a highly fallible human being." Dispute idea that "I'm a bad person for staying in this situation."	Re-do again in group, in a more self-crediting way her announcement to the group that she had spoken to her lover and that she and her boss had had a good talk about ways of setting job priorities. Continue to request of lover changes in his behavior.

170

4	Arrived in group more relaxed than in previous sessions. Spoke to lover about giving her more clitoral stimulation, since she never orgasmed with him, and credited herself (without qualifications, for the first time). Getting impatient about other of her lover's behaviors.	Dispute belief that "it's awful when things don't go my way right away;" that "I am an inadequate person if I can't get my lover to treat me better;" and that "I couldn't stand it if my lover left me."	Continue to give feedback to lover about her wishes and feelings and attempt to keep her assertions from escalating into rage. Go to party and talk to three interesting-looking people (to get practice in initiating relationships should she decide to leave her lover).
5	Continued to report positives and to talk about negatives without attacking self. Asked for and got more sexual stimulation, and let self enjoy it even though she did not achieve orgasm.	Read *Intelligent Women's Guide to Dating and Mating* (Ellis, 1979) and dispute idea that she "couldn't stand it" if she didn't have a man in her life.	Go to one event alone or with a woman friend. Continue to assert self with lover and boss. "Brag" about self three times this week about something good she has done.
6	Reported in enthusiastic, positive terms first orgasm with partner. Confronted him (without anger) about not calling to let her know he was going to be late, and he responded well. "He's really changing... listens more."	Continue to remind self that "I have the right to express my feelings and to make mistakes" and that "my lover's not acting the way I want does not make me a worthless person."	Continue reading *Intelligent Woman's Guide*. Continue behaving assertively with lover, boss, and others. Speak to boss about job advancement. Complete a written exercise on her work skills and interest (to brainstorm possible new career options).

Focus on Environmental Resources and Societal Change

RET women's groups go beyond the traditional boundaries of therapy and include all efforts and resources that can be mustered to provide women with corrective socialization experiences, new options, and tools for institutional or societal change. A woman may be encouraged to contact an organization that provides help with sexual harrassment or to set up a meeting in her building to discuss pooled daycare. Extensive lists of resources, including battered women's shelters, women's professional organizations, and nonsexist gynecologists are kept by feminist rational therapists to help women work at changing some of the societal conditions they have successfully "antiawfulized" about.

CASE STUDY

Table 12.1 indicates week-by-week work with Gena, a member of a six-session assertiveness group that combined RET and behavioral practice.

SUMMARY

To function effectively in the complex environments of today requires a variety of skills, realistic self-appraisal, and self-acceptance. Women traditionally have been discouraged in their efforts to develop the kinds of behaviors and attitudes that promote optimal functioning. Cognitive behavior therapy and RET in particular teach women how to set their own goals, how to conceptualize and solve practical and emotional problems, handle anger, and increase self-acceptance. RET women's groups offer a highly effective model for women's self-empowerment and growth.

REFERENCES

Blechman, E. (1980). Ecological sources of dysfunction in women: Issues and implications for clinical behavior therapy. *Clinical Behavior Therapy Review*, 2(1), 1–18.

Burns, D. (1980). *Feeling good: The new mood therapy.* New York: New American Library.

Ellis, A. (1956, August). *Rational psychotherapy.* Paper presented at the session on "Recent Innovations in Psychotherapeutic Strategy" at the American Psychological Association Convention, Chicago.

Ellis, A. (1962). *Reason and emotion in psychotherapy.* Secaucus, NJ: Citadel Press.

Ellis, A. (1979). *The intelligent woman's guide to dating and mating.* Secaucus, NJ: Citadel Press.

Ellis, A., & Bernard, M. (1985). What is rational-emotive therapy (RET)? In A. Ellis & M. Bernard (Eds.), *Clinical applications of rational-emotive therapy.* New York: Plenum Press.

Ellis, A., & Harper, R. (1975). *A guide to rational living.* North Hollywood, CA: Wilshire Books.

Oliver, R. (1977). The 'empty nest syndrome' as a focus of depression: A cognitive treatment model based on rational-emotive therapy. *Psychotherapy: Theory, Research, and Practice, 14*(1), 87–94.

Paris, C., & Casey, B. (1976). *Project you: A manual of rational assertiveness training.* Vancouver, WA: Bridges Press.

Russianoff, P. (1982). *Why do I think I'm nothing without a man?* New York: Bantam.

Walen, S., & Wolfe, J. (1983). Sexual enhancement groups for women. In A. Freeman (Ed.), *Cognitive therapy with couples and groups* New York: Plenum Press.

Wolfe, J. (1975, August). *Rational-emotive therapy as an effective feminist therapy.* Paper presented at the American Psychological Association Convention, Chicago.

Wolfe, J. (1980, September). *Rational-emotive therapy in women's groups.* Paper presented at the American Psychological Association Convention, Montreal, Canada.

Wolfe, J. (1985). Women. In A. Ellis & M. Bernard (Eds.), *Applications of rational-emotive therapy* . New York: Plenum Press.

Zachary, I. (1980). RET with women: Some special issues. In R. Grieger & J. Boyd (Eds.), *Rational-emotive therapy: A skills based approach.* New York: Van Nostrand.

■ four
SPECIAL PROBLEMS AND POPULATIONS OF WOMEN

■ 13
Group Treatment for the Homeless and Chronic Alcoholic Woman

BARBARA J. GRAHAM and MARSHA M. LINEHAN

This chapter will address two problem areas for women that often overlap with those of men: alcoholism and homelessness. Both are areas that have a paucity of information on treatment, specifically with women. We will include a brief review of the literature and then describe a group treatment strategy that we have found useful in working with homeless women, with emphasis on problems with alcoholism. The chapter is directed towards helping the clinician who is interested in working with women who obviously do not have the resources of the average middle-class therapy client but who, nonetheless, can benefit from a therapeutic milieu. We believe these women can provide the clinician with a rewarding and satisfying work experience. It is a population of women that can appear intimidating and discouraging, but it is our contention that group treatment is a viable approach toward helping such women begin to take the steps to improve their living conditions and that progress can be made. Clinicians might be required to examine their treatment goals and criteria for treatment success but, within such limitations, should find it possible to justify involvement with a segment of women who currently receive very little professional attention, even though they perhaps could most benefit from interactions with highly skilled and trained clinicians.

DOWN AND OUT

"Down and out." Three words that convey much in the way of human misery and hopelessness. Add to that phrase the word "woman" and it would seem difficult to imagine anyone with fewer advantages, certainly in our culture. Currently, if we are to believe the media, down-and-out women are receiving a great deal of attention and therefore help from the rest of society. Articles appear in the popular press about displaced homemakers, battered wives, the aged female, single mothers, and the rise in the numbers of alcohol- and drug-addicted women. Add to these, feature articles about the chronically mentally ill and homeless, many of whom are female, and one would imagine that women, as evidenced by all this attention, have finally found their place in society. It would logically follow that their problems are also receiving the serious attention they deserve. One is left with the comforting notion that a woman with few or no resources, faced with turning to our accepted cultural institutions for assistance would no longer have to worry about being doubly disadvantaged by virtue of her gender. This is what the general reader might start to believe is the case. It is disturbing therefore to undertake a review of the social science literature in some of the above-mentioned areas and to continually find researchers decrying the serious lack of research in general (much less well-designed and controlled studies) that would address the specific concerns of women particularly when the problems overlap with those of men.

ALCOHOLIC WOMAN

It has been estimated that 7% of the general United States population has alcohol-related problems and that approximately 20% of these are women, with the numbers increasing as it becomes more and more acceptable for women in our culture to drink (Beckman, 1975; Kay, 1985). To date most research in alcoholism has been done on males with the assumption that the findings could be generalized to the female alcoholic population. This state of affairs changed somewhat in the early 1970s. The concurrent interest in feminism provided a climate that encouraged the examination of a sexist bias in scientific research, and a larger proportion of government funding was earmarked for studies of alcoholism that related to women in particular. This research is, for the most part, still in the early descriptive stages, a necessary condition in order to provide a solid base from which to design further studies with better controls. Despite the early financial limitations, thoughtful researchers have provided useful information that can help the clinician formulate appropriate strategies. Corrigan (1974) found that women alcoholics tend to be much more secretive about their drinking than males. They most frequently drink alone rather than in the social settings of bars and even when at home tend to drink when no one else is present. Corrigan theorized this could partially be the result of the greater social disapproval the female alcoholic experiences, not only from others, but from herself. The fact that alcoholism is frequently viewed as a moral problem and women are expected to have higher moral standards than men in our culture and the lack of information about the physical effects of alcohol dependence, according to Corrigan (1980), all contribute to the differential effects of alcoholism in women. In general, the accepted thinking on women and alcoholism has been that women have a later onset of uncontrolled drinking and a more rapid progression than men. They have fewer legal difficulties as a result of their drinking behavior, are less likely to lose jobs as a result of drinking, and are less likely to be hospitalized with medical complications that result from drinking (Tamerin, Tolor, & Harrington, 1976). Curlee (1970) concluded that women alcoholics exhibit a greater degree of psychiatric dysfunction than males, although it is unclear whether this is representative of a true difference between men or women or the fact that women are generally much more open in talking about their emotional concerns. Women alcoholics tend to have a higher incidence of depression than male alcoholics (Schuckit, 1972).

An area that has received considerable attention is the notion that women drink for very different reasons than men. Wilsnack (1976) after reviewing the literature and conducting her own independent studies concluded that women who drink often have problems with sex-role identification. Drinking is seen as a way for women to increase their feelings of femininity, which for these women is somewhat diminished. Other researchers have concluded that female alcoholics can more frequently identify a specific life stressor that triggered their problem drinking as opposed to males who can less readily name a specific starting point. For women, these stressors are more frequently linked to problems with relationships (Schuckit & Morrissey, 1976). Curlee (1967) also observed that the wives of male alcoholics tended to stay with their husbands, whereas the husbands of alcoholic wives tended to leave them, particularly once the wives started treatment. Tamerin (1985) notes that female alcoholics more frequently see themselves as having psychiatric problems without identifying and talking about their alcohol problems, seeing them as secondary. Tamerin suggests a careful evaluation of all female clients in psychological treatment in order to assess whether there is the presence of alcohol-related problems, believing that the complications of alcoholism, such as depression, are all too often treated and the true disorder, alcoholism, is left untreated. Schulte and Blume (1979) emphasized the importance of supplementing any male-female treatment groups female alcoholics might attend with all-women groups. They believe that women's even more negative self-image can only be replaced with a more positive one through focused support from others like themselves. In addition, these researchers also saw the stress alcoholic women faced as primarily related to their home situations, whether it was an unsatisfactory emotional life within the family or social isolation and lack of a family.

ALCOHOLIC HOMELESS WOMAN

In reviewing the literature in the area of alcoholic homeless women, we have found that many, and particularly the earlier studies, focused on the male skid row alcoholic (Halikas, Lyttle, & Morse, 1984; Goldfarb, 1970; Rooney, 1961; Turner, 1979), whereas the more current ones focus on the incidence of mental illness in the homeless population (Bachrach, 1984; Bassuk et al., 1984; Doutney, Buhrich, Virgona, Cohen, & Daniels, 1985). At this time, there appears to be little that focuses on the actual effects of being homeless, the development and duration of the circumstance of being homeless, and the eventual outcome. What is clear, however, is that the alcoholic homeless woman is doubly disadvantaged in receiving treatment.

Why are mental health professionals reluctant to work with the alcoholic homeless woman? Many clinicians prefer not to work with chronic alcoholics, believing that they have inadequate training to work with this population or believing that chronic alcoholics are essentially untreatable. The prevailing wisdom is that only formal treatment approaches are adequate for dealing with alcoholism, and clinicians tend to automatically refer these patients to special programs (Zimberg, 1975). Many clinicians are equally reluctant to work with the homeless as witnessed by chronic lack of well-trained professionals. Homelessness also often appears to be an untreatable problem, particularly at the level of treating the individual. It is our contention that this is not necessarily the case. It is also our contention that within the population of the homeless it is not necessary for the clinician to have extensive experience in treating alcoholism per se, since the central issue is preparing them for the possibility of getting treatment in the first place. This does not minimize the importance of the work, however, since many women who are destitute often are so isolated that standard treatment programs that do exist are essentially unavailable to them. The focus of treatment is helping prepare these women to make contact with and use these services. This in itself is no small, insignificant task. It can be the first step in breaking the destructive pattern of alcoholism and homelessness.

If lack of a supportive family and social structure is a particularly important factor for alcoholic women, then such a stressor is obviously primary for the homeless alcoholic woman who is frequently isolated not only from family but from her fellow homeless as well. Bassuk, Rubin, and Lauriat (1984) found in a survey of 78 homeless men, women, and children in an emergency shelter, that 74% of the overall sample had no family relationships, and 73% had no friends to provide support. In a study funded in 1985 by the National Institute of Mental Health, extensive interviews were completed with 979 homeless people in the state of Ohio. Of these 979, 20.8% were judged to have serious drinking problems and reported 30 as the median number of days since any contact with relatives compared with 14 days for the nonalcoholic group. Rooney (1961) described the "bottle gang" as one way the skid row alcoholic can form affiliations. He likened the bottle gang to a corporate group where funds are pooled to buy a bottle and this resource shared. He concluded that this practice indicated a continuing ability on the part of the skid row alcoholic to form and sustain a relationship with another and viewed this as a positive sign. It is unclear whether the alcoholics in such groups themselves perceive the bottle gang as a supportive group wherein they have "relationships," particularly given the ever changing make-up of the gangs. Rubington (1967) saw the homeless alcoholic somewhat differently from Rooney. Rubington defined the homeless alcoholic as "a person who has no regular membership in a family unit of whatever kind, is socially isolated, is usually jobless, and suffers more injuries than he [sic] causes through excessive drinking."

For the alcoholic homeless woman the issue of whether there is social bonding through drinking within the homeless population is very likely a moot point. For the homeless woman, drunkenness is not much more acceptable than for her counterpart in the suburbs. In our experience working with homeless women, there is a fair amount of disapproval where drinking is concerned. Although many women have drinking problems, these problems are often seen as moral issues by the women themselves as well as their peers, rather than as a problem largely influenced by physiological dependence on the drug itself. To our knowledge there are no studies that have specifically focused on the incidence of alcohol problems in homeless women; thus, it is difficult to say empirically how severe the problem is within the population. In our clinical experience in working with the homeless, however, we found alcohol to be a core issue. We had expected mental illness and psychoses, in particular, to be the most salient issue, and at times this has certainly been the case. It quickly became apparent, however, that we would also have to familiarize ourselves with alcohol problems as related to women in order to be beneficial in helping them to get the help they needed.

At the initial treatment level that will be described here decisions about the type of alcohol treatment and the appropriate theoretical approach are not paramount, since the issues will center on helping the clients accept the need for treatment in the first place. However, it is important to be familiar with the general psychology of the female alcoholic, how she differs from the male alcoholic, and what some fruitful topics of discussion might be in relation to these issues. Also, there is a small body of literature, generally in the form of descriptive studies, dealing with the homeless. Our emphasis will be on this literature and how it applies specifically to the homeless female and to the development of our treatment strategy.

TREATMENT OF ALCOHOLISM

As stated earlier, extensive knowledge of the specific techniques for the treatment of alcoholism is not a prerequisite for work with the alcoholic homeless population as described here. It might be useful, however, to be familiar with some of the issues concerning treatment. It is the contention of some workers in the field of alcoholism that many physicians, psychiatrists, and other mental health professionals have had little success in treating alcoholics and, therefore, have lost interest. These workers contend that this state of affairs is the result of therapists and other professionals being exposed to the physical and psychiatric complications of alcoholism while not being familiar with the diagnosis and treatment of the disorder itself (Zimberg, 1985). However, when one begins to read the alcoholism literature it can be surprising to find a broad range of well-described and clearly defined treatment approaches. These include various forms of individual therapy, family therapy, group therapy, and peer support groups such as Alcoholics Anonymous (AA) and Women for Sobriety.

Theoretical approaches include psychoanalytic theories of alcoholism (Blum, 1966), theories of traits that contribute to the development of alcoholism (McCord & McCord, 1962), cognitive behavioral approaches (Sanchez-Craig, Annis, Bornet, & MacDonald, 1984; Sobell & Sobell, 1973), and systems theory as it applies to "alcoholic" families (Bowen, 1974; Jackson, 1958). There is also controversy in relation to the basic treatment goal for alcoholism itself. This controversy centers around the issue of whether it is better to advocate complete abstinence from alcohol for the rest of one's life (which is the approach strongly espoused by AA) or whether it is possible for an alcoholic to actually learn controlled drinking skills and thus learn to drink in moderation (Marlatt, 1983). At present, the controversy still rages with support available for both sides (Foy, Rychtarik, & Nunn, 1982; Pendery, Maltzman, & West, 1982; Sanchez-Craig et al., 1984). In addition, to confuse the issue further, numerous studies have found that many alcoholics treated according to the abstinence model later, of their own accord, acquire normal, moderate drinking habits with long-term success (Davies, 1962; Emrick, 1974; Polich, Armor, & Braiker, 1981; Sanchez-Craig & Walker, 1982). At this point, it appears that whether controlled drinking is a viable treatment option depends more on client characteristics than the treatment modality. In other words, controlled drinking techniques might be more successful in individuals with less severe drinking problems, and individuals with very severe alcohol problems would be best treated with the abstinence model (Maisto, Sobell, & Sobell, 1980; Polich et al., 1981).

In our experience, most of the alcoholic homeless would fall in the category of individuals with severe alcohol problems. The abstinence model would, therefore, at least for the present, be the treatment model of choice for this population. A clinician working with the homeless should be familiar with the available treatment programs in the community and, of course, be ready to refer individuals to the most appropriate programs. This should only be done after working with someone for a period of time and laying the groundwork to prepare them for the referral. This period of preparation is as important for the eventual completion of a treatment program as the treatment itself.

TREATMENT OF THE DOWN AND OUT ALCOHOLIC

Although the literature is sparse, some treatments specifically for the homeless alcoholic have been developed. Turner (1979) wrote a very detailed description of a community residential treatment for skid row alcoholics that discusses how a community clinic outreach team eventually developed a comprehensive approach to getting this population into alcohol treatment. The component of the strategy as described by Turner that most applies to the subject of this chapter is the finding that in order to reach the alcoholic homeless and draw them into treatment, the clinic and the clinician must go out to them. The lives of the homeless are unstructured, and they tend to be suspicious of formal institutions and their representatives. Given this, it is unlikely that the clinician who decides to work with this population can merely advertise through the usual channels and attract these clients. It will be necessary to go to where the homeless are, to emergency shelters and satellite health care clinics directly in the homeless neighborhoods. With this proviso, we believe that it is possible to establish ongoing treatment with this population. It is then up to the clinician to decide what form this treatment will take.

In our experience, and as reported by others (Turner, 1979), often the best way to involve the homeless and, particularly, the alcoholic in any form of treatment is to arrange for them to gather informally for some type of social interaction. The first step towards reaching the isolated individual is to provide them with positive experiences in interacting with other individuals, both with their comrades in the streets and also with representatives of the larger community. This was the first goal of our own group strategy. This conforms with an accepted strategy for treating alcohol problems in general and not just in the homeless population in particular. Many alcoholics first begin treatment by affiliating with a supportive group, often AA but often other groups as well.

Levine and Gallogly (1985) identified three kinds of outpatient alcoholic groups:

1. clients who are unmotivated for treatment and who deny their alcoholism
2. clients who have some capacity for situational insight
3. clients who are chronic and have been unresponsive to past treatment

Levine and Gallogly believe that group therapy can help clients in any of these three conditions but that the three types should not be mixed in treatment groups. They state that the three types want and need different types of help and support and go on to outline the different strategies. In dealing with the homeless, the clinician often does not have the luxury to do careful screening of clients but must work with everyone who shows for the session. Given Levine and Gallogly's recommendations, what does a clinician do when faced with a group in which the individuals are not only at varying levels in terms of problems with drinking but also have a mix of psychiatric and personality disorders instead of or in addition to alcoholism? Our experience of what seems to work was similar to that described by Turner (1979) in the community residential treatment model and mirrors the group treatment strategy outlined by Levine and Gallogly (1985) for dealing with the chronic alcoholic who has been unresponsive to treatment in the past. Their strategy, as well as ours, is to minimize as much as possible the group's discussion of drinking and alcoholism. Instead, the focus is on building personal connections among group members and building rapport with the group leaders in order to provide a positive experience of working with people other than those on the street. The objective is to keep the topics practical and nonthreatening, keep the members interested and, with time, create the kind of atmosphere that builds trust and hope. With trust and some sense of hope established, members are then willing and able to begin to look for ways to change a lonely and difficult lifestyle and to begin to believe that things can be different and that they can have some influence on that process.

THE DESC TREATMENT GROUP FOR WOMEN

What follows is a description of a treatment group for alcoholic homeless women that we hope will be useful for clinicians who might be interested in working with this population. Individual clinicians could develop such groups without being part of a larger institution. Initiative and motivation are the resources required here.

Setting

The setting was the Downtown Emergency Services Center (DESC) in Seattle, Washington. The DESC is a place for people to sleep when they have nowhere else to go. Located in an old downtown Seattle hotel, it provides mattresses on the floor on a first-come, first-serve basis for about 225 people. On average, only 30 to 40 are women. People under 18 are excluded from this shelter, and few services other than social service referral and minimal counseling by overworked floor staff are available. Use of the DESC as a permanent residence is actively discouraged but, despite this, the shelter definitely has its regular boarders who stay for fairly extended periods of time. Most good-sized cities have emergency shelters similar to the DESC, community health clinics, churches, or soup kitchens where street people tend to congregate. This is where the clinician should go with outreach attempts. We believe outreach is a crucial part of this approach. As a starting point, the best strategy is to contact staff members at the facility chosen and find one or two staff members interested in the idea of a group and who are also interested in participating. Staff know the population and usually have established some rapport. They are invaluable when it comes time to recruiting group members. At this stage it is important to have some clear ideas in mind about what the purpose of the group will be and who one would like to attend so that one can communicate this to the staff. In our case, a staff DESC member had, on her own initiative, started a women's group. Several crises during early group sessions, however, made her aware that she needed support from leaders with more training and expertise than she had. The DESC initiated community outreach in the opposite direction—to the clinicians.

Composition of the Group

From the very beginning, it was apparent that homeless women had issues that were important to address, these issues were different from those facing the men, and more resources existed, in terms of outreach and otherwise, for the men. There is very little of similar quality for the women. This is not to say that resources for the homeless are in any sense adequate, but, of what is in existence, little is geared towards addressing problems unique to homeless women. Our goal was, in a small way, to change this.

Five to 20 women attended group sessions on any given night. There was a core of "regulars" and a subgroup of women who stayed only brief periods of time or attended irregularly. The women came from a variety of backgrounds. The educational level varied from little schooling to master's degrees. Most reported some sort of physical or sexual abuse in the families of origin or in their adult lives. Their ages ranged from 18 to 70 years. A number of women once had husbands and families and were well-functioning until their 40s or 50s when divorce or other financial difficulties forced them onto the streets. Others have known only the streets, mental hospitals, or half-way houses. Most of the women had children who, if minors, were either wards of the state or were living with relatives. Although formal psychiatric assessments were never done, we estimate that from 40% to over 70% of the group had severe psychiatric disorders at any given time. Besides alcoholism, these included schizophrenia, other active psychoses, personality disorders, and some depression. In any given week, at least one woman was pregnant, and several had serious physical disorders. Many women reported problems with alcohol, often talking about what a problem it was on the streets rather than making it a more personal issue. Problems with other drug addictions were less evident, at least in the population at this shelter.

Attracting Members

We believe a crucial aspect of our strategy was that we individually approached every woman in the shelter on the evenings of the meetings to invite them to participate. No matter how many times they had refused in the past, we would invite them again the next week. This was done in a casual and friendly manner without any attempt to coerce them. Over time, many women became less suspicious and eventually participated. Some reported that our persistent interest made the difference in allowing them to feel their presence really mattered.

Another important strategy was to offer snacks (usually fruit, not often served with free meals) and coffee during meetings. These are small luxuries hard to come by on the streets and difficult to pass up. In addition, it was a way for some members to save face with skeptical boyfriends, husbands, or other individuals by stating that it was really the free food they were going for. Stability is also key with a group such as this.The meeting was held without fail at the same time and place every week. Members knew when to show up and did so with regularity. It is recommended that there be at least two leaders so that if one cannot be present there is always backup.

Treatment Goals

As described earlier, treatment goals for a group such as this should be focused on building trust and rapport; dealing with the specifics of uncontrolled drinking should only be done as the opportunity arises. The homeless alcoholic usually recognizes that alcohol only adds to an already difficult situation. Alcohol, however, is a large part of the street culture and the only means through which many street people have social contact with other individuals. In addition, alcohol also is often the only means of escape from their problems, and unless there is something more worthwhile to replace it with, it is difficult to justify taking away what is often seen as one of few pleasures in life, regardless of the cost. The purpose of the treatment group is to do exactly that—to provide social contact, to increase awareness of each other as resources and means of emotional support, and to begin to replace an isolated lifestyle with one where other humans are seen as people who can also help rather than just harm. Alcoholism is often a symptom of this isolation and at this early stage of treatment to focus on drinking behavior at the expense of dealing with the more crucial issue of relationships with other people only serves to alienate group members further. Therefore, the treatment goals described below will focus on issues we saw as useful in enhancing trust and rapport.

Trusting Other Women.   Women on the streets are extraordinarily isolated from other women. Their most common affiliation is with a man who can protect them and take care of them. Homeless women see themselves and other women as helpless and incompetent and generally see men as the main source of support, if they look for support at all. As a consequence, homeless women often see each other as in competition for men. This, of course, has been said about all women, but considering the desperate situations homeless women are in, the stakes would appear to be higher. Therefore, an important goal of our group was to increase the level of trust by discussing these issues and by emphasizing the skills, resources, and knowledge unique to women that they have to offer each other. The focus was not on minimizing the importance of men but on highlighting their awareness of each other as competent individuals too.

Enhancing Self-Esteem.　Homeless women are often treated with derision, hostility, and much disrespect during a day on the streets. In addition, their dependence on men as well as frequent emotional, physical, and sexual abuse from men do little to enhance their belief in their own capabilities and integrity. Most of the women come from chaotic, violent families and have little opportunity to develop a sense of competence and self-worth. These women not only do not trust each other, they do not trust themselves. An important goal of the group was to take every opportunity to enchance the women's sense of self-esteem.

Independence From Men.　Another goal of sessions was to foster a certain amount of independence from men. Progress here required skill and diplomacy in order to not alienate the men, who could then prevent the women from attending future sessions, while at the same time introducing sound feminist principles, such as working toward financial independence/security. In many ways, street culture is very traditional and sexist. The women are often paralyzed in terms of making decisions for themselves and are very child-like when interacting with males. When invited to the group, it often happened that the women had great difficulty deciding whether to come, turning to their husband or boyfriend for help in making this decision. However, the women were also often aware, at some level, of the pitfalls of being too dependent. The opportunity to discuss this with other women in their same difficult situation was welcome.

Planning for the Future.　In some ways, it is foolish to think much of the future when living on the streets, but giving up all hope of things getting better is equally so. Exploring this issue was sometimes painful, anger-inducing, but hope-inspiring as well. Living on the streets can become a lifestyle like any other. Often the process of getting back into the mainstream of society is more difficult than staying homeless. The culture of the streets can, in many ways, be more tolerant and accepting than what the homeless and, particularly, alcoholic woman is faced with as she struggles to learn to interact with and survive in the rest of society. An awareness on her part of this process is useful in helping her cope with the inevitable feelings of awkwardness and inadequacy as they arise.

Self-Care. A chronic problem with homeless and severely alcoholic women is the serious deterioration of rudimentary health care and hygiene that often develops. Many psychotic and alcoholic women prematurely discontinue use of medications necessary to treat their condition. Alcoholic and pregnant women often have poor nutrition. Many have physical ailments requiring the attention of a physician, and some have problems with hygiene and body lice that are readily handled if the individuals know about the resources available to them. Thus, an important goal was education about these issues. We also encouraged the women to share their knowledge and experience of the medical resources in the community.

Sexual Responsibility. As mentioned earlier, during every group session there was at least one group member who was pregnant. Often the pregnancy was intentional. It is difficult to feel womanly while living on the streets, and pregnancy is the ultimate proof of womanhood. Just as frequently, the pregnancies were accidental. Sexual relationships with men are frequently engaged in impulsively and because the man in question expected it and not necessarily because the woman desires it. Also, engaging in sexual behavior is not something that is very easy when one is homeless, so sex is often infrequent. This leads many women to rationalize that they cannot get pregnant "since it's just this one time." Issues of intimacy and pregnancy are obviously as important to homeless women as to any woman. Their financial status makes them particularly vulnerable to high-risk pregnancies due to lack of good prenatal care, nutrition, and education (e.g., the effects of alcohol on the human fetus). They also frequently have to give up the care of their babies to others if they do give birth. The opportunity to discuss these issues and think through the consequences is rare when a woman is isolated from others. An important goal of the group was to provide this opportunity.

Reducing Resistance to Professional Help. The experience of many homeless and alcoholic women is that professionals and institutions are to be avoided. They have been patronized, preached at, ordered about, and ignored. They themselves often feel shame about their situation and have little ability to assert themselves when abused by the system. The group was therefore an opportunity to expose them to leaders who made an attempt to understand, respect, and learn from them. The survival skills of homeless women are impressive. Their ability to continue on in the face of very difficult circumstances and still appreciate and find joy in life is worthy of respect. Therefore, a goal for the group was to allow them to teach as well as learn in order to enhance their sense of self-respect in relation to the group leaders who they often saw as being better, smarter, and different in a way that they could never hope to attain. Such an experience would do much toward reducing the sense of alienation and awe that is often directed toward people who are in positions of authority.

Unrealistic Goals

Getting Women Off the Streets.　It is useless to expect that a weekly group in and of itself can affect such a major change. Using this as a criteria for measuring the success of treatment is foolhardy. The group is best seen as laying the groundwork for gradual change and for allowing the members to learn to turn to others and themselves for help. It is teaching the process of change. Once a woman learns that she is able to decide for herself, the rest is often much easier.

Getting the Women off Alcohol.　Again the focus is on preparing the women to work with others. This skill can then be transferred to specific groups for alcohol abuse or for work with individual therapists. The immediate issue at hand is not the drinking problem but the isolation from which the alcohol is a welcome escape. Once a woman makes contact with others, she can then begin to attend to more concrete problems.

Treatment Strategies

What follows is a description of some of the strategies we use to structure and run the group. There is also a brief list of topics and questions for discussion that we found useful in terms of encouraging group interaction. Group leaders must assess at the beginning of each session the overall level of functioning of the group and what the members can handle. Sometimes topics should be kept very concrete and practical; at other times the discussion can be more philosophical and abstract.

Providing Structure.　There are certain characteristics that provide structure for the group. The time limit is one hour for our group, and despite the often large size, this seems to be the optimal time. It is difficult for many of the women to attend for more than an hour. Every session begins with formal introductions if there are any new members. The best option is to have a current member introduce a newcomer if possible. Then everyone in the group introduces herself, giving her name and whatever information she thinks would give others a sense of who she is. It is important to go to each member of the group and encourage her to talk, giving her plenty of time to collect her thoughts but also being careful not to appear to push unnecessarily. A group member then communicates the rules of the group to the new members. This is also useful as a reminder to the older members. One firm rule is that only one person at a time can speak. Any fighting or out of control behavior is prohibited, and, if this occurs, the parties involved have to leave that session. Sometimes women have been drinking prior to the group. If they can control their behavior and do not disrupt the group, they, of course, are allowed to remain. Demanding sobriety at this stage would only exclude the women who are most in need of what the group has to offer.

In this type of group, there will always be very quiet members and highly verbal ones. It is the leader's responsibility to be sure all group members have a chance to participate. This applies to choosing the topic for discussion also. Often the highly verbal members have issues they wish to address and which often do not apply to everyone. It is important to see that the topics are representative of the group as a whole as much as possible.

A formal end to the group is just as important as a formal beginning. Our group ends by joining hands and expressing appreciation for the group as a whole. This seems like a small thing, but to women who experience little in the way of intimacy this becomes very important. For many it is the only time that week they will touch or be touched by another person. It is also a way to end the group on a warm note and to highlight the fact that the group is a source of support.

Inclusion Strategies.   Given that building trust and rapport is an important goal of the group, it is important to take every opportunity to help the group members feel included and involved. Some of the techniques used to provide structure for the group also enhance these feelings of inclusion (e.g., group introductions, formal ending). In addition, we involve the women in the process of preparing for the group. They help set up chairs, set out food, and get each other coffee. Everyone is encouraged to help clean up at the end. The purpose is to communicate that this is their group, not just something the group leaders are doing for them. Group members are constantly encouraged to talk about the group with other women they encounter on the streets and to invite them to attend.

Group discussion is structured around the circle technique. Everyone has to participate by contributing, and the best way to insure this is to go around the circle and have each member talk in turn. As group leaders, we also participate. This is a good way for the group members to get to know us, too, and we have found it very helpful for establishing rapport. Group members are very patient, tolerant, and understanding of each other and are willing to give even the actively psychotic women attention and time to speak. This is important to guarantee that everyone feels valued.

There are also certain questions that help members interact and feel a common bond. They generally involve the more practical and concrete issues facing the women day to day but also include some issues about quality of life that apply to them all. Below is a brief list of some of the questions that we have posed when using the circle technique:

1. Where to go when the shelter is closed? What to do during the day?

2. What places provide free or low-cost food, clothing (especially good clothing for job interviews), medical care, psychological services, alcohol treatment, showers, laundry facilities, temporary jobs, housing?

3. Personal safety. Where can women safely go? How do they protect themselves? Group members welcomed the idea of someone coming to discuss self-defense techniques. These women are often victims of violence.

4. What is the thing in life (this week, today) they are most grateful for?

5. Any good or positive event that happened to each woman during the past week.

6. How do they stay happy even though times are so hard?

7. How have they successfully quit alcohol/drugs? What do they think will help, if they haven't quit yet? Address this issue only if the group members express the interest. (They will, eventually.)

8. After major holidays, what was the best meal, best gift, best thing that happened to them?

9. Past history, childhood, where they grew up. Many of the women never talk about these things with each other. There are inevitable commonalities, which increase bonding with each other.

Discussion Topics. The topics suggested in the section on inclusion strategies are useful when there are many new members and everyone has to get to know each other. Even though the older members have heard the information before, it provides them with the opportunity to show off their knowledge and skills and to be supportive. These topics are also useful when the group has a high proportion of dysfunctional individuals. It is important for the group leaders to assess the overall level of functioning of the group in order to help in the decision about what to focus on in each session. This is usually done during group introduction, when possible discussion themes often become apparent. When the group is composed of a high proportion of well-functioning individuals, the group can choose the topic for discussion. At other times, it is more appropriate for the group leaders to take responsibility for this. When the group is functioning at a generally higher level, it is possible to tackle less concrete issues about their lives and to be more abstract and philosophical. Listed below are some topics that have worked well for the DESC women's group:

1. children; a very important and emotional issue
2. any goals they might have for the week (month, year)
3. issues with men; feminist issues are not lost on these women
4. sexuality/birth control; approach this one carefully
5. something they like about themselves, each other
6. how to be feminine while living on the streets (a very successful topic; this one carried over into the next week)
7. problems with the shelter, organizations in general; this should not degenerate into a "bitch" session, however.

These are suggested topics that worked well for this group. Through creative experimentation and listening carefully to group members it is possible to come up with new and different topics that will more closely address the needs of other groups.

Leader Characteristics

It is probably apparent at this point that not every clinician can lead a group of this type. Experience with psychotic and highly dysfunctional individuals is useful. Also, experience in running groups is essential. This is not the type of group to learn group therapy with unless there is also an experienced co-leader. A group leader has to be prepared to be directive and provide a great deal of structure. An attitude of "I am here to save the homeless" will only lead to therapist burnout *if* the group manages to stay intact longer than one session. Group leaders working with this population cannot be judgmental and autocratic. This population has too much experience with such individuals, and exposure to one more is definitely not therapeutic.

In terms of clinical skills, they are put to use not only during the group but also when interacting with the staff at the shelter. Staff members often do not have the formal training of the experienced clinician, yet they are the ones who know the residents and their problems. Some staff members will be defensive if not treated with care (and some clinicians will be highhanded). It is important to use this resource to the advantage of the group.

Good clinical skills go far in helping further the treatment goals outside the group, as well as during the sessions.

Therapist burnout is a particular problem when working with this population. A key factor in minimizing this is remembering to be content with minimal goals. Another is being aware that being in a new environment is always stressful. Most mental health professionals find themselves as part of the middle class. Homelessness is usually not a familiar state of existence. Yet when one begins to get to know people instead of just stereotypes, it becomes clear that their problems could, given the right circumstances, be our problems. This is certainly true of alcoholism and can be true of homelessness. One must deal with these fears on some level, or they will serve to discourage the clinician from continuing to work in this problem area. These fears are one of the reasons most mental health professionals work only with members of the middle class. The people who are most in need of quality mental health services are ignored. Our strong belief is that fear is one of the major reasons for this state of affairs. It keeps people from seeking funding, doing research, developing treatments, and providing the impetus and motivation to get things done. This fear can be dealt with. Systematic desensitization does not only work with clients but can be put to use helping clinicians improve the scope of their professional work as well.

On a more practical level, it is necessary to have at least two therapists so that one can have a break when needed without the group itself being disrupted. Running such a group is demanding because of the frequent need for structure and the high demand for creative use of clinical skills in a very nontraditional setting. This can lead to burnout, but it can also lead to highly rewarding therapy situations. If the clinician models the good self-care skills she is attempting to teach the homeless women, she will see to it that she monitors herself carefully and does the things that are necessary to get respites when called for, get outside supervision when appropriate, and be conscious of her mental state.

Problems

Funding.   Often such groups are run strictly by volunteers. It is rewarding and satisfying work and obviously necessary. Many homeless individuals do have funding, however, in the form of social security insurance, welfare, and private resources. Community clinics also have financial resources that can be earmarked for such treatment groups. In addition, private sources are often willing to contribute funds in the form of charitable contributions. The effort expended is a little more than usual, but the personal rewards can make it well worthwhile.

Group Turnover. Turnover in such a group is high. Traditional psychotherapy and traditional goals are unrealistic as a result. The clinician must be flexible in terms of treatment. Long-term goals have to be kept in mind to offset what often appears to be short-term failure. It helps to keep in mind the notion of the group as a separate entity that is in itself stable and unchanging. This offsets the ever changing faces within the group itself.

Confidentiality. This can prove to be a more difficult area and can at times threaten the existence of the group. Life on the streets is not very private, and the street community is often small. People know each other. The likelihood of secrets getting out is sometimes great. Confidentiality should be stressed at the beginning of every session, and if members breach it, this should be discussed. In addition, it is wise to remind the women they are each taking risks in confiding. Taking risks is good and useful at times, but each must weigh the costs versus the benefits, and they must keep in mind that confidentiality can never be guaranteed, so they must function accordingly.

CONCLUSION

We hope this chapter will prove useful in encouraging other clinicians to begin working with a population of women that is too often denied the benefits of treatment by experienced mental health professionals. We have found the group experience described here to be enjoyable (to our initial surprise, given our apprehension about whether we would be accepted) and very rewarding. For those therapists who are interested, we encourage you to take some chances and use your skills where you might think they are not needed or warranted. Our own experience has been to the contrary.

REFERENCES

Bachrach, L. L. (1984). Asylum and chronically ill psychiatric patients. *American Journal of Psychiatry, 141*(8), 975–978.

Bassuk, E. L., Rubin, L., & Lauriat, A. (1984). Is homelessness a mental health problem? *American Journal of Psychiatry, 14*(12), 1546–1550.

Beckman, L. J. (1975). Women alcoholics: A review of social and psychological studies. *Journal of Studies on Alcohol, 36*(7), 797–824.

Blum, E. M. (1966). Psychoanalytic views of alcoholism: A review. *Quarterly Journal of Studies on Alcohol, 27*(2), 259–299.

Bowen, M. (1974). Alcoholism as viewed through family systems theory and family psychotherapy. *Annals of the New York Academy of Sciences, 233,* 115.

Corrigan, E. M. (1974). *Problem drinkers seeking treatment. Rutgers Center of Alcohol Studies, Monograph No. 8,* New Brunswick, NJ: Rutgers Center of Alcohol Studies.

Corrigan, E. M. (1980). *Alcoholic women in treatment.* New York: Oxford University Press.

Curlee, J. (1967). Alcoholic women: Some considerations for further research. *Bulletin of the Menninger Clinic, 31*(3), 154–163.

Curlee, J. (1970). A comparison of male and female patients at an alcoholism treatment center. *Journal of Psychology, 74*(2), 239–247.

Davies, D. L. (1962). Normal drinking in recovered alcoholic addicts. *Quarterly Journal of Studies on Alcohol, 23*(1), 94–104.

Doutney, C. P., Buhrich, N., Virgona, A., Cohen, A., & Daniels, P. (1985). The prevalence of schizophrenia in a refuge for homeless men. *Australian and New Zealand Journal of Psychiatry, 19,* 233–238.

Emrick, C. D. (1974). A review of psychologically oriented treatment of alcoholism: I. The use and interrelationships of outcome criteria and drinking behavior following treatment. *Quarterly Journal of Studies on Alcohol, 35*(2), 523–549.

Foy, D. W., Rychtarik, R. G., & Nunn, B. L. (1982). *Controlled drinking training effects for chronic veteran alcoholics: A randomized trial.* Paper presented at the American Psychiatric Association Convention, Toronto.

Goldfarb, C. (1970). Patients nobody wants— Skid row alcoholics. *Diseases of the Nervous System, 31*(4), 274–281.

Halikas, J. A., Lyttle, M. D., & Morse, C. L. (1984). Skid row alcoholism—An objective definition for use in detoxification and treatment planning. *Journal of Clinical Psychiatry, 45*(5), 214–216.

Jackson, J. K. (1958). Alcoholism and the family. *Annals of the American Academy of the Political and Social Sciences, 315,* 90–98.

Kay, R. (1985). The homeless mentally ill. *ADAMHA News, 11*(10), 12–13.

Levine, B., and Gallogly, V. (1985). *Group therapy with alcoholics: Outpatient and inpatient approaches.* Beverly Hills, CA: Sage Publications.

Maisto, S. A., Sobell, M. B., & Sobell, L. D. (1980). Predictors of treatment outcome for alcoholics treated by individualized behavior therapy. *Addictive Behaviors, 5*(1), 259–264.

Marlatt, G. A. (1983). The controlled-drinking controversy. *American Psychologist, 38*(10), 1097–1110.

McCord, W., & McCord, J. (1962). A longitudinal study of the personality of alcoholics. In D. J. Pittman & C. R. Snyder (Eds.), *Society, culture and drinking patterns.* New York: Wiley.

Pendery, M. L., Maltzman, I. M., & West, L. J. (1982). Controlled drinking by alcoholics? New findings and a reevaluation of a major affirmative study. *Science, 217*(4555), 169–174.

Polich, J. M., Armor, D. J., & Braiker, H. B. (1981). *The course of alcoholism: Four years after treatment.* New York: Wiley.

Rooney, J. A. (1961). Group processes among skid row winos. *Quarterly Journal of Studies on Alcohol, 22,* 449–450.

Rubington, E. (1967). The halfway house for the alcoholic. *Mental Hygiene, 51*(10), 552–553.

Sanchez-Craig, M., Annis, H. M., Bornet, A. R., & MacDonald, K. R. (1984). Random assignment to abstinence and controlled drinking: Evaluation of a cognitive-behavioral program for problem drinkers. *Journal of Consulting and Clinical Psychology, 52*(3), 390–403.

Sanchez-Craig, M., & Walker, K. (1982). Teaching coping skills to chronic alcoholics in a coeducational halfway house: I. Assessment of programme effects. *British Journal of Addiction, 77*(1), 35–50.

Schuckit, M. A. (1972). The alcoholic woman: A literature review. *Psychiatry in Medicine, 3*(1), 37–43.

Schuckit, M. A., & Morrissey, E. R. (1976). Alcoholism in women: Some clinical and social perspectives with an emphasis on possible subtypes. In M. Greenblatt & M. A. Schuckit (Eds.), *Alcoholism problems in women and children.* New York: Grune and Stratton.

Schulte, K., & Blume, S. B. (1979). A day treatment center for alcoholic women. *Health and Social Work, 4*(4), 222–231.

Sobell, M. B., & Sobell, L. C. (1973). Individualized behavior therapy for alcoholics. *Behavior Therapy, 4*(1), 49–72.

Tamerin, J. S. (1985). The psychotherapy of alcoholic women. In S. Zimberg, J. Wallace, & S. B. Blume (Eds.), *Practical approaches to alcoholism psychotherapy* (2nd ed.). New York: Plenum Press.

Tamerin, J. S., Tolor, A., & Harrington, B. (1976). Sex differences in alcoholics: A comparison of male and female alcoholics' self and spouse perceptions. *American Journal of Drug and Alcohol Abuse, 3*(3), 457–472.

Turner, S. (1979). Community residental treatment for skid row alcoholics. *Health and Social Work, 4*(4), 163–180.

Wilsnack, S. C. (1976). The impact of sex roles and women's alcohol use and abuse. In M. Greenblatt & M. A. Schuckit (Eds.), *Alcoholism problems in women and children.* New York: Grune and Stratton.

Zimberg, S. (1975). New York State Task Force on alcohol problems: Position paper on treatment. *New York State Journal of Medicine, 75*(10), 1794–1798.

Zimberg, S. (1985). Principles of alcoholism psychotherapy. In S. Zimberg, J. Wallace, & S. Blume (Eds.), *Practical approaches to alcoholism psychotherapy* (2nd ed.). New York: Plenum Press.

■ 14
Group Treatment of Adult Women Incest Survivors

JUDITH E. SPREI

The mental health profession has only recently recognized the full dimensions of the problem of intrafamilial sexual abuse of children. Incest was formerly believed to be rare (in 1955, Weinberg estimated an incidence of one case per million population); a more recent study reported a conservative estimate of 14% of women experiencing intrafamilial sexual abuse before the age of 18 and 12% before the age of 14 (Russell, 1983). Until recently, the aftereffects of incest were often ignored or discounted, and the incest experience was rarely addressed in therapy. However, recent research has graphically documented its potential for destructive and pervasive consequences in many areas of the incest victim's life. To ameliorate these destructive effects, treatment specifically addressing the incest experience and its aftereffects has been developed.

Incest is taboo in most cultures. It is broadly defined as sexual contact with a person who would be considered an ineligible partner because of his blood and/or social ties to the victim and her family (Benward & Densen-Gerber, 1975). Its occurrence is surrounded by denial, secrecy, and guilt.

This stigma, which according to Browne and Finkelhor (1984) is one of the main sources of trauma for incest victims, is reinforced both societally and within the family.

The societal denial and neglect serve two functions. They allow the abuse to become chronic, the typical pattern being a compulsive/addictive one including onset in prepuberty, duration of several years, and progressive sexual activity over time ranging from fondling to intercourse. Denial and secrecy also serve to compound reactions to the abuse, causing a secondary victimization or second injury. As a consequence of the abuse and the lack of response, the individual internalizes a sense that something is wrong with her, that she is bad, or that she caused the abuse. The negative self-concept and sense of shame have yet another consequence: the development of secondary effects such as poor interpersonal skills and relations, sexual problems, self-abusive behavior, and vulnerability to revictimization (Courtois & Sprei, 1987).

The consequences of incest are compounded by its occurrence within the family, sometimes in the context or under the guise of love and affection. A pattern of secrecy, rivalry, guilt, and power is maintained by family members, and because the disclosure of the incest is so disruptive to family functioning, the victim is under intense pressure to remain silent. Moreover, "because the betrayal by sexual misuse is often embedded within the broad context of a caring relationship, the victim may be left with both tender and negative feelings towards the perpetrator and with guilt and self-doubt" (Sprei and Courtois, 1987).

The long-term effects of incest, exacerbated by the denial, secrecy, and shame surrounding its occurrence, are pervasive. Peters (1976) compares the aftereffects to "psychological time bombs" that, as with acute stress responses precipitated by other types of intense trauma, may be set off without warning. Courtois (1979) classifies these effects into eight life spheres: (1) social, including vocational; (2) psychological/emotional; (3) physical; (4) sexual; (5) family; (6) sense of self; (7) relations with men; and (8) relations with women.

This chapter presents a model of time-limited retrospective group treatment of adult women incest survivors based on the author's experience in facilitating over a dozen such groups and a long-term (4 years duration) group. Short-term groups are conducted by the author as a consultant to several local sexual assault centers. This makes it possible to offer groups at no direct cost to the client and to provide training and supervision to sexual assault center counselors. The long-term group is conducted in a private practice setting.

Specific descriptions of retrospective incest survivors' groups are sparse in the professional literature (Cole, 1985; Gordy, 1983; Herman & Schatzow, 1984; Tsai & Wagner, 1978), although there is general agreement that group treatment is a particularly effective treatment modality for incest survivors. There are many benefits derived from a group setting. In particular, the issues of shame, isolation, negative self-concept, and guilt can be more quickly and thoroughly addressed in group rather than individual therapy. Each modality allows different issues to be addressed, different transferences to arise, and different types and levels of interventions to be made. Therefore, the combination of individual and group therapy, either concurrently or consecutively, may be the most effective and complete method of treating adult incest survivors. The benefits of group treatment with this population, the group structure and process, topics and themes discussed in group sessions, the role of the therapist, and transference and countertransference issues are discussed below. For a more complete discussion of client dynamics, transference/countertransference issues, treatment conceptualizations and approaches, and the therapy process in the individual retrospective treatment of incest the reader is referred to Courtois and Sprei (1987) and Sprei and Courtois (1987). Summit (1983) is also essential reading for anyone working with child or adult incest survivors.

BENEFITS OF GROUP TREATMENT

Identification with Other Members

One of the more persistent effects of childhood sexual abuse is the victim's sense of being different and isolated from other people. A group setting can instill a sense of identification with other survivors. Morrissey (1982) notes the sense of accomplishment, hope, energy, and pride that results from the group's collective appreciation for and identification with all its members' struggles. In hearing each survivor describe her experiences and watching each one struggle to survive and grow, each member learns to appreciate her own strengths.

Recognition of Commonalities Among Members

In the group, members come to realize that they share similar problems regarding self-esteem, guilt, self-destructive behavioral patterns, control, intimacy, and sexual functioning. Rather than internalizing and seeing these problems and the abuse itself as resulting from their personal character defects, members are able to externalize and recognize the abuse as the cause of those problems. Thus, the group has a consciousness-raising effect, helping members gain new perspectives on their experiences.

Acknowledgment of the Abuse

Because of the presence of other members, the group allows for a more complete resolution of the issue of secrecy than in an individual setting. After sharing their secret in the group, many women find it easier to talk to close friends, spouses, or other family members about it. In the group, members prepare for and rehearse disclosures to their families and anticipate possible outcomes. The participants are encouraged by the disclosures of other group members and the support provided by the group.

Support Network

Members often develop friendships with each other, learning perhaps for the first time to create intimate, trusting, and mutually satisfying relationships. The group can also serve as a "new family" for members. Both siblings and parental transferences occur and can be explored; this occurs more frequently in a long-term than a short-term group. Further, in contrast to the member's family of origin, the group models a family in which the conflicts can be openly discussed and worked through without the member being rejected or abused.

Catalyst for Exploration

The group is a powerful catalyst for identifying and exploring feelings and beliefs and breaking through denial. The client is given the opportunity, either directly or by listening to other group members, to focus on areas that previously may have been too threatening. However, the power of the group to break through denial must be carefully monitored lest it overwhelm the client. Using the analogy of a brick wall, the goal is to take out one brick at a time, not to dynamite the whole wall. As Gelinas (1983) states, "sometimes the client will send out a clear mesage to the group that the material being addressed represents so painful an issue that they cannot relinquish the defense mechanism of denial. . . . The group must respect these feelings but can also encourage the victim to face the issue rather than continue to evade it (p. 327)." As therapists, we need to constantly remember how extremely frightening and painful the therapy process can be for clients. We need to respect clients' rights to regulate their own pacing of the therapy process.

Challenging of Beliefs and Childhood Messages

The group is an ideal setting for challenging long-held beliefs. For example, although a member may believe that she is responsible for her own abuse, she rarely will believe that the other group members caused or deserved their own abuse. Members also help each other differentiate childhood messages from facts. Once the client identifies these faulty internalized perceptions, she can choose which beliefs to maintain and which to replace with more positive self-messages.

Observation and Exploration of Client Dynamics

In a group, the therapist has the opportunity to observe directly the client's mode of interaction with a number of individuals, her defense systems, the ways in which she protects herself, and how these defenses affect others. Thus, client dynamics and interactional patterns can be explored as they are manifested.

Development of Social Skills

A group provides a safe environment in which to practice social skills, explore interpersonal relationships, and deal with intimacy issues. Healthy expression of emotion, particularly anger, and exploration of conflicts are modeled in the group.

TIME-LIMITED GROUP

The time-limited group does not attempt to resolve all the issues and problems surrounding the incest experience; rather, it provides a safe, supportive environment in which members can become knowledgeable about those issues and gain a sense of direction for their continuing therapeutic work.

The time-limited group has several initial advantages over long-term therapy for adult incest victims. Participants may find it easier to make a shorter time commitment than an ongoing one. The limited life-span of the group promotes goal-oriented work, focusing attention on common themes relating to incest and minimizing interpersonal conflicts within the group. It provides structure and consistency that can support the members through the intense disorganizing aspects of treatment. Finally, the group's limited duration fits the schedules and organizational structures of most crisis service agencies.

Goals

Goals for the short-term group include acknowledging the abuse; reattributing responsibility for the abuse; recognizing, labeling, and expressing such emotions as guilt, shame, anger, fear, and grief; gaining knowledge about incest and family dynamics; breaking feelings of isolation; gaining insight; making behavioral changes; and deciding on a future course of action.

Group Structure

The time-limited group for adult incest survivors meets for 10 1½-hour sessions for 10 consecutive weeks. It is designed for adult women over 20 years of age who are former victims of incest. That is, they are no longer in the incestuous relationship and/or are out of the home where the incest occurred. It is a closed rather than a drop-in group to enhance the development of cohesiveness and trust. A minimum of four members and a maximum of six members is recommended.

Two female co-leaders conduct the 10 sessions. The format of the group is for the most part unstructured, although outside readings, homework assignments, and exercises are used where appropriate. No formal follow-up is planned; however, during the last two sessions, members assess their progress, define areas in which to continue working, and plan how to accomplish that work. Many groups decide to hold reunions. In one area, upon termination members are invited to attend a reunion and to join a local chapter of a self-help network, VOICES (Victims of Incest Can Emerge Survivors), organized by participants in previous groups.

Screening of Group Members

A group modality is not appropriate for all incest survivors. It is therefore necessary to assess carefully the client's appropriateness for the group setting, including her needs, motivation, current life situation, and interpersonal skills. Both the group's impact on the client and the client's impact on the group must be considered.

To function constructively in a short-term group setting, the client requires a sufficient level of tolerance to deal both with the painful feelings that may arise and the intimacy of the group, a sufficient level of interpersonal skills, and sufficient energy to focus on the incest. Contraindications to short-term group participation include an active psychosis, intense paranoia, drug or alcohol addiction, life-threatening eating disorder, acute suicidal tendencies, severe self-mutilation, an inability to control strong aggressive and impulsive tendencies, a multiple personality, an inability to discuss the incest without dissocation, and a current severe life crisis.

Intake

An intake interview is important both as a screening device and as an introductory mechanism. It serves to weed out women who are unlikely to benefit from the group, to desensitize clients to the idea of discussing the incest, and to give the client and the therapists an opportunity to meet each other. For the client, seeing a familiar face makes coming to the first group meeting somewhat less frightening. Meeting each group member individually allows the therapists to make an initial assessment of client dynamics, issues, and interpersonal skills.

The intake interview is scheduled approximately two weeks before the first group meeting, allowing time to add new members if some clients are screened out during the intake process. Each interview lasts 50 minutes. When possible, it is preferable to have both therapists present at each interview. Having both leaders present increases the desensitization effect of the interview and minimizes the formation of an alliance between the client and one therapist. If both therapists cannot conduct all intakes together, it is recommended that either each one conduct half the intakes or each client have two interviews, one with each group leader.

Although each intake interview differs depending on the client's responses, needs, and emotional state, they follow a similar pattern. Most clients are very nervous as they come to the intake session. It may be their first disclosure of the incest or their first therapy experience, or they may have had negative therapy experiences in the past. To enable the client to relax and to become familiar with the therapists, general questions are asked at the beginning of the interview. The client fills out an intake form with biographical data, which serve as the basis for a discussion of the client's current life situation. The conversation should be friendly and low-key.

After the initial phase of the interview, discussion turns to the incest experience, and its consequences. The therapists ask such questions as who was the perpetrator, how old the victim was when the incest began and ended, what was the degree of violence involved, how the client survived while the abuse was occurring, what were the reactions of other family members, and how the incest affects her now. The therapists also ask the client what her goals are for group participation and if she has any fears or concerns about being in the group.

In the final phase of the interview, the therapists describe the group, its general goals, structure, and ground rules. They tell the client that during the coming week she may experience some emotional reactions to the disclosure of the incest and that these reactions are normal. The therapists congratulate the client for coming and talking with them and end the interview on a warm and welcoming note.

If the client is presently in individual therapy, it is essential to obtain a release form that gives the group leaders permission to talk to her individual therapist. The client's refusal to sign such a form has many implications. Her desire to keep the group leaders and her individual therapist from speaking may recapitulate the splitting between her parents, may represent a wish to maintain control or secrecy, or may be an indication of her lack of trust in authority and parental figures. One must also recognize that many therapists still deny and minimize the effects of incest, and some therapists even abuse their clients. The group leaders must be alert to possible inappropriate therapy and the client's possible fear of her present therapist and must help her terminate that therapy, if necessary.

Ground Rules

Certain ground rules are essential for the success of any group. Additional ground rules are often suggested by group members, and following these suggestions indicates to the members that their needs are important and are taken seriously. Some common ground rules are discussed below.

Confidentiality. Because of the secrecy and shame surrounding the incest and the lack of trust engendered by it, it is crucial to establish the ground rule of confidentiality. Members agree not to discuss other members' issues, problems, or secrets outside the group.

Termination. If a member decides to drop out of the group, she is asked to announce her decision to the group and to attend at least one more group session to discuss her reasons for termination. Returning to the group to discuss her feelings teaches the client that misunderstanding can be faced and resolved.

Emotional Discharge. Expressing feelings is encouraged, but hurting oneself, another member, or the furniture is not allowed. The therapists pledge not to permit damage to occur and to intervene to protect participants' safety.

Pushing. Members accept that they will be encouraged to disclose information and explore issues surrounding the incest, with the reassurance that if they become too frightened or the material becomes too painful that the group will back off. A member always has the right to refuse to answer a question.

Discussions Outside of Group.   Group members are encouraged to exchange telephone numbers and to contact each other for support. However, they are not permitted to discuss group issues involving other group members or the leaders; these must be dealt with in group.

Unplanned Meetings Outside of Group.   Members discuss what they would like to do should they accidentally meet another group member outside of the group. They need to be reassured that their confidentiality will be maintained.

TREATMENT ISSUES, TOPICS, AND THEMES

From the wide variety of topics discussed during the sessions, certain common and often interrelated themes tend to emerge. The following discussion is organized according to the life spheres affected by incest (Courtois, 1979). Sprei and Fine (1983) devised a group handout in which members are asked how the abuse affected them as children and how it now affects them as adults in each of these life spheres. Examples of possible effects are included in each category.

Social Issues

These issues include feelings of isolation or of being different from "ordinary" people, difficulties with establishing intimate relationships, an inability to identify and express feelings, and concern about the "false image" the client projects to others.

Psychological/Emotional Issues

Often feeling that the abuse was their fault, members frequently express emotions of guilt, anger, helplessness, and fear. They may direct their anger toward themselves or to significant others who failed to protect them, such as the nonabusing parent, siblings, relatives, teachers, or therapists. Initially, they seldom direct feelings of anger toward the perpetrator.

  Defense systems used to survive before, during, and after the incest and to protect themselves from other people are discussed. Such coping strategies include denial, detachment, isolation, withdrawal, intellectual-izing, blocking, passive/aggressive behavior, splitting, personalizing, per-fectionistic drives, eating disorders, substance abuse, self-mutilation, and suicide attempts. Clients often berate themselves for their behavior. In-stead, they can be taught to reconceptualize these behaviors as survival mechanisms that may have been very functional during the abuse. As Sum-mit (1983) states, "Much of what is eventually labelled as adolescent or adult psychopathology can be traced to the natural reactions of a healthy child to a profoundly unnatural and unhealthy parental environment" (p. 188). The client is encouraged to congratulate herself for her self-sustaining behavior and to explore whether it is now safe enough to let go of these coping mechanisms and replace them with coping skills more adaptive to her current situation.

Physical Issues

Physical complaints include weight problems, migraine headaches, severe backaches, distorted body image, gastrointestinal and genitourinary pro-blems, an inability to concentrate, lethargy, anxiety, and phobic behavior (Courtois & Sprei, 1987).

Sexual Issues

Members frequently present sexual identity conflicts and impairment in sexual functioning (Sprei & Courtois, 1987). Sexual problems range from an inability to function sexually, to an inability to relax or experience orgasm, to self-defined promiscuity and masochistic behavior. Members often report difficulty feeling sexually aroused and emotionally close at the same time. Specific sexual behaviors in the current relationship may act as triggering events leading to flashbacks of the incest experience.

Familial Issues

This category includes issues regarding the member's relationship to her family of origin, both as a child and as an adult, and to her current family. Often as a child, the member was given the role of the caretaker, and she has continued in this role in adult relationships. Members' needs to take care of others selflessly may be evidence of this process of "parentifica-tion" (Gelinas, 1983). In addition, members may express their search, desire, and wait for their parents to show them love. They may express feelings of grief or loss about their lack of nurturing parents. Past and current pressures to remain in an unhealthy family system are also explored. Finally, the member may be concerned for the well-being of particular children in the family who may be vulnerable to the perpetrator. The need for the client, family, or therapists to report the suspected abuse must be emphasized.

An understanding of family dynamics is often important in the clients' search for meaning (Silver, Boon, & Stones, 1983). Recognizing and addressing family dysfunction should not be done in such a way as to minimize or deny the pathology and responsibility of the offender nor in such a way as to blame the nonoffending parent for the abuse. Unfortunately, this has happened in the incest literature and in therapy.

Sense of Self

Often, incest victims report a poor sense of self-esteem, a feeling of power or powerlessness, a distorted body image, fears of being crazy or different, and self-destructive behavior. Clients are helped to see themselves both as victims and as survivors. Seeing oneself as a victim addresses the areas of guilt and responsibility. The therapist's basic assumption must be that the child is never to blame for the abuse. The term survivor emphasizes the client's strength in coping with the abuse and her current ability to control her life. Seeing oneself as a survivor can reduce feelings of helplessness and increase self-esteem.

Interpersonal Relationships with Men and with Women

Issues of being close/distant, trusting, intimate, controlling or controlled in relationships, both past and present, are explored. Often, relationships in general are described as empty, superficial, conflicted, or sexualized (Courtois & Sprei, 1987). Not valuing themselves, victims are often vulnerable to revictimization in adult relationships.

Abuse Itself

In addition to these life spheres, the incest experience itself is discussed in the group. At their own pace, members disclose some of the details of the experience, including who abused them, what type of sexual activity was involved, where and when it occurred, and the method of coercion used. Members sometimes report pleasurable aspects of the abuse, their positive feelings toward the perpetrator, and that they initiated the activity at times; these feelings elicited intense emotions of guilt and shame.

STAGES OF THE GROUP

Because of its limited duration and its focus on incest and its after-effects, the time-limited group follows a set developmental sequence.

Session One: Getting to Know Each Other and Ground Rules

The leaders' task in the first session is to point out commonalities among the members, provide a safe supportive environment, and work toward building cohesiveness.

The session's focus is on the members getting to know each other and the discussion of ground rules. Because the ground rules were briefly described during the intake session and because interaction tends to relieve anxiety and enhance group cohesiveness, it is usually most effective to let members talk with each other first.

Members introduce themselves by telling only as much information as is comfortable for them. This often is followed by a discussion of previous disclosures and reactions to them. Members often discuss their reactions to being in a room with other incest survivors. Their feelings, expectations, and goals for attending the group are aired. During the last half-hour, ground rules are reviewed and homework is assigned. The leaders warn the group members that they may experience increased distress, including flashbacks and memories, as a normal reaction to being in the group. Members often fear that this reaction means they are "going crazy." Instead, they are told it means they are beginning to feel safe enough to relinquish survival mechanisms and to retrieve memories and feelings that were too painful to acknowledge outside of the supportive environment of the group.

Homework Assignments. Assignments are given at the end of most group sessions. The homework after the first meeting usually centers on self-nurturance. Typical assignments are "to do something good to yourself" or "to be good to the little girl inside of you." Because being self-nurturing is unfamiliar to many incest survivors, it is important to give examples of self-nurturing activities, such as taking a bubble bath, buying flowers, reading a favorite book, or taking an hour to relax. Difficulty in completing this assignment often leads to a discussion of the difference between being self-nurturing and being selfish.

In following weeks assignments are based on the topics discussed and each client's individual needs. Members are often asked to devise homework assignments for themselves, giving them a sense of control. Assignments have included (1) ask someone to do you a favor, (2) think about someone with whom you would like to be friends, (3) look at childhood photographs, (4) observe how people around you express anger, (5) write a letter (not to be sent) to your abuser, expressing how you feel, and (6) make a list of messages you were given about yourself as a child.

Sessions Two to Five: Focus on the Past

Pregroup Socializing. When the meeting room is available before the start of the session, leaders may suggest that members go straight to the room, rather than remaining in the waiting area. Having the women talk to each other before the therapists arrive can enhance group cohesiveness and the building of a support network.

Group Go-Around. Starting with the second session, each meeting begins with a brief go-around in which each member has the opportunity to discuss (1) events that occurred during the week, (2) reactions to or unfinished business from previous sessions, and (3) topics she would like to talk about during the session. This technique provides structure and consistency, ensures that each member has some "air time," and encourages the resolution of unfinished issues.

However, certain problems may arise in using the go-around. Some clients have difficulty maintaining brevity in discussing their concerns. Others may feel they need to be in crisis or greatly agitated in order to be heard. Perhaps being in crisis was the only way she could receive attention in her family. In the group, she learns that she can receive attention even when not in crisis. Often, the go-around focuses on current issues and individual concerns, which may result in an avoidance of deeper issues or of discussions of the incest. The leaders need to refocus the discussion by examining the issue, feelings, defenses, and behavioral patterns underlying current problems and by making connections between them and the abuse.

Focus on the Past. The focus of sessions two to five is primarily on the members' past as they describe their parents, siblings, and other relatives; family patterns; faulty childhood messages; and the abuse itself. Noone is forced to disclose more details than she chooses to reveal. The client remains in control of all disclosures. Possible reactions to "breaking the secret," including self-punishment, are discussed and monitored. Common elements of members' feelings and experiences are emphasized by the leaders. In this discussion, the member becomes attuned to the child inside of her and her feelings.

Session Four, Five, or Six: Putting the Wall Back Up

In many groups, the initial opening-up period is followed by a session in which members close up again. This may occur as a fear reaction to the intimacy and intensity of the group. Some members need to test their defenses to ensure that they are still working. Others fear further disclosure. All these reactions are ways by which the members can maintain control. In leading this session, the therapists should be supportive, nonpunitive, and respectful of their clients' right to maintain boundaries while reassuring them that it is safe to let go of past survival mechanisms. If the group cannot progress beyond this point, an evaluation or the introduction of an incest handout (Sprei & Fine, 1983) often helps the members refocus on the goals of the group.

Sessions Six to Eight: Focus on the Present

These sessions explore the members' present lives, including current relationships, problems, and behavioral patterns. Transference issues become more noticeable as members begin to discuss their reactions to other group members. Members may become more action-oriented, confronting family members, enrolling in school, developing support networks, reading books on incest, and starting to take better care of themselves.

Sessions Nine and Ten: Termination

Clients evaluate the progress they have made, the areas in which they wish to continue working, and their plans for continuing therapy. Some may try to avoid dealing with termination by suggesting that the group meet for an additional 10 weeks. Although continued contact among members is encouraged, the leaders must point out that the last session still represents an ending of the group and the members' relationships in their present form. It is important to give closure to the group experience.

THERAPIST ISSUES

Qualifications

In order to facilitate most effectively the time-limited group for adult incest victims, the co-leaders should possess knowledge and experience regarding the treatment of incest survivors, group leadership skills, and a feminist orientation in their overall approach to treatment. The feminist perspective focuses on the experience of the victim and views sexual violence as a logical consequence of women's less powerful status in society. The perpetrator is held responsible for his actions. Although family dynamics, including the possible role played by family members in the occurrence of incest are not ignored nor dismissed, belief in and support of the survivor are most strongly emphasized. Her emotions and experience are given primary consideration, with the goal of providing her safety and relief.

Roles of the Therapists

The co-leaders serve both as competent, appropriate therapists and as facilitators of group process. In performing those functions, the leaders should be nurturing but not indulgent. As discussed by Courtois and Watts (1982), the basic therapy stance should be nurturing and reality-based, as opposed to being abstinent or aloof. The therapists should convey a willingness to deal with all aspects of the abuse in an accepting and nonjudgmental manner. "Skepticism and questions about complicity may well be signs of professional unwillingness to deal with the issue directly" (Courtois & Watts, 1982).

The therapists also function as witnesses to the past abuse; they attest to it and validate it with the survivor. They act as the client's alter ego. Helping the member become attuned to her feelings, the therapists may at times even react for her when she is emotionally blocked. "Often all feelings are denied, despite the contradicting messages of body language and inappropriate affect. In these cases, the leaders need to gently point out that certain feelings would surely be natural in this situation and that such feelings are acceptable. . . . They should even be able to describe in physical terms what various emotions might be like" (Leehan & Wilson, 1985, pp. 86–87).

Finally, the therapists serve as role models and educators. Not only must they be models of understanding, patience, emotional sensitivity, and of fair unbiased authority, they must also be models for parents and other social roles (Leehan & Wilson, 1985).

Countertransference Issues

Because of the painful subject matter dealt with in an incest survivors' group, the therapists can feel overwhelmed when hearing of the abuse. To counter this pain, they may adapt defenses similar to those used by the incest survivor. These defenses include the following:

1. *Avoidance/minimization:* The incest experience might be avoided by encouraging the survivor not to discuss it; by changing the subject when it is brought up; by overgeneralizing the extent to which "we are all victims/survivors"; by muting language, such as avoiding words like abuse, incest, or violation; and by maintaining an overprofessional, aloof position.

2. *Overprotection/rescuing:* The therapists may treat the clients as damaged goods or as overly fragile without appreciating her strengths. Or the client may be treated as very special as the therapists make many special attempts to accomodate her. Doing so may result in overprotection of the client, with the therapists functioning as rescuers.

3. *Therapist anger and rage:* If expressed prematurely or too intensely, therapist rage can be problematic. Although it can be of great benefit to the survivor to have someone be angry about what happened to her, overly strong or mistimed reactions can be overwhelming. Too, that anger may block the client from expressing her ambivalent feelings or any tender or loving feelings she may have for the perpetrator or other family members (Courtois & Sprei, 1987).

4. *Voyeurism:* Privileged voyeurism may lead to an excessive interest in the sexual details of the incest without adequate attention to its aftereffects. The therapists may be so shocked or fascinated by the sexual behavior that they focus on it almost exclusively, leaving the incest victim feeling as if she was on the witness stand, forced to divulge her most embarrassing memories.

TRANSFERENCE ISSUES

In the following discussion, the author does not limit the use of the term "transference" to its traditional Freudian definition. Rather, it includes all projections onto the therapist and other group members arising from relationships with and feelings about people in the client's past. Members gain a clearer understanding of their family relationships by examining their interactions with other group members and leaders. This discussion will be limited to transference issues unique to group treatment. Courtois and Sprei (1987) discuss dynamics of incest and resultant transference reactions including trust/betrayal, negative self-concept, shame and stigmatization, guilt and complicity, loss and mourning, control and power, conflicted and ambivalent feelings, and defenses and survival skills.

Splitting of Therapists

Splitting is the defense mechanism used by the child to cope with inconsistencies in parental behavior. For example, the abuser may have been a loving father who provided attention and nurturance, but he was also abusive. The child, not able to conceptualize how her father could be both loving and abusive, splits the two so that when he is "good," she can block out the bad. The splitting may be transferred to the therapist, who is at times seen as supportive and nurturing (the good parent) and at other times as rejecting and controlling (the bad parent). In a group setting, this split is more often complete with one therapist seen as the good parent and the other one as the bad parent. The therapist who is the bad parent becomes the object of the client's rage.

Sibling Transferences

It is often possible to gain insight into the client's position in her family of origin by examining how she reacts to other group members and the roles she takes in the group. Sibling transferences may be manifested in the following ways: jealousy and rivalry, protecting or taking care of other members (taking the part of the older sister), wanting other members to take care of her and stand up to their abuser (acting the part of the younger sister), resenting that other members cannot protect her, competing for the therapists' attention, and comparing herself negatively to the other members.

Mother–Daughter Transferences

Older members may feel protective of younger members or may resent their needs. Younger members may desire closeness, feel resentful, rejected or disliked, smothered, misunderstood, protective of older members, or see them as helpless. In the safe environment of the group and with the distance that is possible outside the emotionally charged family relationships, clients can begin to understand the needs of their own mothers and children.

Self-Transferences: Projection

Members may project parts of themselves onto other group members. For example, one member projected her "bad, helpless child" onto another group member. As a result, she disliked her intensely. By working through this relationship, the client was able to recognize how much she rejected this part of herself. She began to understand and accept this disowned part.

CONCLUSION

Time-limited retrospective group therapy for incest victims is an effective modality for adult incest survivors. Group therapy can provide a quicker and more complete resolution of the problems of isolation, shame, secrecy, denial, and low self-esteem, which are common after-effects of the incest experience. The short duration of these groups ensures a more focused approach to the incest experience, minimizing interpersonal conflicts among group members. It also fits the schedules and organizational environments of most crisis service agencies. A careful intake process can screen out clients for whom this treatment modality is inappropriate. Through the nurturing, supporting stance of the therapist combined with exercises, focused discussion, and homework assignments, the group members can begin the process of growth and healing.

Conducting short-term therapy groups for incest survivors requires skill, creativity, warmth, compassion, fortitude, and humor. The work is often demanding, exhausting, and emotionally draining. It is also extremely rewarding. In a brief period of time, the therapist shares with the group members the pain of recalling the abuse, the strength of surviving, and the joy of growing and connecting with other women. Being part of this experience is truly inspirational and a gift.

REFERENCES

Benward, J., & Densen-Gerber, J. (1975). Incest as a causative factor in anti-social behavior: An exploratory study. *Contemporary Drug Problems, 4*(3), 323–340.

Browne, A., & Finkelhor, D. (1984). *The impact of child sexual abuse: A review of the literature.* Unpublished manuscript, University of New Hampshire, Family Violence Research Program.

Cole, E. L. (1985). A group design for adult female survivors of childhood incest. *Women and Therapy, 4*(3), 71–82.

Courtois, C. A. (1979). Characteristics of a volunteer sample of adult women who experienced incest in childhood and adolescence. (Unpublished doctoral dissertation, University of Maryland, 1979). *Dissertation Abstracts International, 40,* 3194A.

Courtois, C. A., & Sprei, J. (1987). Retrospective incest therapy for women. In L. E. Walker (Ed.), *A handbook on sexual abuse of children: Assessment and treatment issues.* New York: Springer.

Courtois, C. A., & Watts, D. (1982). Counseling adult women who experienced incest in childhood or adolescence. *Personnel and Guidance Journal, 60*(5), 275–279.

216 : : *Special Problems and Populations of Women*

Gelinas, D. J. (1983). The persisting negative effects of incest. *Psychiatry, 46*(4), 313–332.

Gordy, P. L. (1983). Group work that supports adult victims of childhood incest. *Social Casework: The Journal of Contemporary Social Work, 64*(5), 300–307.

Herman, J., & Schatzow, E. (1984). Time-limited group therapy for women with a history of incest. *International Journal of Group Psychotherapy, 34*(4), 605–616.

Leehan, J. & Wilson, L. P. (1985). *Grown-up abused children*. Springfield, IL.: Charles C Thomas Publishers.

Morrissey, K. (1982). *Self-help for women with a history of incest*. Paper presented at the American Psychiatric Association Convention, Toronto, Canada.

Peters, J. J. (1976). Children who are victims of sexual assault and the psychology of offenders. *American Journal of Psychotherapy, 30*(3), 398–421.

Russell, D. E. H. (1983). The incidence and prevalence of intrafamilial and extrafamilial sexual abuse of female children. *Child Abuse and Neglect, 7*(2), 133–146.

Silver, R. L., Boon, C., & Stones, M. H. (1983). Searching for meaning in misfortune: Making sense of incest. *Journal of Social Issues, 39*(2), 81–102.

Sprei, J., & Courtois, C. (1987). The treatment of women's sexual dysfunctions arising from sexual assault. In J. R. Field & R. A. Brown (Eds.), *Advances in the understanding and treatment of sexual problems: Compendium for the individual and marital therapist*. Jamaica, NY: Spectrum.

Sprei, J. E., & Fine, S. (1983). *Adaptation of Courtois' life spheres for group use*. Howard County Sexual Assault Center, MD.

Summit, R. (1983). The child sexual abuse accomodation syndrome. *Child Abuse and Neglect, 7*(2), 177–193.

Tsai, M. & Wagner, N. (1978). Therapy groups for women sexually molested as children. *Archives of Sexual Behavior, 7*(5), 417–427.

Weinberg, S. (1955). *Incest Behavior*. New York: Citadel Press.

■ 15
Reexamining Women's Roles: A Feminist Approach to Decreasing Depression in Women

MONIKA J. HAUSSMAN
and
JUDITH H. HALSETH

This chapter presents the theoretical context, rationale, participants, structure, content, process, and outcome of a 13-week group for depressed women in a rural area in Michigan.

CONTEXT

Depression is an extremely frequent phenomenon in the United States. More women are depressed than are men; estimates as to the exact ratio range from 2:1 to 10:1 (Radloff, 1978; Weissman & Klerman, 1977). Theoretical explanations regarding the prevalence of depression in women encompass genetic and endocrinological factors, depressogenic variables in women's socialization process, the learned helplessness model,

Reprinted from Lynn Clemmons Morris (Ed.) (1982). *Dignity, diversity, and opportunity in changing rural areas: Papers presented at the Sixth National Institute in Social Work in Rural Areas* (pp. 236–245). Reproduced by permission of the College of Social Work, University of South Carolina.

the cognitive model of depression, effects of marital and occupational roles, and social discrimination against women.

The socialization process for most women encourages nurturant, submissive, and conservative aspects of the female role, whereas assertiveness, achievement, orientation, and independence are explicitly discouraged (Block, Von der Lippe, & Block, 1973). Daughters, more so than sons, continue affiliations and dependencies well into adulthood (Hoffman, 1975). Women learn to vicariously achieve through their husband's and children's accomplishments rather than through their own (Lipman-Blumen & Leavitt, 1978). They tend to be submissive to a male-dominant-other and become economically, socially, and psychologically dependent (Arieti, 1979). Due to social discrimination, women have difficulties in achieving mastery, direct action, and self-assertion, which may lead to increased vulnerability to loss and to clinical depression (Weissman, 1980). Depressed individuals were found to view themselves as more responsible in interpersonal rather than impersonal contexts than nondepressed individuals (Rizley, 1978). High interpersonal responsibility for others' behavior was found to be more typical for women than for men (Alper, 1978). Traditional female roles of wife and mother may contribute to depression (Bernard, 1973; Radloff, 1975).

The combination of these vulnerability variables to depression—lack of direct achievement, high interpersonal responsibility, little actual power and status, psychological submissiveness to a dominant-other plus economic dependency and traditional sex-role attitudes—may partially account for why so many women are depressed in Western cultures.

TREATMENT APPROACHES

Rural, low-income women are especially vulnerable to depression due to lack of social and educational opportunities, inadequate resources in childcare, transportation difficulties, isolation, and traditional family role demands regardless of a woman's employment. Traditional approaches in the treatment of depression consist of medication and individual psychotherapy; though potentially helpful on a short-term basis, these approaches do little to prevent women's depression, which may be due more to societal inequities than to personal failures (Weissman, 1975).

Many community mental health centers are not yet designed to facilitate education and prevention; instead, they are often structured according to the medical model in dealing with individuals, with little consideration for larger societal components in a person's distress. Our concern was how we as mental health practitioners could assist women in decreasing depression within the parameters of a rural community mental health setting.

In a 1980 survey in Michigan, depression in women was found to be associated with perceiving one's partner as dominant, having a low sense of mastery and power, relying on others for achievement, blaming oneself for others' difficulties, and, if employed, having stereotypical attitudes toward women's roles (Haussman, 1981a, b). These factors are learned through sex-typed female socialization. They can be reexamined and unlearned.

A variety of approaches can facilitate such unlearning through a reexamination of women's roles: (1) Assertiveness training can counteract patterns of helplessness and submissiveness; women learn to challenge socialization messages and to develop a belief system about their personal rights (Butler, 1976). (2) Cognitive approaches can facilitate a rational examination of one's own assumptions and those of others about women's roles. Thus, women can acquire self-reliance and learn to distance themselves from cultural prejudices (Beck & Greenberg, 1974). (3) Consciousness-raising groups can facilitate the exploration of identity issues and can help women move from personal individual solutions to group actions (Kravetz, 1980). Women resocialize themselves and each other through role-modeling, opening-up, sharing, analyzing, and abstracting from their personal experiences (Kirsh, 1974). (4) Feminist therapists emphasize societal and personal changes rather than adjustment to the status quo. They view the therapist–client relationship as egalitarian; techniques are employed that enhance a client's sense of personal power, self-nurturance, and ability to express anger. The therapist serves as a role model and uses appropriate self-disclosure (Gilbert, 1980). (5) When dealing with women who have no or very little income, real life problems of economic survival can be addressed through vocational training programs (Messer & Lehrer, 1976). Reentry of women into school, training programs, or employment is a normal transitional stage; support groups are needed in dealing with problems of low self-confidence, role conflict and resulting guilt, and time management (Brooks, 1976). Manis and Mochizuki (1972) developed a Search for Fulfillment program at the Western Michigan University Counseling Center to help reentry homemakers remove psychological blocks that prevent them from changing their lives. This program consists of trust building, realistic assessment of one's own abilities and of available opportunities in the community, decision-making skills, and risk taking. (6) All-women groups are likely to be more effective than individual therapy or mixed-sex groups, because women then tend to become less dependent on one person and they learn to receive and give support and protection from and to other women (Carter, 1977).

The facilitators decided to offer an all-woman group, based on feminist principles and designed to decrease depression. The group consisted of an examination of women's roles, assertiveness training, consciousness-raising, and mutual support.

GROUP PARTICIPANTS

The group for depressed women was sponsored by Van Buren Community Mental Health, Paw Paw, Michigan. Van Buren County is a rural county in Southwestern Michigan, with agriculture, fruit farming, and wineries among the main sources of employment. The population is 66,000 and the largest town has 6,000 inhabitants. Approximately 20% of the county residents receive some form of welfare. About 11% of the residents are black, and there is a significant seasonal and "settled out" migrant population of Mexican-Americans and whites. There are more female clients than male clients at Van Buren County Community Mental Health, and many of the women clients are depressed.

In order to meet the needs of these depressed women, the facilitators designed a group, "Coping with Depression." The group was planned to last for seven weeks (two hours, one evening a week) and was expanded to 13 weeks at the clients' request. The 14 group participants were all clients at Van Buren County Community Mental Health. The facilitators encouraged other agency staff to refer women who were presently depressed, had some communication skills, and were not overtly psychotic at the time of the referral. Eleven participants have been seen individually by the co-facilitators.

Because no minority women participated, it is not known which parts of this group model would be effective with minority women. The mean age of the participants was 35. All have been married at one time, all had children, and all except one were economically dependent on a husband or on Aid for Dependent Children (ADC). Most of the women had completed high school, and their job skills and experience were minimal.

GROUP STRUCTURE, CONTENT, AND PROCESS

The co-facilitators' roles were to be responsible to the needs of individuals and the group, to suggest group activities, to provide resource materials, and to participate fully in the group activities. By listening, being supportive, and offering feedback, the co-facilitators served as role models for open communication.

Before the first group meeting, materials and themes were developed and collected. The facilitators both conducted for the first time a group specifically designed to assist women in coping with depression. Therefore, they allowed two hours for emotional preparation immediately prior to each group meeting, in addition to ample preparation time during the week, and debriefing time after each meeting. The two-hour time period prior to the meeting helped the facilitators relax, gain a break from a full day's work as individual therapists, and focus on the past week's group meeting. The plan for each specific session was developed week by week in order to be responsive to the needs and energy flow of the participants.

Basic materials used each session included easel and chart paper, marking pens, 3 × 5″ cards, and pencils. The women sat in an open circle of chairs. Each session began with an "opener" of an incomplete sentence such as "During the past week I felt depressed (or happy, or sad) when ...." In this and all other activities, participation was voluntary. The closure each week was also structured to encourage quieter women to participate. Open-ended statements were posted including "Tonight I learned ...," "I was pleased ...," and "I was displeased ..." (Manis, Lockwood, Nutter, Mochizuki, & Pattison, 1977a).

Brainstorming was frequently used, followed by posting of the ideas on chart paper and processing the feelings and the learning (Pfeiffer & Jones, 1979). Brief lectures and handouts were given on socialization messages girls and women receive (Jakubowski, 1977), depression (Gilmore, 1973), assertiveness (Manis, Lockwood, Nutter, Mochizuki, & Pattison, 1977b), anger (Bienvenu, 1976; Jones & Banet, 1976), and sexuality. Short homework assignments were given at many sessions.

A refreshment break each week encouraged mutual contact and support. Information was shared on community resources and women's activities. There was discussion of the value of continuing education and of paid employment outside the home. A book table was used one evening to display the facilitators' favorite books on women's development, assertiveness, and sexuality.

During the first seven weeks the activities were semistructured. The women brainstormed, posted, and processed the theme, "What we mean when we say 'I'm depressed' "; "Why people get depressed"; and "Why *women* get depressed." From individual and personal goals, group goals were developed, with the following themes emerging: (1) understand depression, (2) get support and reassurance from the group that I'm not always wrong, and (3) learn to stop feeling apologetic or guilty for asking or expecting partner to share responsibilities.

Anger was a significant issue for many women, and some were able to move from being afraid to feel or express anger toward allowing themselves choices about expressing anger in a variety of ways. Assertiveness, aggressiveness, and nonassertiveness were defined (Lange & Jakubowski, 1976), and the women encouraged each other to move assertively toward getting some of their own needs and rights met without violating the needs and rights of others. They discovered that they had rights that they had allowed others but not themselves; they learned to give themselves permission to nurture themselves and to speak in more positive terms about themselves.

After the first seven sessions, most participants expressed a strong desire to continue the group. Suggestions for improvement of the group were to allow more time to examine one's own difficulties, to role play more problem situations as they occur at home, and to spend more time sharing, discussing, and integrating new learning.

Therefore, the facilitators designed the next sessions to work in depth on individual concerns and kept structure and materials to a minimum. The group as a whole was expected to bring up and deal with highly personal issues. The utmost importance of confidentiality was reaffirmed. Participants dealt with a wide variety of intimate issues and shared previously kept family and personal secrets. The initial enthusiasm and risk-taking was followed by a session characterized by anxiety and withdrawal. The women examined the crucial question whether they could trust each other. Following this probing period, group members worked on problems with single mothering, unequal power distribution in one's marriage, value conflicts regarding women's roles, and the "empty nest" experience. From this work, the sense of trust and safety within the group reemerged. A commonly shared theme surfaced: The exploration of societal double standards regarding expectations of women and men. The group posted two lists, "A Good Woman Should ... ," and "A Good Man Should ... ." The group was amazed and concerned with the results. For the "good woman," 37 expectations were listed such as "put him first, let the man win, do as he says, always ask permission, not get sick—stay on feet even when sick, keep husband happy ... " For the "good man," only 10 expectations were listed, such as "not use all his money for his wants, show his feelings more, communicate with wife, take interest in children." The group discussed how attempting to fulfill the impossible masses of "good woman expectations" would make anyone depressed. The women realized the importance of developing realistic self-expectations based on one's own needs and wants, rather than living in an attempt to fulfill others' expectations.

The poster on the wall, a quote by Jean Baker Miller (1976), received renewed understanding and importance:

It is only when the woman can move away from thinking first of pleasing another and conforming to his desires and expectations that she can ever begin to know herself (p. 110).

The women worked on affirming their rights as individuals, explored career and lifestyle choices and options, and built increased assertiveness. They became aware of and confronted their tendencies to decrease their positive sense of self by discounting compliments and acknowledgments. Themes of gaining self-respect emerged: accepting and expressing feelings, owning pride in one's accomplishments, and understanding and choosing how to deal with one's anger. The participants recognized the sense of freedom that comes from taking charge of one's own life rather than asking one's partner to do so. Throughout the group, women were building an informal network system with each other and planned ways of continuing these networks. When the group closed after 13 sessions, the women noted an increased sense of personal power and a significant decrease in depression and helplessness. This resulted from a sense of belonging and trust in their value as women, individually as well as a group.

OUTCOME

Ten weeks after termination of the group, the facilitators mailed a group evaluation form. Excerpts from the members' written evaluations follow: "I liked the outward openness of all participants, having ideas tossed at you from all angles—brainstorming—to work with and improve on where *you* feel necessary"; "Having contact with other women who are depressed was important to me, and realizing that others have needs such as mine"; "We are helping each other outside the group, and we plan to go to school together"; "I'm not the only one with problems: just because you're married doesn't mean you're happy"; "I was able to obtain courage from the support in the group; I've become stronger in dealing with my problems and if it becomes necessary I can go off and live on my own without guilt"; "What I learned in the group was pretty scary at times; things were brought out that I didn't like at all, and I really didn't know the feelings were inside; but—it was good for me; now it's much easier to cope with problems; I feel a lot better about myself and everyone around me; I can state my feelings without being afraid of anger ... All in all what's really important for me is knowing I have a mouth and a brain and they both work! That makes me feel good!"

RECOMMENDATIONS

In addition to the subjective evaluation of the group process by the participants, the facilitators attempted to objectively measure the group members' varying levels of depression. A self-report depression scale, the CES-D scale (Radloff, 1977), was administered to the group members at the initial session, after the seven semistructured sessions, and at the closing session. As some group members chose to fill out the questionnaire at home and failed to complete and return the questionnaires, the available data are inconclusive. Preferably, group participants would be asked to complete the questionnaires at the beginning of certain predetermined sessions to accurately measure variations in levels of depression throughout the group process.

Another suggestion is to initially plan a 10- to 16-session group; thus, more time would be allowed for the shift from a semistructured, socioeducational approach to a dynamic, personal growth oriented group, which required more trust and personal openness.

Some women mentioned difficulties in making childcare arrangements. It would be advantageous to offer childcare within the agency for the period of the group sessions.

CONCLUSION

For many depressed women, their environments and lifestyles play an intricate part in their depression; thus, the larger interpersonal and societal context must be addressed. In this 13-session group, we examined and worked on many issues in the lives of previously depressed rural women: challenging female role stereotypes, developing self-reliance rather than depending exclusively on a man, exploring and expressing anger, asserting oneself, learning to nurture oneself, and networking with each other to decrease isolation and increase female bonding and support.

Based on the positive responses of the women to this group, we believe that women can be assisted in decreasing their depression through a nontraditional feminist approach. Important in this process is learning to challenge societal role expectations and to develop a healthy definition of one's self. And this can be done in the supportive context of a women's group.

REFERENCES

Alper, T. (1978). Achievement motivation in college women: A now-you-see-it-now-you-don't phenomenon. In L. S. Hansen & R. S. Rapoza (Eds.), *Career development and counseling of women.* Springfield, IL: Charles C Thomas.

Arieti, S. (1979, April). The roots of depression: The power of the dominant other. *Psychology Today,* pp. 54, 57–58, 92–93.

Beck, A. T., & Greenberg, R. L. (1974). Cognitive therapy with depressed women. In V. Franks & V. Burtle (Eds.), *Women and therapy: New psychotherapies for a changing society.* New York: Brunner/Mazel.

Bernard, J. (1973). *The future of marriage.* New York: Bantam.

Bienvenu, M. J., Sr. (1976). Inventory of anger communication. In J. W. Pfeiffer & J. E. Jones (Eds.), *The 1976 annual handbook for group facilitators.* San Diego, CA: University Associates.

Block, J., Von der Lippe, A., & Block, J. H. (1973). Sex-role socialization patterns: Some personality concomitants and environmental antecedents. *Journal of Consulting and Clinical Psychology, 41,* 321–341.

Brooks, L. (1976). Supermoms shift gears: Re-entry women. *The Counseling Psychologist, 6*(2), 33–37.

Butler, P. A. (1976). *Self-assertion for women: A guide to becoming androgynous.* San Francisco: Harper & Row.

Carter, D. K. (1977). Counseling divorced women. *Personnel and Guidance Journal, 55*(9), 537–541.

Gilbert, L. A. (1980). Feminist therapy. In A. M. Brodsky & R. T. Hare-Mustin (Eds.), *Women and psychotherapy: An assessment of research and practice.* New York: Guilford Press.

Gilmore, S. K. (1973). If you're depressed, you're probably sub-assertive. In. J. R. Leppaluoto (Ed)., *Women on the move: A feminist perspective.* Eugene, OR: University of Oregon.

Haussman, M. J. (1981a). Women's roles and vulnerability to depression (Doctoral dissertation, Western Michigan University, 1981). *Dissertation Abstracts International, 42,*2130B. (University Microfilms, No. 81-24, 216).

Haussman, M. J. (1981b). *Women's roles and vulnerability to depression.* Paper presented at the Eighth Annual National Conference on Feminist Psychology, Association for Women in Psychology, Boston. (ERIC Document Reproduction Service NO. ED 216 250).

Hoffman, L. W. (1975). Early childhood experiences and women's achievement motives. In M. T. S. Mednick, S. S. Tangri, & L. W. Hoffman (Eds.), *Women and achievement.* Washington, DC: Hemisphere.

Jakubowski, P. A. (1977). Assertive behavior and clinical problems of women. In E. I. Rawlings & D. K. Carter (Eds.), *Psychotherapy for women: Treatment toward equality.* Springfield, IL: Charles C Thomas.

Jones, J. E., & Banet, A. G., Jr. (1976). Dealing with anger. In J. W. Pfeiffer & J. E. Jones (Eds.), *The 1976 annual handbook for group facilitators.* San Diego, CA: Univeristy Associates.

Kirsh, B. (1974). Consciousness-raising groups as therapy for women. In. V. Franks & V. Burtle (Eds.), *Women in therapy: New psychotherapies for a changing society.* New York: Brunner/Mazel.

Kravetz, D. F. (1980). Consciousness-raising and self-help. In A. M. Brodsky & R. T. Hare-Mustin (Eds.), *Women and psychotherapy: An assessment of research and practice.* New York: Guilford Press.

Lange, A. J., & Jakubowski, P. A. (1976). *Responsible assertive behavior: Cognitive/ behavior procedures for trainers.* Champaign, IL: Research Press.

Lipman-Blumen, J., & Leavitt, H. J. (1978). Vicarious and direct achievement patterns in adulthood. In. L. S. Hansen & R. S. Rapoza (Eds.), *Career development and counseling of women.* Springfield, IL: Charles C Thomas.

Manis, L., Lockwood, K., Nutter, S., Mochizuki, J., & Pattison, M. (1977a). *Assertiveness training workshop.* Kalamazoo, MI: Susan B. Anthony Press.

Manis, L., Lockwood, K., Nutter, S., Mochizuki, J., & Pattison, M. (1977b). *Leader's handbook for one-day assertiveness training workshop.* Kalamazoo, MI: Susan B. Anthony Press.

Manis, L. G., & Mochizuki, J. (1972). Search for fulfillment: A program for adult women. *Personnel and Guidance Journal, 50*(7), 594–599.

Messer, S. B., & Lehrer, P. M. (1976). Short-term groups with female welfare clients in a job-training program. *Professional Psychology, 7*(3), 352–358.

Miller, J. B. (1976). *Toward a new psychology of women.* Boston: Beacon Press.

Pfeiffer, J. W., & Jones, J. E. (1979). *Reference guide to handbooks and annuals* (3rd ed.). San Diego, CA: University Associates.

Radloff, L. S. (1975) Sex differences in depression: The effects of occupation and marital status. *Sex roles, 1*(2), 249–265.

Radloff, L. S. (1977). The CES-D scale: A self-report depression scale for research in the general population. *Applied Psychological Measurement, 1*(3), 385–401.

Radloff, L. S. (1978). *Sex roles, helplessness, and depression.* Unpublished manuscript, Center for Epidemiological Studies, National Institute of Mental Health, Rockville, MD.

Rizley, R. (1978). Depression and distortion in the attribution of causality. *Journal of Abnormal Psychology, 87*(1), 32–48.

Weissman, M. M. (1975). *Depressed women: Traditional and non-traditional therapies.* Paper presented at the Eighth Annual Symposium, Effective Psychotherapy, Texas Research Institute of Mental Sciences, Houston, TX.

Weissman, M. M. (1980). Depression. In. A. M. Brodsky & R. T. Hare-Mustin (Eds.), *Women and psychotherapy: An assessment of research and practice.* New York: Guilford Press.

Weissman, M. M., & Klerman, G. L. (1977). Sex differences and the epidemiology of depression. *Archives of General Psychiatry, 34*(1), 98–111.

■ 16
Preorgasmic Group Treatment: Marital Adjustment and Sexual Function in Women

**ANNIE L. COTTEN-HUSTON and
KATHERINE A. WHEELER**

Despite some changes in sexual attitudes in recent years, little progress appears to have been made in the reduction of female orgasmic dysfunction. Kinsey, Pomeroy, Martin, & Gebhard (1953, p. 513) reported that 10% of married American women and 30% of sexually active unmarried women never experienced orgasm. Only 40% of married women were orgasmic in 90 to 100% of their coital experiences (p. 403). Twenty years later roughly the same figures were reported in surveys by Hunt (1974) and Hite (1976). Along with contemporary media attention to women's rights to pleasure and demands for increased human rights and privileges, there has appeared a change in ideas about female sexuality. Undoubtedly, the Women's Movement has influenced this change (see, for example, Cassell, 1984; Dodson, 1975; Hite, 1976; Laws & Schwartz, 1977; Seaman, 1972).

The first major contribution to scientific data regarding human sexuality was that of Kinsey and colleagues (1953) who openly collected a substantial objective body of facts about sexual behavior. It was not until the landmark work of Masters and Johnson (1966, 1970), however, that basic

Published in a shortened version in *Journal of Sex and Marital Therapy,* 1983, 9(4), 296–302.

data on the physiology of human sexual response were made available. Masters and Johnson (1966) demonstrated in the laboratory that physiologically there is essentially only one kind of female orgasm with both vaginal and clitoral components. More recently it has been shown that vaginal orgasms can result from manual or coital stimulation of the Grafenberg spot, a remnant of the prostate gland found in the vagina behind the symphisis pubic bone (Perry and Whipple, 1981). This research has not been pursued by Masters and Johnson and has gathered some controversy in scientific circles. It thus appears that sexual dysfunctions in women are still shrouded with confusion and misunderstanding (Cassell, 1984; Faulk, 1973; Heinrich, 1976; Kaplan, 1974, 1979; LoPiccolo, 1978; Masters and Johnson, 1970; Masters, Johnson, & Kolodny, 1985; Mead, 1949; Scherfey, 1972). Controversy surrounding types of female orgasm (Bohlen, Held, Sanderson, & Boyer, 1982; LoPiccolo & Heiman, 1978; Schneiderman & McGuire, 1976; Schulman, 1972; Sherfey, 1972; Singer & Singer, 1972), the variant capacities of women to experience coital orgasm (Brindley & Gillan, 1982; Kaplan, 1974; Wilcox & Hager, 1980), the role of the muscles surrounding the vagina in orgasm (Graber, 1982; Sultan & Chambles, 1982; Trudel & Saint Laurent, 1983), and the connection between orgasm and female sexual satisfaction (Waterman & Chiauzzi, 1982) give evidence of continuing uncertainty.

The term "preorgasmic" was introduced by Barbach (1975) to substitute for primary orgasmic dysfunction. "Preorgasmic" provides a more positive, optimistic connotation and implies that women simply have not yet learned how to achieve an orgasm. Preorgasmic group treatment is defined here as an eclectic approach (Carlson & Wheeler, 1980) combining Barbach's (1980) group method, the nine-step program prescribed by LoPiccolo and Lobitz (1972) and Masters and Johnson's (1970) intensive sex therapy program.

Vicarious learning is the process of learning through modeling or through reports of others. The most important aspect of the preorgasmic group treatment process is the format of a small group of women meeting to discuss their sexual dissatisfaction and working together to overcome their orgasmic difficulties. Research by Berzon, Pious, and Parson (1963) showed that the main curative mechanism of their short-term therapy was the interaction among group members. They found that the influence of the therapist was less important than the interpersonal feedback, which enabled patients to reconstruct their self-images in part because they realized that their problems were not unique.

The group format provides significant reduction in therapist time and patient costs and makes sex therapy accessible to a greater number of people. Wallace and Barbach (1974) pioneered preorgasmic women's groups at the University of California Medical Center in San Francisco. They designed these groups specifically to provide short-term group treatment for anorgasmic women. The women were treated without their partners present, thus making treatment available to any woman regardless of her current partner situation. Up to that time, treatment for women without partners, who were willing to participate, was not readily available.

The two primary components of the treatment were the use of the direct masturbation program developed by LoPiccolo and Lobitz (1972) and the supportive, desensitizing experience of being with a group of women having the same sexual difficulty. The groups were run by two female co-therapists and met for 10 two-hour sessions. The co-therapists actively assisted the women in realizing that they had a right to sexual pleasure and that their bodies and their sexuality were positive. In addition to this verbal retraining and relearning, at each session the women were assigned homework to be practiced for an hour a day at home. During the following session, each women related in detail her experience with her assignment. After the first few sessions, assignments were given according to the specific needs of individual women.

Unlike most of the sex therapy approaches, no restriction was ever placed on sexual intercourse. However, there was an initial prohibition placed on efforts to have orgasm during intercourse. Rather than stressing orgasm through intercourse, or any other "ideal" sexual response, the treatment was aimed at allowing the woman to expand her repertoire of sexual activities in ways that met her unique needs and capabilities.

Preorgasmic group treatment was available in the private practice of Drs. Sumner, Wheeler, and Smith of the Ob-Gyn Group of Manchester, Connecticut, for 64 women with either primary or secondary orgasmic dysfunction who completed a course of treatment. Many of the women kept in touch over the past years through biannual reunions, which were held at one of the co-therapists' homes. Participatory women have demonstrated many positive changes in their lives; however, enough divorces and separations have occurred to cause some concern. There are several hypotheses one might make concerning the reasons for this. First, it may be that some of the women were involved in relationships that were troubled when they entered the program and perhaps saw this as a "last resort." Second, it may be that as the women became more assertive sexually, and/or in general, they may have decided that they did not want to stay in a relationship that did not meet their needs. Third, their new assertiveness and sexual independence may have been too threatening to their partners. This risk of separation or divorce was pointed out to the women at the beginning of each course of treatment. Research concerning this group treatment approach yielded some important treatment effects (Cotten-Huston & Wheeler, 1983) concerning the following hypotheses.

HYPOTHESES

I

Subjects in the treatment group would report higher frequency of orgasm, in a variety of situations, than those in the control group as measured by the General Information Questionnaire (Heinrich, 1976).

II

Following treatment, subjects in the treatment group would rate their general frequency and pleasure of sexual activities higher than subjects in the control group.

III

Subjects in the treatment group would have higher scores in the Dyadic Adjustment Scale (Spanier, 1976) than those in the control group indicating a harmonious, stable relationship.

IV

Subjects in the treatment group would have higher scores in the Sexual Arousal Inventory (Hoon, Hoon, & Wincze, 1976) than those in the control group, indicating a change in attitude and perception.

V

Subjects in the treatment group would have become more assertive than those in the control group, as measured by the Gambrill–Richey Assertion Inventory (Gambrill & Richey, 1975).

METHOD

Subjects and Design

At the Ob-Gyn Group of Manchester, 64 women had completed the 10-week course of preorgasmic group treatment. Of these 64 women, 38 participated in the study. Some had moved away, and some never returned the questionnaires. Of the mailing list of 60 women who had expressed an interest in joining the group, 32 women participated as a comparison group. Information was collected either in small groups or by mail over a period of four months. If a woman wished to remain anonymous, she was asked to put an identification number on her questionnaire. The women in both groups were contacted by telephone, and the project was explained to them. They were asked if they wanted to participate, and all of them agreed. Twenty sets of questionnaires were never returned by mail.

The control versus treatment group method was used. The length of time between completion of the course and participation in the study varied from one week to five years, a factor that could have been controlled for with pre- and posttest design. All the women in both groups were heterosexual and shared the presenting complaint of either primary or secondary orgasmic dysfunction, making the two groups matched in that respect. Other similarities in the two groups included geographic location, education, economic, religious, and racial backgrounds. All the women were white, with an average income of $25,000. Fifty-one (73%) were married; 10 (14%) were divorced; seven (10%) were single; two (3%) were separated. The average length of time married was 12.3 years. The mean number of children was 1.8, with 20 women having no children. Fifteen (23%) were high school graduates, whereas 22 (33%) had attended college; 19 (28%) held Bachelor's degrees, and 8 (12%) had graduate degrees. One had special training for her job, and two were diploma R.N.'s. Fifty-one (73%) were working outside the home, whereas eight (12%) said they were students.

The range in age was 21 to 55 for the total sample. The mean for the control group was 31 years of age, whereas the treatment group mean was 34. There were 14 women under the age of 30 in the control group, and only 7 under that age in the treatment group, indicating that the treatment group was slightly older. The control group was slightly smaller than the treatment group. Age was the only significant difference between the two groups on demographic analysis: $t(68) = 2.24$; $p < 0.03$.

Measures

Three of the measures selected were used in a dissertation by Heinrich (1976): General Information Questionnaire, Survey of Sexual Activity, and the Locke–Wallace Marital Adjustment Scale (Locke & Wallace, 1959). Heinrich analyzed three groups of preorgasmic women ($N = 44$) who were randomly assigned to three conditions: Group Treatment (15 subjects), based on the standard treatment approach; Education Treatment (one-time meeting in which all the information and materials needed to self-direct the program at home were presented to 15 subjects); and a Waiting List (14 subjects). The General Information Questionnaire and the Survey of Sexual Activity were designed by Heinrich and were especially relevent to the investigation. Because of its current validity and reliability, the Dyadic Adjustment Scale (adapted by Spanier, 1976) replaced the original Locke-Wallace Marital Adjustment Scale (Locke & Wallace, 1959) that Heinrich used. The Sexual Arousal Inventory (Hoon, Hoon & Wincze, 1976) was selected for its ease of scoring the appropriateness, and the Gambrill-Richey Assertion Inventory (Gambrill & Richey, 1975) was deemed relevant because of its capacity to analyze a subject's behavior and desire to work on situations to become more assertive.

RESULTS

Analysis of variances revealed sigificant differences between the two groups in several areas. On three of the measures, findings yielded significant t-test scores related to the General Arousal Inventory. Although the Dyadic Adjustment Scale and the Assertion Inventory did not show significant differences between the two groups, some implications for treatment were revealed.

Hypothesis I

It was predicted that subjects in the treatment group would report a higher frequency of orgasms, in a variety of situations, as measured by the General Information Questionnaire. Women in the treatment group did report frequency of orgasm through masturbation significantly more often than women in the control group, $t(68) = 6.34$, $p < 0.001$. In fact, 77% of the treatment group women reported orgasm through masturbation more than once a week, whereas 60% of the control group women reported this sexual activity less than once a month or not at all, $t(7) = 28.82$, $p < 0.0002$. Of the women in the treatment group, 62% reported ability to reach orgasm through masturbation all (100%) of the time, whereas in the control group only 28% reported this same competency, $t(6) = 17.35$, $p < 0.008$. However, there was no significant difference between the two groups in orgasm frequency during partner related activities, such as coitus, with or without clitoral stimulation. This hypothesis received only partial support, therefore, in that while women in the treatment group did report significantly higher frequency of orgasm through masturbation, this frequency did not generalize to a variety of situations.

Hypothesis II

Following treatment, it was predicted that subjects in the treatment group would rate their general frequency and pleasure of sexual activities higher than subjects in the control group.

The Survey of Sexual Activity (SSA) was divided into two parts: (1) How often does the activity occur? and (2) How pleasant do you find the activity?

SSA Part One.   Women in the treatment group found themselves able to talk about their sexual concerns with other women more often, $t(67) = 3.19, p < 0.002$. They also felt like "a desirable sexual partner" more often, $t(67) = 2.50, p < 0.015$. Treatment group women were able to tell their partners specifically what feels good during foreplay and coitus more often, $t(66) = 4.53, p < 0.001$ and reported having more sexual fantasies, $t(67) = 1.94, p < 0.05$. Further treatment effects revealed the ability to (1) demonstrate more often to their partners how they reached orgasm, $t(67) = 3.42, p < 0.001$, and (2) to feel more comfortable and accepting of their own sexuality than the control group women, $t(67) = 3.86, p < 0.001$. In addition, they reported appreciating their own unique capacities for sexual pleasure and enjoyment more often than the control group women, $t(66) = 4.52, p < 0.001$.

SSA Part Two.   Women in the treatment group found it more pleasant to look at themselves both dressed, $t(67) = 2.78, p < 0.007$, and nude, $t(66) = 2.11, p < 0.035$, in a full length mirror. Treatment group women also found more pleasure in washing their bodies during a bath or shower, $t(66) = 2.58, p < 0.012$, and looking at their genitals in a hand mirror, $t(66) = 4.51$, $p < 0.001$. They found pleasure in caressing and stimulating their own breast, $t(66) = 2.77, p < 0.007$. They were also more pleased when their partner saw their genital area, $t(66) = 2.76, p < 0.007$. It was more pleasant for them to anticipate having coitus and sex play with their partner than the control group, $t(66) = 2.45, p < 0.017$, and they reported more pleasurable sexual fantasies, $t(67) = 3.35, p < 0.001$, and enjoyment of erotic materials, $t(66) = 3.28, p < 0.001$. It was more pleasurable too for them to give themselves or have their partner give them clitoral stimulation during intercourse, $t(64) = 3.38, p < 0.001$. They further enjoyed experiencing themselves as sexual beings with sexual likes and dislikes, $t(64) = 5.01, p < 0.001$, and thinking of their desirability as a sexual partner, $t(67) = 2.53$, $p < 0.014$, significantly more than the control group. In conclusion, there was very strong support for this hypothesis. The difference between the two groups indicated a positive change in the behavior and attitude of the women in the treatment group toward themselves and their partners.

Hypothesis III

It was predicted that women in the treatment group would have higher scores on the Dyadic Adjustment Scale than those in the control group. No significant difference was found on t-test scores on this measure; therefore, the hypothesis could not be supported.

Hypothesis IV

The prediction of this hypothesis was that the women in the treatment group would have higher scores on the Sexual Arousal Inventory than those in the control group, perhaps indicating some change in attitude and perception as a result of the treatment.

The treatment group did have significantly higher scores on this measure, $t(68) = 3.11, p < 0.003$. The mean for the control group was 68, and the mean for the treatment group was 87. The mean for the validation sample was 80.9. Women who participated in the validity sample were somewhat younger than the women in this study; however, it was apparent from this study that women who sought treatment for orgasmic dysfunction frequently had arousal dysfunctions as well. It was also apparent that this form of treatment was effective for these women. Of all the measures used in this study, the Sexual Arousal Inventory was the one that seemed most effective in showing the women themselves how much they had changed in 10 weeks' time. Treatment group women reported feeling more aroused during foreplay, $t(67) = 2.90, p < 0.005$, and coitus, $t(66) = 2.51, p < 0.015$. Additionally, in response to their partner's sexual advances, treatment group women said they usually respond with pleasure, $t(65) = 2.98, p < 0.004$.

Hypothesis V

This hypothesis predicted that the Assertion Inventory would show the women in the treatment group to be more assertive than those in the control group. While the t-test did not show any significant differences between the two groups, there were some indications that the treatment group women became slightly more assertive.

To establish average scores of "normal" people, the Assertion Inventory was administered to 313 male and female college students. It was found that the average discomfort score was 95, and the average response probability score was 104. These scores were subsequently used as general averages. A higher than normal discomfort score (96 and above) and a higher than average response probability score (105 and above) placed a person in the "nonassertive profile." Being in this profile meant that a person reported high discomfort for most of the 40 situations on the Assertion Inventory and low likelihood in engaging in assertive behavior.

The mean score for discomfort of the control group in this study was 107 (above 96 = high), and the treatment group mean was 101 (also above 96), indicating more anxiety in the control group. Moreover, the mean scores for response probability of the control group was 109 (above 105 = low probability with the score reversed so that the higher the score the lower the probability of response). The score for response probability for the treatment group was 107, only a slight difference but nonetheless in the direction of the predicted hypothesis. In conclusion, then, even though these *t*-test scores were not significant, they were in the direction of the predicted hypothesis, suggesting that further research with a larger sample might provide evidence to support the hypothesis.

Of interest particularly was the finding that both groups were nonassertive. At the end of the Assertion Inventory all participants were asked to go back and circle any of the 40 items they would like to work on. The items they selected most often were described as "Item Cluster Three" or "Expressing negative concerns." This cluster includes such items as "Tell a person with whom you are intimately involved when he or she does something that bothers you," "Tell a person when you feel that he or she has done something that is unfair to you," and "Ask a person who is annoying you in a public situation to stop." Assertiveness, thus, appeared to be a part of the total problem that these women have.

Additional evidence of the role of assertiveness was found in the Survey of Sexual Activity. In response to the question, "Can you tell your partner specifically what feels good to you during foreplay and intercourse?," the control group had significantly more difficulty than the treatment group, $(66) = 4.53, p < 0.001$. Furthermore, treatment group women initiated sex more often than the control group women, $t(66) = 3.56, p < 0.001$. These findings suggested increased assertiveness as a result of treatment.

Along with assertiveness one might expect to see changes in self-esteem. Two findings did lend support to that theory: Treatment group women felt more knowledgeable about their bodies, $t(68) = 2.98, p < 0.004$, and reported more satisfaction with their overall self-image, $t(68) = 2.80, p < 0.005$.

DISCUSSION

Clearly, there were many significant differences between the two groups in this study. The demographic similarities in the two groups contribute strong support for the theory that preorgasmic group treatment was responsible for those differences.

The first hypothesis stated that subjects in the treatment group would report higher frequency of orgasm in a variety of situations than those in the control group as measured by the General Information Questionnaire. The findings in hypothesis I indicate a significant increase in the frequency of orgasm through self stimulation, thus supporting the finding of Heinrich (1976) that orgasm frequency was statistically significant following treatment. It is of interest that Heinrich also reported increased self esteem and improved ability to communicate sexually with a partner. Although it might be dissapointing that orgasm frequently was not increased in a variety of situations, it is important to note that similar findings were reported by Heinrich (1976) and others (Wallace & Barbach 1974; Kinsey et al., 1953; LoPiccolo & Lobitz, 1972). There seems to be a consensus that orgasm during intercourse has a lower probability of occurrence than through masturbation. It is also worth noting that, in spite of this, many women listed orgasm during intercourse as their only acceptable goal. Self-stimulation with the partner presence (for the purpose of instruction) was the only partner-related activity in which a significant increase in orgasmic frequency was found in the present study. Thus, orgasm through masturbation may be a transitional step for orgasm through sexual intercourse.

This group treatment approach challenged the notion that orgasm during coitus is the only "authentic" orgasm for women and activity established alternative orgasmic patterns. The treatment structure stressed working on sexual response independent of the partner as well as providing the women with the necessary education and the techniques to change their behavior. Thus, taking responsibility for one's own sexuality was an important concept in treatment and could be viewed as a way for women to "catch up" with men sexually, since most men know how to reach orgasm before they begin to share sexual activity.

The second hypothesis stated that, following treatment, subjects in the treatment group would rate their general frequency and pleasure of sexual activities higher than subjects in the control group. In hypothesis II, women in the treatment group did rate their general frequency and pleasure of sexual activities significantly higher than women in the control group. Further, treatment group women felt like a "desirable sexual partner" more often and were more comfortable with clitoral stimulation during sexual activity. They were able to demonstrate to their partners what felt good to them during a sexual encounter. It appeared that communication improved, since they were able to tell their partner what felt good to them during foreplay and intercourse. They were able to enjoy sexual fantasies and erotic materials more often, an apparent indication of increased comfort with their sexuality. More of them found it pleasant to look at themselves both dressed and nude in a mirror, perhaps an indication of increased self-esteem. They also took more pleasure in washing their own bodies and looking at their genitals in a hand mirror and were more pleased when their partner saw their genital area. It was more pleasant for them to anticipate having coitus and sex play than for the control group women and they took more pleasure in experiencing themselves as sexual beings. All of these findings indicate that feeling better about their own bodies helped them to feel better about their sexuality.

Results appeared to support the Wallace and Barbach (1974) evaluation of a group of 17 women who had been treated for anogasmia—treatment during which several additional aspects of the women's lives, such as a general level of happiness and relaxation, appeared to change.

It should be pointed out that the initial concern of the researchers about divorces or separations amoung treatment group women found no support, since there was no significant difference between the two groups on marital status. Further, the finding of no significant difference between the two groups on the Dyadic Adjustment Scale added to the reassurance that the treatment did not influence the relationship significantly. However, the Dyadic Adjustment Scale, being a stable measure, may not be sensitive to flexibility or change in a relationship, as in transitional sexual dysfunctions.

It should be noted that of all the measures used in this study, the Sexual Arousal Inventory (SAI) appeared to be the most sensitive intrument for assessment of the women's change over time. One important earlier finding was that women who had more sexual experience had higher scores on sexual arousal (Hoon, Hoon, & Wincze, 1976). Overall findings in the present study supported that finding and suggest the SAI as a valuable aid in preorgasmic group treatment.

Even though the treatment group did not reflect significantly higher scores on the Assertion Inventory, there was some evidence from survey findings that this hypothesis might have found significant support in a larger sample. For example, assertiveness may play an important role in learning to communicate sexually with a partner, as in questions about what feels good during love-making. Sexual communication, however, as well as assertiveness and dyadic adjustment, are undoubtedly influenced by partner reponse.

Of particular interest was the finding of masturbation as an aid to learning adequate sexual response. However, generalization of these results is limited by the part played by emotions and sex guilt in transferring masturbation experience to love-making with a partner.

Important research for the future, then, needs to include partner attitudes toward and behavioral responses to female increases in sexual arousal, activity, and pleasure.

REFERENCES

Barbach, L. G. (1975). *For yourself: The fulfillment of female sexuality.* New York: Doubleday & Co.

Barbach, L. G. (1980). *Women discover orgasm.* New York: Free Press.

Berzon, B., Pious, G., & Parson, R. (1963). The therapeutic event group psychotherapy: A study of subjective reports by group members, *Journal of Individual Psychology, 19,* 204–212.

Bohlen, J. G., Held, J. P., Sanderson, M. O., & Boyer, C. M. (1982). Development of a woman's multiple orgasm pattern: A research case report. *Journal of Sex Research, 18*(2), 360–363.

Brindley, G. S., & Gillan, P. (1982). Men and women who do not have orgasms. *British Journal of Psychiatry, 140,* 351–356.

Carlson, B., & Wheeler, K. (1980). Group counseling for pre-orgasmic women. *Topics in Clinical Nursing, 1*(4), 9–18.

Cassell, C. (1984). *Swept away: Why women fear their own sexuality.* New York: Simon and Schuster.

Cotten-Huston, A. L., & Wheeler, K. (1983). Pre-orgasmic group treatment: Assertiveness, marital adjustment and sexual function in women, *Journal of Sex and Marital Therapy, 9*(4), 296–302.

Dodson, B. (1975). *Liberating masturbation: A meditation in self-love.* New York: Bodysex Designs.

Faulk, M. (1983). Frigidity: A critical review. *Archives of Sexual Behavior, 2*(3), 257–266.

Gambrill, E. D., & Richey, C. A. (1975). An assertion inventory for use in assessment and research. *Behavior Therapy, 5*(4), 550–561.

Graber, B. (Ed.) (1982). *Circumvaginal musculature and sexual function.* New York: Karger.

Heinrich, A. G. (1976). The effect of group and self-directed behavioral-treatment of primary orgasmic dysfunction in females treated without their partners. (Doctoral dissertation, University of Colorado, 1976). *Dissertation Abstracts International, 37,* 1902B. (University Microfilm NO. 76-23, 623).

Hite, S. (1976). *The Hite report.* New York: Macmillan.

Hoon, E. F., Hoon, P. W., & Wincze, J. P. (1976). An inventory for the measurement of female sexual arousability: The SAI. *Archives of Sexual Behavior, 5*(4), 291–300.

Hunt, M. (1974). *Sexual behavior in the 1970's.* Chicago: Playboy Press.

Kaplan, H. S. (1974). *The new sex therapy.* New York: Brunner/Mazel.

Kaplan, H. S. (1979). *Disorders of sexual desire.* New York: Brunner/Mazel.

Kinsey, A. C., Pomeroy, W. B., Martin, C. E., & Gebhard, P. H. (1953). *Sexual behavior in the human female.* New York: Simon & Schuster, Pocket Books.

Laws, J. L., & Schwartz, T. (1977). *Sexual scripts: The social construction of female sexuality.* Hinsdale, IL: Dryden Press.

Locke, H., & Wallace, K. (1959). Short marital and adjustment tests: Their reliability and validity, *Marriage and Family Living, 21*(3), 251–255.

LoPiccolo, J., & Heiman, J. (1978). The role of cultural values in the prevention and treatment of sexual problems. In C. B. Qualls, J. P. Wincze, & D. H. Barlow (Eds.), *The Prevention of Sexual Disorders.* New York: Plenum Press.

LoPiccolo, J., & Lobitz, E. C. (1972). The role of masturbation in the treatment of orgasmic dysfunction. *Archives of Sexual Behavior, 2*(2), 163–171.

LoPiccolo, J., & LoPiccolo, L. (1978). *Handbook of sex therapy.* New York: Plenum Press.

Masters, W., & Johnson, V. (1966). *Human sexual response.* Boston: Little, Brown.

Masters, W., & Johnson, V. (1970). *Human sexual inadequacy.* Great Britain: Churchill/Livingstone.

Masters, W., Johnson, V., Kolodny, R. (1985). *Human sexuality* (2nd ed.). Boston: Little, Brown.

Mead, M. (1949). *Male and female.* New York: William Morrow.

Perry, J., & Whipple, B. (1981). Pelvic muscle strength of female ejaculators: Evidence in support of a new theory of orgasm. *Journal of Sex Research, 17*(1), 22–39.

Schneidman, B., & McGuire, L. (1976). Group therapy for non-orgasmic women: Two age levels. *Archives of Sexual Behavior, 5,*(3), 239–247.

Schulman, A. (1972). Organs and orgasms. In V. Gornick & B. K. Moran (Eds.). *Women in Sexist Society.* New York: Basic Books.

Seaman, B. (1972). *Free and female: The sex life of the contemporary woman.* Greenwich, CT: Fawcett.

Sherfey, M. J. (1972). *The nature of evolution of female sexuality.* New York: Random House, Vintage Books.

Singer, J., & Singer, I. (1972). Types of female orgasms, *Journal of Sex Research, 8*(3), 255–267.

Spanier, G. (1976). Measuring dyadic adjustment: New scales for assessing the quality of marriage and similar dyads. *Journal of Marriage and the Family, 38*(3), 15–31.

Sultan, F. E., & Chambles, D. L. (1982). Pubococcygeal function and orgasm in a normal population. In B. Garber (Ed.), *Circumvaginal musculature and sexual function.* New York: Karger.

Trudel, G. & Saint Laurent, S. (1983). A comparison between the effects of Kegel's exercises and a combination of sexual awareness relaxation and breathing on situational orgasmic dysfunction in women. *Journal of Sex and Marital Therapy, 9*(3), 204–209.

Wallace, D., & Barbach, L. (1974). Pre-orgasmic group treatment. *Journal of Sex and Marital Therapy, 1*(2), 146–154.

Waterman, C.K., & Chiauzzi, E. J. (182). The role of orgasm in male and female sexual enjoyment. *Journal of Sex Research, 18*(2), 146–159.

Wilcox, D., & Hager, R. (1980). Toward realistic expectations for orgasmic response in women. *Journal of Sex Research, 16*(2), 162–179.

■ 17
Curative Factors in Groups for Women with Bulimia

Kathy Hotelling

With the increased prevalence of bulimia in the last decade (Garner & Garfinkel, 1985), practitioners have intensified their search for effective treatment models for those suffering from bulimia. A review of the literature indicates that a variety of groups have been beneficial to women with bulimia: psychoeducational groups (Johnson, Connors, & Stuckey, 1983), experiential-behavioral groups (White & Boskind-White, 1981), cognitive-behavioral groups (Starkey, 1982), a "bulimics anoymous" format (Hornak, 1983), eclectic groups (Lacey, 1985), feminist-support groups (Lindsey, Gauchet & Ricker, 1984), and traditional interpersonal process groups (Kelly & Liter, 1984), among others.

While the techniques utilized in these group models may be quite different, the amelioration of the bingeing and purging behavior has been cited by the proponents of each type of group. It appears, then, that there may be something about these groups in general, regardless of the theoretic orientation of the leaders, that contributes to the change in behavior of women with bulimia. Yalom (1970) has asserted that by disregarding the techniques and language of a certain school of therapy and considering only the actual method of effecting change in group members, one will find similar mechanisms of change ("curative factors").

I would like to gratefully acknowledge the suggestions of Lin Breeden and the patience of Rita Stewart who typed this manuscript.

The operation and significance of these factors on the process of change in groups for women with bulimia is the basis of this chapter. An analysis of curative factors lends organization to exploring how it is that these groups can be and are helpful. Some curative factors seem to "naturally " evolve from having a group of people together, whereas others require explicit intervention on the part of the leader to elicit desired change.

Each of the 10 curative factors will be reviewed in terms of its particular relevance to women with bulimia, with suggestions for specific leader interventions. Although the significance and operation of the curative factors are described singly for clarity's sake, it is important to recognize that these factors neither occur nor function separately. They are intimately tied to one another as the group progresses and aids in the recovery of group members.

UNIVERSALITY

Yalom (1970) described people entering therapy as having "the foreboding thought that they are unique in their wretchedness, that they alone have certain frightening or unacceptable problems, thoughts, impulses, and fantasies" (p. 10). The disconfirmation of this feeling of uniqueness is universality, which helps clients feel that they are not so inhuman after all.

At the conclusion of groups for women with bulimia that this therapist has led, the concept of universality is by far the most often cited answer to "What was the most important aspect of the group for you?" A significant step in overcoming bulimia successfully is discarding the shroud of secrecy that pervades the syndrome and contributes to a feeling of negative uniqueness; many women with bulimia have not shared their "secret" with anyone before entering treatment. Once the anticipatory fear of identifying themselves as having bulimia to a group of strangers has dissipated, the women are relieved that they are not alone with their problem. Because of the recent media attention on eating disorders, group members cognitively recognize that there are others experiencing similar eating behaviors; however, it is often not until hearing others "tell their story" in a face-to-face setting that the women actually integrate the fact that they are not the only ones suffering from bulimia. They are consoled that others can identify, because of shared experience, with the feelings and thoughts associated with bulimia.

While universality occurs "naturally" through the process of getting women with bulimia together in a group, it is important for the leader to help members thoroughly explore their similarities before moving into individual differences; this sense of "we-ness" helps members feel that they are fighting a common enemy (women with bulimia describe themselves as being controlled by bulimia, almost as if it were an animate being hovering overhead) and also enhances the curative factor of cohesiveness, described below. By leader-initiated questions, such as "Have others experienced this?," "How is this similar to how you react in a similar situation?," similarities are not only reinforced, but the leader demonstrates that asking for validation of experiences is expected in group.

IMPARTING OF INFORMATION

Yalom (1970) pointed out that the imparting of information in groups can function as the initial binding energy until other curative factors begin to operate. Nonetheless, the explanation of behaviors can be curative in and of itself.

While most group therapists do not explicitly give information to members (Yalom, 1970), educating clients about different aspects of bulimia can be very helpful as a first step in learning to take control of undesirable behaviors. In the early stages of a group, members can benefit from learning about the sociocultural factors operational in the development and maintenance of bulimia by reading *The Obsession: Reflections on the Tyranny of Slenderness* (Chernin, 1981) and/or *Fat is a Feminist Issue* (Orbach, 1978). When women with bulimia consciously realize that both they and others often equate one's worth with physical appearance, their frustration and anger with this superficial barometer can provide impetus for changes as they begin to question these values. In addition, an explanation of the dieting–bingeing–purging cycle (Garner, Rocket, Olmsted, Johnson, & Coscina, 1985) as self-perpetuating points out the futility of the behavior. Understanding the medical consequences of bingeing and purging can change the attitude that this behavior is just a bad habit to its being seen as a harmful and potentially fatal method of not caring for oneself.

In order to establish the link between eating and emotions (to go beyond the "I just want to be thin" explanation of bulimia), having members chart their eating is vital. The chart should include all circumstances of their eating: time, amount, and content of eating; thoughts and feelings just before eating; significant events of the day; and whether purging occurred. By writing down all eating, regardless of whether it is defined as a binge, patterns of feelings and thoughts related to a binge versus "normal" eating can be established. This process is related to developing care for oneself: to know what one needs, to assert oneself to fulfill these needs, and to begin to realize that one can maintain relationships without sacrificing onself.

Once the woman is aware of her individual process (which often includes "swallowing" anger, loneliness, hurt, and/or "positive" feelings that she feels she does not deserve), she can begin the task of developing healthy ways of dealing with these emotions. Although this process of developing a conscious awareness of the role that eating plays in one's life must be initiated early in the group, understanding develops throughout the life of the group.

As members grapple with not bingeing, information regarding how people know they are actually hungry must be discussed. Because of their erratic eating, women with bulimia have lost touch with their own bodily cues of hunger. Often this information is appropriately given midway through the group when the members have developed an understanding of the function of eating for themselves.

Imparting of information also includes members sharing with each other how they have begun to change their own behavior, as well as making suggestions to others. Since it is often easier to see what others need to do than seeing the same for oneself, giving suggestions is often a first step in recognizing changes for oneself. The process of sharing conveys caring about self and others.

INSTILLATION OF HOPE

Yalom (1970) asserted that the instillation and maintenance of hope is decisive in keeping clients in therapy so that the other curative factors can operate, as well as being effective therapeutically in and of itself.

In many ways, a group based on a commonality such as bulimia can take the most advantage of this curative factor. Members of a group will be at various stages of symptomology, which will encourage members as to their own recovery. It is important for group leaders to actively point out the progress of individuals and to encourage this feedback among group members. By creating a climate of trust and encouragement, the group will reinforce changes and indicate strengths to individuals.

While instilling hope is especially important in the beginning of the group to encourage members to remain, its import throughout the group cannot be diminished: there will be periods of regression where hope is vital to group members in proceeding with their recovery. It is at these points that the leader will need to be very active in encouraging conscious awareness of changes that have occurred and the possibility of additional changes.

COHESIVENESS

Group cohesiveness was defined by Yalom (1970) as the attraction that members have for their group and other members, an analogue of "relationship" in individual therapy. Cohesiveness, a sense of "we-ness," can be viewed as both a determinant and effect of the acceptance members show each other. Often women with bulimia have not experienced this sense of solidarity with others, especially with women; by accepting traditional female stereotypes, women may dislike, not trust, and view with contempt other women (Bernardez-Bonesatti, 1978). These feelings stem not only from cultural views of women as inferior, but also from the competition among women for men, a valued commodity in a society where a women's partner is symbolic of her worth.

In this therapist's observations of facilitating groups for women with bulimia, it appears that the most cohesive groups have members who are successful in eliminating bulimic symptoms, and less cohesive groups often have members who prematurely terminate and who say that the group is not helpful. In addition, cohesive groups seem to have members who can express anger toward one another and the leaders. In exit interviews, members often cite the expression and successful resolution of anger toward someone in the group as the most impactful incident in the group that affected personal change. This is vital for women with bulimia, since unexpressed anger is often a precipitating emotion in a binge and is related to the women placing the care of others and how they will react over care of self.

Sharing repugnant parts and experiences of oneself and still being accepted by group members is a powerful healing force in establishing self-worth. This, of course, is related to the concept of universality. Women are less harsh on others with the same symptoms than they are on themselves. By being aware of their acceptance of others similar to themselves, they can begin to accept themselves in spite of their own rejected parts.

Leaders can enhance cohesiveness by modeling acceptance of each individual and by encouraging members to actively support each other both inside and outside of the group. Whereas contact among members outside of group is often implicitly discouraged in groups, such contact to discuss an impending binge and alternative behaviors (much as Alcoholics Anonymous utilizes sponsors) can draw members together, as well as provide new learning. If a member merely waits until the next group to describe the binge, the cycle is reinforced and not averted. Even if another member cannot be reached, members often report avoiding a binge by imagining what might be or already has been said to her. In either case, this process allows for continued caring for others, an important part of women's identity, and developing caring for self by asking for and/or recreating support. The belief that one is either totally independent (and often, metaphorically, hungry) or totally dependent (a child) is challenged; the concept of interdependence is reinforced.

ALTRUISM

Altruism operates throughout the course of a group and consists of members offering each other support, insight, suggestions and the like. Leaders can elicit and reinforce this process by diverting direct questions from themselves to members of the group. Although leaders may understand the process of the development and maintenance of bulimia (see Imparting of Information above), members themselves have valuable insights to offer one another and themselves. This is important for several reasons. It strengthens the idea that one can be "a responsible actor rather than a powerless victim" (Bart, 1971, p. 126) of an eating disorder that has strong sociocultural roots. Perhaps even more importantly, altruism allows members to care for and to be connected to others. As Gilligan (1982) illustrated, this is an important dimension of women's identity, which if completely nonexistent would be devastating to women. There is, however, a caveat in encouraging altruism in these groups. Some women may use the group to continue their life goal of serving others at the expense of self. The leaders must carefully assist group members in being aware of when they are helping others to the detriment of themselves and/or to avoid examining their own behavior. After the leaders have monitored and addressed this potentially destructive behavior, group members will do the same, as evidenced by members stating at the start of a session that they need group time, by recognizing that another member appears very preoccupied in spite of her attempts to focus on another, etc. Helping women temper their care of others with care for themselves is a delicate, but vital task, in the recovery of women with bulimia.

IMITATIVE BEHAVIOR

Bandura, Ross, and Ross (1963) have shown that vicarious learning is a powerful force. Often women can hear suggestions given to and acted upon by others that they themselves have not been able to integrate into their own thinking and behavior. The group provides an influential setting for members to observe others develop new coping mechanisms and then emulate these behaviors themselves. Although some behavior may be imitated and later rejected, this process is still helpful in learning who one is through understanding who one is not.

Leaders are also imitated, and, therefore, their behavior toward each other and group members must be consistent with what they are advocating to group members. For example, conflict between co-leaders can be processed within the group, and members can learn that conflict need not end a relationship, and that, indeed, it can enhance mutual respect and caring between people.

One concern about putting nonpurging women with bulimia in a group with those that purge is that the purging behavior will be imitated. It seems that, although there may be this tendency, the purging individuals actively seek to discourage this behavior in their nonpurging counterparts: those who purge fear others getting into this self-perpetuating cycle and are quite convincing in their testimony against it, although they themselves may feel helpless to prevent their own behavior.

DEVELOPMENT OF SOCIALIZING TECHNIQUES

The development of social skills occurs in all groups, although the explicitness of this may vary among types of groups (Yalom, 1970). Often women with bulimia have been very popular, but, in fact, have superficial social skills.

For example, members are often able to chat about classes, activities, etc. before the group formally begins. Once the group is underway however, they often will interrupt other members and respond inappropriately or change the subject completely. This behavior appears to be motivated by three factors, which often interact. First, the women may not know how, from a skill point of view, to maintain a conversation on the same topic by drawing the other person out and by responding with one's own comments. Second, often members are scared by the emotional content of what is being said, partly because it is so close to their own experience. Third, one of the women's greatest fears is that they have nothing to offer another in a relationship, that they have a hollow self. Thus, by facilitating self-understanding, by leader modeling of appropriate responses to emotional material, and by actively teaching and giving feedback on suitable ways of interacting, the precursors of inappropriate behavior in the group can be addressed and behavior modified. In addition, role playing can be employed for situations outside of the group, with feedback serving to refine potential interactions.

INTERPERSONAL LEARNING

Yalom (1970) defined the broad curative factor of interpersonal learning as the group therapy analog of the operation of factors such as insight, transference, and corrective emotional experience in individual therapy. As pointed out earlier, relationships with others are critical to one's life, especially for women. Thus, this aspect of group therapy is of utmost therapeutic value to women with bulimia.

Perceptions of others are often distorted (Sullivan, 1953) and based on both the transference of attitudes of others in one's experiences and on intrapersonal needs. If one views a group as a social microcosm wherein members interact with others as they do in the outside world, these distortions will be exhibited in the group.

It is often these distortions that cause women with bulimia great concern and elicit the "swallowing" of one's feelings through bingeing. For example, if the expression of anger was met with punishment by a parent, the woman may inhibit all or most forms of anger, such as resentment and frustration. Thus, in the group, this woman may experience the frustration of not being understood, not express this feeling at the time, and leave the group and binge. If she brings this matter to the next group session, discussion can lead to insight, feedback, and emotional experiences that ameliorate the effect of previous experiences (the "corrective emotional experience," Alexander & French, 1946) and heighten understanding of oneself in relationship to others. As this occurs, a spiral is set in motion whereby self-worth improves and the need to conceal oneself (and push away previously unacceptable parts) decreases, resulting in decreased bingeing.

This process of receiving validation for one's feelings can be extended to the importance of learning about interdependence and the value of giving *and* receiving. As the group accepts and gives feedback to individuals regarding their need for others and the expression of this need, the misinterpretation of the need to totally care for others can be replaced and will detract from the emotional need to eat.

Of course, for this process to be set in motion, group leaders must help to establish a trusting and supportive group atmosphere.

CORRECTIVE RECAPITULATION OF THE PRIMARY FAMILY GROUP

Closely tied to the curative factor of interpersonal learning is the recapitulation of the primary family group, which Yalom (1970) described as having the capacity to be corrective in that "maladaptive, growth-inhibiting relationships are not permitted to freeze into the rigid, impenetrable system that characterizes many family structures" (p. 13).

The analogies between a therapy group and the primary family of each group member are striking: dependence on the leader, perceived as having unrealistic power and information; members "grow up" painfully in the group; and individuals separate at the group's ending to be on their own (Yalom, 1970). Although not necessary, a male/female therapy team can heighten this similarity.

The family is the earliest and most impactful group influencing an individual's view of how one "should" be in the world. Yet, many individuals experience their family as unsatisfactory. For women with bulimia, this is initially manifested by the association of their own dissatisfaction with their body and the emphasis of their mothers on attractiveness and thinness for their daughters, which is translated into perceiving worth as primarily related to how one looks. Furthermore, many women with bulimia suffer from a conflict between the image of their mothers (many of whom live by values currently being called into question and whose lives often have not been fulfilled) and the "new" image of women, who can conquer the world and be all things to all people at home and work (Chernin, 1985). They feel it necessary to protect their mothers and support how they have chosen to live their lives, which in turn leads to difficulty in separating enough to make their own choices. This conflict is often played out with the female therapist, who for many clients is a women unlike their mothers, but to whom they transfer their mothers' attributes at the same time. To successfully help the client work through this transference, the female therapist must be, like the ideal mother, nurturing, while also establishing herself as unlike the mother and a person in her own right. This, in turn, gives the client permission to be unlike the therapist *and* mother. The therapist is a transitional object who allows the client to merge with and then separate from her; successfully completed, this process then allows the client to reunite with her mother in a new way that validates the uniqueness of both.

Women with bulimia often perceive their fathers as not being there, both physically and emotionally, for them. Thus, with a male therapist, they will first deny his caring, then reject it as nongenuine. Part of the corrective experience is for the client to see herself as worthy of the emotional support of a man, personified by the therapist. Often not feeling worthy of a healthy relationship with a male has led to the bulimic woman's involvement in abusive relationships. Through reality testing, exploring of male/female relationships, and behaving in different ways in the group, these women increase their capacity to seek and experience nonabusive relationships with men outside the group.

In a like manner, working through unfinished issues with siblings (other group members), such as competition for the therapists' time and caring, can validate the woman's worth as an individual, separate from whether others are accepted or rejected.

Appropriate and sensitive handling of the transference and counter-transference issues that arise as part of the process described above is of paramount importance to the resolution of the issues relevant to the recovery of women with bulimia. Again, the balance of both giving and receiving in relationships can be modeled and discussed in this context.

CATHARSIS

Catharsis, the expression of strong emotion, is a part of the curative process of groups (Yalom, 1970). It promotes cohesiveness and is intimately tied to interpersonal learning and the corrective recapitulation of the primary family group. Because it is part and parcel of these other curative factors and, thus has been integral in the discussion above, little needs to be added to its valuableness in these groups. Suffice it to say that through the experience of catharsis, women with bulimia can learn not to be scared of their feelings and how expression of one's emotion need not lead to the isolation that they fear. Rather, emotional experiences promote our connectedness to others.

CONCLUSION

Active facilitation of the emergence and maintenance of the curative factors described by Yalom (1970) can lead to the personal growth and behavior change of women with bulimia in groups. While utilizing the group format as an extension of the importance of women's connection to others, leaders can encourage each member to also care for herself, develop an understanding of who she is as an individual, to act in accordance with this understanding, and to replace her binge/purge behavior with self-nurturing acts. In order to do this, the leader must have both an understanding of the dynamics of those with bulimia, as well as how the group process works to promote change.

REFERENCES

Alexander, F., & French, T. (1946). *Psychoanalytic therapy: Principles and applications.* New York: Ronald Press.

Bandura, A., Ross, D., & Ross, S. (1963). Vicarious reinforcements and imitative learning. *Journal of Abnormal and Social Psychology, 67*(6), 601–607.

Bart, P. B. (1971). The myth of a value-free psychotherapy. In W. Bell & J. Mau (Eds.), *The sociology of the future.* New York: Russell Sage Foundation.

Bernardez-Bonesatti, T. (1978). Women's groups: A feminist perspective on the treatment of women. In H. H. Grayson & C. Loew (Eds.), *Changing approaches to the psychotherapies.* New York: Spectrum.

Chernin, K. (1981). *The obsession: Reflections on the tyranny of slenderness.* New York: Harper & Row.

Chernin, K. (1985). *The hungry self.* New York: Times Books.

Garner, D. M., & Garfinkel, P. E. (1985). *Handbook of psychotherapy for anorexia nervosa and bulimia.* New York: Guilford Press.

Garner, D. M., Rockert, W., Olmsted, M. P., Johnson, C., & Coscina, D. V. (1985). In D. M. Garner & P. E. Garfinkel (Eds.), *Handbook of psychotherapy for anorexia nervosa and bulimia.* New York: Guilford Press.

Gilligan, C. (1982). *In a different voice.* Cambridge, MA: Harvard University Press.

Hornak, N. (1983). Group treatment for bulimia: Bulimics Anonymous. *Journal of College Student Personnel, 24*(5), 461–462.

Johnson, C., Connors, M., & Stuckey, M. (1983). Short-term group treatment for bulimia. *International Journal of Eating Disorders, 2*(4), 199–208.

Kelly, S., & Liter, S. (1984). *Group treatment of bulimia: A Yalom-type approach.* Paper presented at annual meeting of the American Association of Counseling and Development, Houston, TX.

Lacey, J. H. (1985). Time-limited individual and group treatment for bulimia. In D. M. Garner & P. E. Garfinkel (Eds.), *Handbook of psychotherapy for anorexia nervosa and bulimia.* New York: Guilford Press.

Lindsey, R., Gauchet, D., & Ricker, K. (1984). *A feminist approach to the group treatment of builimia.* Paper presented at the annual meeting of the American Association of Counseling and Development, Houston, TX.

Orbach, S. (1978). *Fat is a feminist issue.* New York: Berkeley.

Starkey, R. (1982). *Cognitive-behavioral group treatment of bulimia: A pilot study.* Paper presented at the Colorado Personnel and Guidance Association, Colorado Springs, CO.

Sullivan, H. S. (1953). *The interpersonal theory of psychiatry.* New York: W. W. Norton.

White, W., & Boskind-White, M. (1981). An experiential-behavioral approach to the treatment of bulimarexia. *Psychotherapy: Theory, Research and Practice, 18*(4), 501–507.

Yalom, I. D. (1970). *The theory and practice of group psychotherapy.* New York: Basic Books.

Index

n denotes text citation in footnote

T indicates tabular listings

Italicized page numbers indicate reference listings

In multiple author references, senior authors are indexed